Moder of emploitment

THE POLITICAL STYLE OF CONSPIRACY

Rhetoric and Public Affairs Series

The Political Style of Conspiracy

Chase, Sumner, and Lincoln

Michael William Pfau

Michigan State University Press
East Lansing

∞ The paper used in this publication meets the minimum requirements of
ANSI/NISO Z39.48<hy>1992 (R 1997) (Permanence of Paper).

Michigan State University Press
East Lansing, Michigan 48823<hy>5245
Printed and bound in the United States of America.

11 10 09 08 07 06 05   1 2 3 4 5 6 7 8 9 10

LIBRARY OF CONGRESS CATALOGING-IN-PUBLICATION DATA

Pfau, Michael.
  The political style of conspiracy : Chase, Sumner, and Lincoln / Michael
William Pfau.
      p. cm.—(Rhetoric and public affairs series)
  Includes bibliographical references and index.
  ISBN 0-87013-760-3 (casebound : alk. paper)
  1. United States—Politics and government—1815–1861. 2. Slavery—Political
aspects—United States—History—19th century. 3. Conspiracies—United States—
History—19th century. 4. Chase, Salmon P. (Salmon Portland), 1808–1873—
Language. 5. Sumner, Charles, 1811-1874—Language. 6. Lincoln, Abraham, 1809-
1865—Language. 7. Rhetoric—Political aspects—United States—History—19th
century. 8. English language—Discourse analysis. 9. Political culture—
United States—History—19th century. I. Title. II. Series.
  E415.7.P64 2005
  815'.0103093553—dc22

                                                    2005027199

Cover and book design by Sans Serif, Inc.
Cover art: Library of Congress, Prints and Photographs Division [reproduction
number, e.g., LC-USZ62-945].

Martin J. Medhurst, Series Editor, *Baylor University*

g green
g press
INITIATIVE Michigan State University Press is a member of the Green Press
Initiative and is committed to developing and encouraging ecologically
responsible publishing practices. For more information about the Green Press
Initiative and the use of recycled paper in book publishing, please visit
www.greenpressinitiative.org.

Visit Michigan State University Press on the World Wide Web at:
www.msupress.msu.edu

Contents

Acknowledgments

Many assisted in the germination, gestation, and birth of this book. Foremost among them was David Zarefsky. His careful scholarship inspired the project, and his encyclopedic knowledge, diligence, and personal commitment over a period of many years enabled it to grow to completion. Michael Leff nourished the study with numerous disputations and a commitment to rhetorical criticism that kept me focused on elucidating the inner life of texts, and Dilip Gaonkar brought to the project a theoretical sophistication that kept me reevaluating my assumptions. Others in the Northwestern University community provided essential intellectual and personal support at many stages of its development. So, too, my colleagues at the University of Minnesota–Duluth provided a highly supportive environment that enabled me to improve and expand the book manuscript. Reviewers from the editorial board of the Michigan State University Press, Rhetoric and Public Affairs Series, offered invaluable assistance that substantially strengthened the book. Finally, along with each of these intellectual midwives, I must acknowledge the debts I owe to previous scholars—debts that I can only repay in the currency of the footnote.

1

Problems of Interpretation: Approaching Conspiracy in Text and Discourse

Occasionally . . . conspiracy arguments will become credible to the political mainstream, being advanced by moderates as well as extremists and commanding widespread adherence. For example, the argument that President John F. Kennedy's assassination was the work of a conspiracy has passed beyond the bounds of fantasy and almost become the conventional wisdom. The same pattern of "mainstreaming" the conspiracy argument was evident in the late 1850s.

—David Zarefsky, *Lincoln, Douglas, and Slavery: In the Crucible of Public Debate*

Conspiracy, the secret cooperation for the achievement of some base design, has been a frequently recurring topic of political discussions since ancient times. But it has been the turbulent history of the United States that has provided the most fertile ground for conspiracy discourse. From the time of the Revolution to the present day, conspiracy discourse—that is, linguistic and symbolic practices and artifacts revolving around themes, claims, or accusations of conspiracy—has pervaded diverse forums and genres of American political discourse. For many critics and commentators, the ubiquity of conspiracy theories in American history and the increasing appeal of such theories at the beginning of the twenty-first century are a cause for concern and even alarm. Such apprehension is frequently expressed in the imagery of disease. Widespread belief in conspiracies is described as a political "pathology" or as a metastasizing "cancer" threatening the body politic. The language of disease is certainly pejorative and may indicate an excessive paranoia of conspiracy discourse, but thinking about conspiracy discourse in terms of disease does possess the undeniable advantage of suggesting a highly productive avenue of inquiry. From the perspective of the art of medicine, eliminating a disease from the body requires particular knowledge of its strategies for survival and replication. While this author is not yet convinced of the need to wholly rid the body politic of conspiracy discourse, this study's primary goal is precisely to understand the means by which conspiracy theories replicate themselves.

Just as a virus propagates by hijacking one cell at a time, so, too, conspiracy theories may be said to replicate by changing one mind at a time. The precise process by which conspiracy theories colonize minds, of course, is a rhetorical process. "Rhetoric" is a contested term that is difficult to define precisely, but most recognize that the rhetorical perspective is concerned with persuasive discourse and with language or symbolic systems in practice—especially within political settings. The centrality of rhetoric to belief in conspiracy theories is indicated by the observation that absent such a discursive vehicle, conspiracy theories would remain confined to the life of individual minds rather than populating the imaginations of whole polities and cultures. As such, the rhetorical perspective seems to lie at the heart of the larger conspiracy phenomena, and it promises to elucidate the manner in which conspiracy theories, for better and for worse, replicate and reproduce themselves. More specifically, the dominant orientation of this study is rhetorical criticism—that is, it seeks to elucidate the manner in which rhetorical texts become vehicles to transform the perspective of others by way of interpreting, describing, and analyzing such texts.

Previous scholars considering conspiracy from a rhetorical perspective have used a number of terms, often conflicting or overlapping, to describe the phenomenon. In this study, "conspiracism" refers to belief in conspiracy and "conspiracist" to a believer in conspiracy. This study understands "conspiracy rhetoric" to be a text or other discrete artifact purporting to reveal the existence of a conspiracy. "Conspiracy argument" is a narrower category, referring to the logical or rational operations and techniques by which a discourse operates on a given audience or audiences. By contrast, "conspiracy discourse" is a broader category that includes concrete instances of persuasion as well as the wider intertextual, ideological, cultural, political, and social context within which these texts are produced and consumed. This study is concerned with each of these components, for analyzing and interpreting conspiracy rhetoric will require attention to textual practices such as argument and to the broader contexts within which conspiracy texts are situated.

Selecting among the large number of conspiracy theories is difficult, but this study focuses upon an especially virulent conspiracy theory that swept throughout the antebellum North in the mid to late 1850s. Opposition to the "slave power" conspiracy—an alleged cabal of nineteenth-century slaveholders who sought to use the national government to expand their peculiar institution and thereby to aggrandize their political and economic power—was a key component of antislavery rhetoric, and it was in opposition to a slave power conspiracy that the Republican Party rose to power in 1860. Precisely due to its pervasiveness in the 1850s, slave power conspiracy discourse is a promising place to begin searching for answers regarding how conspiracy theories reproduce themselves. This conspiracy theory also questions many of the assumptions of the dominant approach to conspiracy, the paranoid style.

The Paranoid Style and Its Legacy

Richard Hofstadter's work on the "paranoid style" provides the foundation for contemporary conspiracy scholarship. While this study will find fault with how Hofstadter's approach has been applied, it also takes inspiration from this first, and perhaps most successful, attempt to grapple with conspiracy theory from a critical perspective. Hofstadter's sensitivity to the rhetorical dimension of conspiracy discourse is evident in his understanding of style: "When I speak of the paranoid style, I use the term much as a historian of art might speak of the baroque or the mannerist style. It is above all a way of seeing the world and expressing oneself." Hofstadter posits no merely ornamental or literary understanding of style, however, but an understanding of style as constitutive of thought and experience, for the paranoid style is not only a "way in which ideas are believed and advocated" that can be observed within rhetorical texts, it is also a "style of mind" that populates human consciousness. Hofstadter's constitutive understanding of rhetoric and discourse is also evident in his concern with judgment: "distorted style is . . . a possible signal that may alert us to a distorted judgment, just as in art an ugly style is a cue to fundamental defects of taste."[1] For Hofstadter, then, the "style" in paranoid style is not just a shorthand term to characterize a bundle of textual characteristics, it is an analytical tool of great breadth and depth that reflects and anticipates more contemporary understandings of the complex relationship among the categories of language, thought, and reality. Since this study draws on Hofstadter even as it critiques, reworks, and delimits this category's applicability to conspiracy discourse, it is important to consider the paranoid style in some detail.

Hofstadter's understanding of style resonates with the traditional interests of rhetorically minded scholars, as does his basic method. He develops the paranoid style category on the basis of the study of a broad range of rhetorical texts generated over a period of more than a century by a number of social movements throughout U.S. history (each opposing different conspiratorial enemies as varied as the Jesuits, Freemasons, international capitalists, international Jews, and Communists). The "content" of the paranoid style is difficult to summarize due to the wide-ranging nature of Hofstadter's essay, but it is possible to piece together a few of his clearest statements. Readers are first informed that the "paranoid" in "paranoid style" is not intended to be descriptive in the clinical sense. Rather, Hofstadter indicates, "I call it the paranoid style simply because no other word adequately evokes the qualities of heated exaggerations, suspiciousness, and conspiratorial fantasy that I have in mind." Essential to the paranoid style is a sense of persecution that is "systematized in grandiose theories of conspiracy."[2] Indeed, the "central image" of the paranoid style is:

> that of a vast and sinister conspiracy, a gigantic and yet subtle machinery of influence set in motion to undermine and destroy a way of life. . . . One may object that there are conspiratorial acts in history, and there is nothing paranoid about taking note of them. This is true. All political behavior requires strategy, many strategic acts depend for their effect upon a period of secrecy, and anything that is secret . . . may be described as conspiratorial. The distinguishing thing about the paranoid style is not that its exponents see conspiracies or plots here and there in history, but that they regard a "vast" or "gigantic" conspiracy as the motive force in historical events. History is conspiracy, set in motion by demonic forces of almost transcendental power, and what is felt to be needed to defeat it is not the usual methods of political give and take, but an all out crusade. The paranoid spokesman sees the fate of this conspiracy in apocalyptic terms—he traffics on the birth and death of whole worlds, whole political orders, and whole systems of human value.[3]

This passage gestures in a number of directions that are later clarified and elaborated in the essay and which serve as trajectories for subsequent scholarship. Prior to considering how Hofstadter's concepts have been received and elaborated, however, it is important to note several additional components of the paranoid style.

The manner in which the conspiratorial enemy is described and portrayed is one essential element of the paranoid style. In addition to using phrases like "vast and sinister conspiracy" and "demonic forces of transcendental power" to describe conspiratorial enemies, we are told that within paranoid rhetoric, "The enemy is clearly delineated: he is a perfect model of malice, a kind of amoral superhuman: sinister, ubiquitous, powerful, cruel, sensual, luxury-loving." This enemy is the "motive force" in history—all of history is said to bend to the will of the conspirators: "He is a free, active, demonic agent. He wills, indeed he manufactures, the mechanism of history itself, or deflects the normal course of history in an evil way. . . . The paranoid's interpretation of history is in this sense distinctly personal: decisive events are not taken as stream of history, but as the consequence of someone's will." Both the profound evil of the conspiratorial enemy and its great power contribute to the "apocalyptic and absolutist framework" characterizing the paranoid style.[4]

This characteristic demonization of the all-powerful conspiratorial enemy recalls an important prequel to conspiracy scholarship. As early as the 1930s, Kenneth Burke, in his essay "The Rhetoric of Hitler's Battle," outlined Adolph Hitler's use of what was undoubtedly a form of conspiracy rhetoric. For Burke, Hitler's *Mein Kampf* was an instance in which this terrible leader found, in the identification of a conspiratorial enemy, a source of unity and purpose. Hitler's anti-Semitic conspiracy theory, according to Burke, provided not only a scapegoat that allegedly explained the difficulties that had been faced by the German people in the post–World War I period but also enabled the "symbolic rebirth" of individuals and the nation. Over the years, Burke continued to refine and apply the scapegoat concept, noting its importance in all societies as a way of encouraging unity against a common enemy in the face of division. Perhaps most relevant for the purposes of the paranoid style, however, is the tendency Burke notes toward the "perfecting of the scapegoat." The symbolic function of the scapegoat—both individual and collective—is said to be enhanced insofar as the scapegoat's evil and power are emphasized or exaggerated. This imperative may indeed help to explain the paranoid style's tendency to portray the conspiratorial enemy as particularly sinister and powerful.[5] Given

this important connection, it seems appropriate to consider the scapegoating function—and the perfection of the scapegoat—as an essential component of the paranoid style.

Consideration of the nature of the conspiratorial enemy within the
paranoid style suggests not only the importance of scapegoating, it also
lends itself to a number of figural and narrative-based interpretive strategies that enable critics to unlock the "poetics" of conspiracy discourse. Hofstadter's essay only hints at such formal or literary interpretive strategies,
but it deals extensively with the logical and argumentative characteristics
of conspiracy discourse. Hofstadter insists that he is concerned with "the
way in which ideas are believed and advocated rather than the truth or falsity of their content." Nevertheless, there is an epistemological assumption
underlying the paranoid style—that the conspiracies in question are fundamentally false. Hofstadter assumes from the outset that paranoid rhetoric
reflects "distorted judgment," and he is interested in the "possibility of
using political rhetoric to get at political pathology." Presumably in order to
compensate for such epistemological shortcomings, rhetors within the
paranoid style are said to show an elaborate, almost "scholarly" concern
with demonstrating the existence of the conspiracy, as the rhetor "carefully
and all but obsessively accumulates 'evidence.'" Hofstadter writes that the
"typical procedure of the higher paranoid scholarship is to start with such
defensible assumptions and with a careful accumulation of facts, or at least
of what appear to be facts, and to marshal these facts toward an overwhelming 'proof' of the particular conspiracy that is to be established." But
while much of the evidence and initial assumptions may appear sound,
"[w]hat distinguishes the paranoid style is . . . the curious leap in imagination that is always made at some critical point in the recital of events." Despite such curious leaps, the conspiracy may nonetheless gain a modicum
of plausibility to audiences for two major reasons. First, conspiracy arguments camouflage themselves with the appearance of rationality: "The
plausibility the paranoid style has for those who find it plausible lies, in
good measure, in this appearance of the most careful, conscientious, and
seemingly coherent application to detail, the laborious accumulation of
what can be taken as convincing evidence for the most fantastic conclusions, the careful preparation for the big leap from the undeniable to the
unbelievable." Second, conspiratorial interpretations construct a world
that, although fantastic, is in many respects more coherent than the real
world. The conspiratorial explanation "is nothing if not coherent—in fact,
the paranoid mentality is far more coherent than the real world, since it

leaves no room for mistakes, failures, or ambiguities. It is, if not wholly rational, at least intensely rationalistic . . . leaving nothing unexplained and comprehending all of reality in one overreaching, consistent theory."[6]

The paranoid style is a profoundly rhetorical category. It is a style of mind and a style of expression and provides the rudiments of a number of interpretive strategies that later scholars could refine and elaborate in their attempts to understand both the logic and poetics of conspiracy discourse. But while Hofstadter's influential essay is primarily concerned with describing and analyzing characteristics of conspiracy texts, it also discusses a number of extrinsic considerations—exploring the manner in which the paranoid style is connected to social, political, and cultural contexts. First and foremost, the paranoid style is an outgrowth of social movements and as such can be considered in the context of the aspirations, needs, and functions of groups as various as anti-Masons, nativists, and Goldwaterites. But this contextual move is only nascent in Hofstadter's essay. What is emphasized, rather, is the ahistorical nature of this category: "the paranoid style . . . represents an old and recurring mode of expression in our public life which has frequently been linked with movements of suspicious discontent and whose content remains the same even when it is adopted by men of distinctly different purposes." Hofstadter provides tentative explanations for the periodic recurrence of the paranoid style in U.S. history, asserting that "the paranoid disposition is mobilized into action chiefly by social conflicts that involve ultimate schemes of values and that bring fundamental fears and hatreds, rather than negotiable interests, into political action." He notes that the occurrence of catastrophic events may also encourage expressions of the paranoid style.[7]

In addition to sharing a common stylistic "content," groups expressing the paranoid style in the United States are also said to share a common status as "minority movements." Little or no explanation is provided for this consignment to the fringe, leaving readers to assume that the failure of the paranoid style to enter the political mainstream is the result of the fact that such groups hold extreme views not held by the moderate and pragmatic majority. But it is possible to tease out at least one reason for the failure of such groups to thrive, a reason that, unlike Hofstadter's explanation for the periodic recurrence of the paranoid style, is concerned with the rhetorical stance of paranoid rhetors. The paranoid style, apparently, breeds pessimism: "The apocalypticism of the paranoid style runs dangerously near to hopeless pessimism, but usually stops short of it. . . . Properly expressed, such warnings . . . portray that which impends but which may still be avoided. They are a secular and demonic version of adventism."[8] One might imagine that a social movement founded on pessimism is unlikely to succeed, yet this sense of pessimism—presumably associated with the immense power of the conspiratorial enemy—seems a logical consequence of the paranoid style.

Historical and Rhetorical Elaborations of the Paranoid Style

Richard Hofstadter's paranoid style has served as a template for most subsequent studies of conspiracy. Two studies in particular have helped to flesh out and reshape the paranoid style. David Brion Davis was among the first to follow up on Hofstadter's insights, and while he for the most part extends and elaborates the paranoid style, he also makes original contributions that enable one to begin moving beyond Hofstadter's relatively ahistorical construct toward an understanding of conspiracy discourse within its historical context.

Like Hofstadter's, Davis's work is based on his reading of a wide range of conspiracy texts appearing over a period of decades and centuries. Davis's initial work actually preceded Hofstadter's and identified the campaigns of anti-Masons, anti-Catholics, and anti-Mormons in terms of a category he called the "literature of counter-subversion." Davis's work here anticipates Hofstadter's in a number of ways. First, he notes that the literature generated by these groups is almost indistinguishable. Second, he focuses on the psychological and social roles played by conspiracy discourse, noting that the literature of countersubversion was a symptom of the more general problem of ideological unity and diversity in a rapidly changing society. Under conditions of uncertainty and conflict, he suggests, conspiracy discourse served the functions of promoting unity, clarifying national values, and nurturing a sense of self-righteousness. Davis's later writings explicitly elaborate and refine the paranoid style, as he seems to fuse Hofstadter with Burke in identifying the paranoid style as a "psychological device for projecting various symbols of evil on an opponent and for building emotional unity through a common sense of alarm and peril." Such a device, according to Davis, is especially prominent at times and places where the rapidly changing nature of society causes confusion about the nature of social roles and the differences between social appearances and realities. While Davis generally lacks the sensitivity shown by Hofstadter toward style and text, he does note the recurrence of a number of metaphors—revolving around disease, evil spirits, entering wedges, Trojan horses, blueprints, and so forth—within the conspiracy texts he examines.[9]

For the most part, Davis refines and elaborates the paranoid style, but he also points in a direction that enables one to move away from this category toward a richer and more complex understanding of conspiracy discourse in the United States. Davis attempts a less prejudiced account of conspiracy discourse, insisting that he does not share Hofstadter's pejorative attitude or assumption that conspiracists are abnormal and maintaining that conspiracy discourse is as likely to be attached to good causes as bad. Davis also moves beyond Hofstadter's assumptions about the paranoid style as the province of angry minorities. Not only does he note the extent to which conspiracy discourse has been an important part of the American political tradition since before the Revolution, he also shows that conspiracy rhetors have not always been the paranoid fringe types that Hofstadter would lead us to expect. Rather, he observes that conspiracy rhetors have come from a variety of backgrounds, have utilized conspiracy discourse for a number of different purposes, and have often been among the most respectable of citizens. Further, Davis suggests that at particular times and places, belief in conspiracy is far from pathological and instead is not an unreasonable response to current events.[10] Each of these insights is important for the tack this study will take with conspiracy discourse.

While Davis may be said to have taken the paranoid style in the direction of history, Earl Creps initially steered the paranoid style firmly in the direction of rhetorical criticism. Creps's dissertation considered the "conspiracy argument" as "rhetorical genre" and surpassed even Hofstadter's sensitivity to textuality and discursive form. Creps's thesis, drawn from the work of Kenneth Burke and Richard Hofstadter, is that conspiracy arguments serve an essential psychological function—especially during times of crisis and rapid social change—as secular theodicies that help to resolve the problem of evil in the world. Of greater moment for the purposes of this study are Creps's insights regarding the textual features of conspiracy arguments, which he characterizes as representing a fusion of "poetic and dialectic, drama and syllogism." Creps's findings may be succinctly summarized along these two dimensions—of poetics and argument. In terms of the "poetics" of conspiracy, Creps's study makes several important findings—that conspiracy arguments are "dramatic in form," that they employ "exaggerated and lurid imagery," and that they personalize and symbolize evil in terms of a conspiratorial plot. From the perspective of argument, Creps notes that conspiracy arguments assume minimal argumentative burdens, that they make causal claims, that they present evidence en masse, and that they exhibit a deductive logic (though they often appear to be inductive in form). While the vast majority of Creps's findings represent elaborations of the paranoid style, he moves in a direction that is important for the purposes of this study. Creps acknowledges that he, like Hofstadter, considers mainly paranoid or fringe texts; but he hints that the conspiracy argument might take on a different shape in the hands of mainstream rhetors or within mainstream forums.[11]

The Paranoid Style's Rhetorical Trajectory: Conspiracy as Argument

Hofstadter's essay, combined with the elaborations and extensions of Davis and Creps, may be said to have established a paradigm by which most rhetorical scholars—with a few notable exceptions—approach conspiracy discourse. Within rhetorical studies, the paranoid style seems to have been received primarily in the terms of the argumentative dimension concerning Hofstadter's claims about the logical structures undergirding the paranoid style. This emphasis should come as no surprise. Not only has argument been a traditional focus of rhetorical studies, but paranoid conspiracy texts, because they seek to "prove" propositions that are fundamentally false, pose an intriguing challenge to scholars of argument. The 1970s saw quantitative studies of conspiracy texts—studies that tended to emphasize the slippery and deceitful character of paranoid rhetoric.[12] Several qualitative studies of conspiracy arguments in the 1980s confirmed their dubious character. G. Thomas Goodnight and John Poulakos's study of the conspiracy rhetoric surrounding Watergate found that conspiratorial interpretations tend to elide the "traditional proofs" of the pragmatic frame, resulting in a "paranoid quality." David Zarefsky's analysis of the argumentative techniques by which Lincoln and Douglas sought to make their conspiracy positions credible in the Lincoln-Douglas debates found claims of conspiracy to be strategically shrewd yet logically problematic. Finally, Marilyn J. Young, Michael K. Launer, and Curtis C. Austin's study of conspiracy argument concurs with Goodnight and Poulakos and Zarefsky that conspiracy arguments are, if not outright false and deceptive, at least slippery and questionable within the parameters of traditional argument theory. This is a serious problem for Young, Launer, and Austin, for "audience-centered" approaches like the narrative paradigm are said to give critics little evaluative purchase. Following Hofstadter, Young and her colleagues suggest that the logical structures within conspiracy texts serve only as a form of rationalistic camouflage for fundamentally irrational claims. Conspiracy arguments are, in the terms of C. H. Perelman and L. Olbrechts-Tyteca, "quasi-logical arguments"—arguments that are persuasive because they appear to have the form of rational arguments.[13]

While most rhetorical studies of conspiracy discourse have focused upon the argumentative dimension—often finding fault with the rationality of a given conspiracy claim—others have used the paranoid style in a more general manner as a device to elucidate and interpret particular conspiracy texts and fragments. Such is the case with Charles Griffin's analysis of Jedediah Morse's claims regarding the illuminati. Griffin uses the paranoid style, along with the jeremiad, to illuminate and interpret Morse's text. Most recently, Marouf Hasian's study of the role of *The Protocols of the Elders of Zion* within a number of anti-Semitic conspiracy claims adopts the sensibility, if not the precise interpretive strategies, of the paranoid style. Hasian, like Hofstadter, assumes the stance of a physician diagnosing and providing curatives for a pathological and very dangerous body of conspiratorial thought.[14]

While a rhetorical perspective seems best suited to understanding how conspiracy theories replicate themselves, and hence to comprehending the larger conspiracy phenomena, most rhetorical scholarship has been hampered by excessive devotion to the assumptions of the paranoid style. The appeal of the paranoid style is not surprising. Hofstadter's category—alongside Burke's concept of scapegoating—has provided rhetorical scholars with a ready-made package of interpretive strategies that promise to unlock both the logical and poetic dimensions of most, if not all, conspiracy texts. But even as rhetorically minded scholars were utilizing and elaborating the paranoid style's interpretive insights in order to comprehend the rhetorical operations animating conspiracy texts, a number of historians and a few rhetorical scholars were fundamentally questioning the paranoid style's assumptions about the social, political, and cultural context in which conspiracy discourse appears.

Critiques of the Paranoid Style: Conspiracy in the Mainstream

While the paranoid style has thrived as an interpretive apparatus in rhetorical studies, it has been subject to a good deal of criticism from a number of historians who point out the extent to which Hofstadter's category overlooks the pervasiveness of conspiracy rhetoric in the early American

republic. Bernard Bailyn's pivotal study of the pamphlet literature associated with the American Revolution established beyond a doubt that conspiracism has "deep and widespread roots—roots elaborately embedded in
American political culture." Bailyn's explanation for the pervasiveness of
conspiratorial thinking is ideological—it was the civic republican–inspired
works of influential English opposition writers that contributed to the tendency of the American revolutionaries to see conspiracies in politics. Whatever its source, for Bailyn, conspiratorial thinking has become entrenched
within American culture.[15]

Historian Gordon Wood has also challenged the conventional wisdom
that conspiratorial thinking has always been the province of deranged
fringe types. Wood notes, in fact, that conspiratorial interpretations were
extremely common in the world of ancient politics, where they possessed
"a matter-of-fact quality. They were not imagined or guessed at; they hap-
pened. Catiline actually plotted to take over Rome; Brutus and Cassius really did conspire against Caesar." But while such premodern conspiracy
theories were accompanied by an understanding of the contingent nature
of events, by the time of the Enlightenment, conspiratorial interpretations
of politics were part of a scientific impulse to explain all social and political
outcomes in terms of human agency and will. Paradoxically, this Enlightenment tendency toward conspiratorial interpretations came at precisely
the time when the rise of the nation-state and economic modernization
were making the world much too complex to be explained in such a manner. Indeed, the Western intellectual tradition, spurred by the Scottish Enlightenment, eventually came to understand more fully the complexity of
its world, rendering conspiratorial interpretations "so out of place that . . .
they can be accounted for only as mental aberrations, as a paranoid symptom of psychological disturbance."[16]

Bailyn and Wood, as well as their colleagues in historical studies, have
done much to dispel the presumption that conspiracy discourse has always
been the strategy of the fringe or marginal elements of society.[17] At least in
the eighteenth and nineteenth centuries, conspiracy discourse was perva-
sively entwined with the ideological assumptions of the new republic. Centuries of political history, the English opposition tradition, and the very
intellectual currents of the Enlightenment encouraged Americans to be
wary of various kinds of political conspiracies. In each of these respects,
historians have done a great deal to dispel the ahistorical assumption of
marginality underlying the paranoid style category.

Conspiracy in the Mainstream:
Rhetorical and Historical Connections

Corresponding to the insistence of historians that conspiratorial thinking has been a prominent feature of American political rhetoric has been the realization among a few rhetorical scholars that conspiracy discourse may be a significant phenomenon within the political mainstream. Earl Creps was the first to move in this direction. While most of his study concerned the conspiracy arguments from the fringe of society, he speculates that conspiracy arguments addressed to mainstream audiences might well possess their own distinct characteristics. Goodnight and Poulakos also suggest that "the 'paranoid style' no longer can be said to characterize only political extremists, a theory of conspiracy discourse must account for the usefulness of this appeal to mainstream speakers and audiences" and "account for the possibility that those upholding an unpopular or presumably lunatic point of view may be participating in the restructuring of social consensus." For Goodnight and Poulakos, then, the paranoid style is a contagion that occasionally breaks out and captures the imagination of mainstream audiences and speakers. David Zarefsky's study of the Lincoln-Douglas debates also recognizes that, despite the general skepticism toward conspiracy arguments, "[o]ccasionally . . . the arguments are taken seriously, are advanced by moderates as well as extremists, and command widespread adherence." Accordingly, Zarefsky asks, "Under what social circumstances do conspiracy allegations become sufficiently believable that they are used by moderates as well as extremists? And what techniques of argumentation help to make the conspiracy charge credible?" The answers to the first question are, for the most part, reiterations of Hofstadter's and Davis's positions: conspiracy arguments become generally accepted when they "explain an otherwise ambiguous evil" or "pattern of anomalies," when "polarizing positions helps to resolve ambiguity," or during "times of social strain." Zarefsky's answers to the second question focus on the strategic advantage that conspiracy claims provided to Lincoln and Douglas, especially the capacity of these arguments to "shift the burden of proof to one's opponent while minimizing one's own burdens" and the advantage of a countercharge as the most effective response to an opponent's conspiracy claim. Several years later, Nicholas Burnett's study of the conspiracy discourse surrounding the Revolution confirmed the undeniable presence of conspiratorial interpretations in the American mainstream.[18]

Each of these scholars challenges Hofstadter's category insofar as they suggest that the paranoid style occasionally breaks out into the American mainstream, but what is of primary import for the purposes of this study are the rhetorical implications of the undeniable presence of conspiracy discourse in the political mainstream at particular times and places in U.S. history. Zarefsky's work was the primary inspiration for this study's attempt to develop a means of understanding the differences between conspiracy texts at the fringe and those in the mainstream within a given discursive formation like that developed in opposition to an alleged slave power conspiracy in the antebellum period. Zarefsky's study suggested the possibility of "mapping" conspiracy discourse from the perspective of the fringe and center of the mainstream.

While Zarefsky's work has served as a foundation for the present study's attempt to "map" conspiracy discourse, another study is especially worthy of note. The promise of "mapping" conspiracy discourse is endorsed by Robert Goldberg's study of a number of postwar conspiracy theories revolving around the New World Order, communism, UFOs, and anti-Semitic themes. Goldberg finds that many of these conspiracy theories have gained an alarming presence in the American mainstream. His major contribution to the conspiracy literature is to develop the rudiments of a scheme by which we may understand the how and why of a given theory's migration from the fringe to the mainstream and back again. His study finds that while each conspiracy theory is most strenuously advocated by a "core" or "nucleus" of absolutely committed countersubversives (corresponding to Hofstadter's notion that conspiracy theory is generally the province of fringe groups), a given theory frequently finds adherents well beyond these audiences of true believers. Goldberg reads the postwar history of most of these conspiracy theories as one of oscillation from belief solely by a "core" group of believers, outward toward a "periphery" of believers within the political mainstream, and eventually back again to the "nucleus" of the countersubversive community. A number of factors are said to explain this periodicity of belief. First, Goldberg finds that belief in a given conspiracy theory increases according to its correspondence with historical events as well as "personal and group histories." Second, he focuses on the credentials of the "messengers" of conspiracy. In addition to committed countersubversives at the "core," a variety of society's more credible actors—ministers and leaders of other social institutions, politicians and bureaucrats, media elites in news and entertainment, and many others—contribute to "conspiracy imaging." Goldberg finds important differences between believers at the "core" and "periphery." With "distance from nucleus, suspiciousness lessens along with commitment to the specifics of the plot," while "at the periphery, where the subculture joins the mainstream, receptivity and only a vague, seamless account of conspiracy remains [*sic*]." Finally, at certain junctures of history, the "message may overflow barriers of class, race and gender and envelop the majority."[19] While Goldberg is not concerned with the rhetorical dimension of conspiracy texts, his basic notion that discourse generated against a given conspiratorial enemy can be productively categorized within an illuminating spectrum provides support for this study's attempt to "map" the diversity of slave power conspiracy discourse.

Filling a Niche:
Mapping Slave Power Conspiracy Discourse

As we have seen, a wide variety of approaches have furthered the study of conspiracy discourse. Some studies have used a broad range of texts to perform a diachronic analysis of the development of conspiratorial interpretations from the early republic to the present or to construct a genre or style of conspiracy discourse. Some studies have focused narrowly on an ideological complex or discursive formation generated against a particular conspiracy. Other studies have narrowed the focus even further, considering the conspiracy discourse of one rhetor or a single conspiracy text or fragment. This study approaches rhetorical discourses revolving around the slave power conspiracy by reading the conspiracy texts of Salmon P. Chase, Charles Sumner, and Abraham Lincoln within their particular contexts. While one aim of this study is textual criticism, it is also concerned with mapping the larger slave power discursive formation. This study proposes that by studying conspiracy texts closest to the center of the political mainstream of the 1850s, it will be possible to elucidate the character of the larger discursive formation centered around charges of a slave power conspiracy.

Within the context of the extensive conspiracy scholarship, this study fills two important gaps. It challenges the continued dominance of the paranoid style category to the study of conspiracy discourse. While this study is one of several to move in this direction, its design and conception render it uniquely suited to test the limits of the paranoid style. In contrast to Hofstadter's category, this study focuses on a conspiratorial interpretation—the slave power conspiracy—that came to occupy the political center and formed the ideological backbone of the ascendant Republican Party in the 1850s. In order to test the limits of the paranoid style even further, the study selects for close textual readings the orations of three of the most influential Republicans of that period—Salmon P. Chase, Charles Sumner, and Abraham Lincoln. In this respect, the study's corpus and design are crafted specifically to provide maximum contrast with the paranoid style. Given the broad academic interest in conspiracy discourse, a study that can effectively fill important gaps left in the wake of the paranoid style will contribute to discussions within several disciplines.

The second kind of gap is of no less importance. While Hofstadter's original study can be criticized on several fronts, its analysis of conspiracy discourse in terms of style is to be commended for its critical sensitivity. Using terms familiar to rhetorical and literary critics, Hofstadter defined the paranoid style in terms of the arguments, imagery, and narratives characteristic of his corpus, providing a series of interpretive strategies by which critics might better understand the manner in which paranoid conspiracy texts seek to persuade audiences. Given its focus on textual readings and persuasive strategies, this study completes what hitherto has been only a partial revision of Hofstadter. Many of Hofstadter's critics have shown that his methods and assumptions are not applicable to all conspiracy texts, especially those appearing within the political mainstream. But for the most part, these critics have not identified and developed alternative interpretive strategies that might help to explain why some conspiracy theories have been more popular than others. Creps tentatively gestures in this direction; Zarefsky provides only a few characteristic argument strategies; and Goldberg shows little or no interest in rhetorical strategies and textual criticism. As such, while the paranoid style provides a hermeneutically productive category for interpreting fringe texts, we are left with a dearth of interpretive strategies for considering conspiracy discourse as it appears in the mainstream of political life. Put another way, we have some idea of how paranoid conspiracy theories reproduce at the fringe of society, but we know very little about the reproductive strategies of the much more virulent strains of conspiracy theory that occasionally break out into the political mainstream.

This study draws upon the rhetorical sensitivity to audience, situation, and text as a means to more systematically understand mainstream conspiracy discourse and is organized around two questions. The first question asks does "place" at the center or fringe of mainstream political institutions, ideologies, and audiences condition conspiracy texts in significant ways? If the paranoid style category was developed on the basis of the study of the rhetoric of fringe groups, what might we find if we study that conspiracy discourse appearing at the center of public discourse? This latter formulation of the question entails both a critical and productive stance. It involves questioning the appropriateness of the paranoid style paradigm to mainstream conspiracy discourse and points to the possibility of a new way to "map" instances of conspiracy discourse according to their location in relation to dominant political institutions and ideologies. This study also has as its goal the close reading and the thick description of rhetorical texts within their political, ideological, and intertextual contexts. Therefore, the second question asks, what rhetorical processes best characterize conspiracy discourse appearing at the center of the political mainstream? Developing interpretive strategies that unpack these rhetorical processes, of course, also provides insight into how they spread. These conspiracy theories, in other words, replicate themselves precisely by way of the very poetic and logical operations with which critics are concerned. One seeking to understand why conspiracy theories occasionally capture the political mainstream is well advised to look beyond the circumstantial explanations of Hofstadter and Davis (having to do with rapid social change and ethnic conflict) and toward the rhetorical dimension of the most successful conspiracy theories and conspiracy texts.[20]

Implicit in this study's design is the assumption that conspiracy discourse generally, and the slave power conspiracy in particular, is properly divided into at least two distinct categories, each with its own unique characteristics. This assumption can be effectively grounded by "mapping" the contours of the slave power conspiracy formation. But the map developed here employs a different cartographic metaphor than did Goldberg. Goldberg focused on the coordinates "nucleus" and "periphery" within the discursive formation generated against a given conspiratorial enemy, in which the "nucleus" corresponds to the most extreme rhetors and the "periphery" to their more mainstream counterparts. One imagines such a discursive formation or body of conspiracy texts as a sphere or globe in which proximity to the nucleus corresponds to an extreme of belief or action among advocates. This study's map aims to grasp a similar kind of spectrum of conspiracy discourse, but its coordinates and guiding metaphor are distinct from Goldberg's. For the purposes of this study, conspiracy discourse will be mapped according to its place—its origin within society and location within the larger system of political discourse. As such, this study recognizes that persons representing the most committed "core" of believers are actually most likely to exist on the fringes or margins of society. By contrast, Goldberg's "periphery" of believers is most likely to correspond to the "center" of society, political life, and institutions. This distinction will become evident as the next section fleshes out the basic coordinates of fringe and center in terms of the antislavery controversy of the 1830s, 1840s, and 1850s, and considers the persuasive strategies that animated some of the most successful slave power conspiracy texts.

Mapping the Slave Power Conspiracy

Allegations populating antebellum political discourse of a slave power conspiracy were many and varied, but it is possible to produce a basic map of this discursive formation, a map that will enable a better understanding of the diversity and complexity of slave power conspiracy discourse and also assist in the generation of contextually sensitive strategies for interpreting conspiracy texts as they appear in the political mainstream. Fortunately, it is not necessary to begin from scratch. The work of David Brion Davis— both in terms of conspiracy discourse generally and the slave power conspiracy in particular—serves as an essential starting point in the present cartographic enterprise. Davis's collection of conspiracy texts and critical commentary, *The Fear of Conspiracy: Images of Un-American Subversion from the Revolution to the Present,* illustrates a more complicated understanding of the context of conspiracy discourse than that shown by the paranoid style. Not only anti-Communists, anti-Masons, and Know-Nothings but more familiar characters closer to the center of the American political tradition—for example, George Washington, Fisher Ames, and Charles Sumner—make this collection of conspiracy texts. Corresponding to this widening of the selection of texts examined is a more complex picture of the producers and consumers of conspiracy discourse. The "inflamed minds" assuming a "messianic role" and the defenders of "traditional values of class structure"—the key constituencies to the paranoid style and literature of countersubversion—continue to play a central role. But different types of conspiracy rhetors appear. Now "political or religious leaders who . . . adopt conspiracy rhetoric largely as a tactical weapon" and those who see "conspiracy as the most reasonable explanation for a progression of facts and events" are included along with the fanatics, crackpots, and reactionaries of the paranoid style. That Davis's later work on conspiracy is beginning to transcend the confines of Hofstadter's paradigm is evident in his attempt at ranking "movements of countersubversion on a scale of relative realism and fantasy" and his observation that "abolitionists . . . had some empirical basis for their perception of a Slave Power." While abolitionists had some foundation for their fears of a slave power conspiracy, however, the more successful version of this conspiracy theory presented by Republicans is said to have been "toned down" relative to those of radical abolitionists.[21]

Davis's *The Slave Power Conspiracy and the Paranoid Style*, despite its incorporation of Hofstadter's category into its title, also exhibits a somewhat more complex understanding of the contexts of conspiracy discourse. Perhaps part of the explanation for this enhanced contextual sensitivity is that Davis here, for the first time, narrows his corpus to discourse directed against a particular conspiratorial enemy rather than considering scores of texts that are separated by decades or centuries and produced in opposition to very different conspiratorial enemies. In any event, Davis's work on the slave power conspiracy makes a general point that, while underdeveloped and still relatively insensitive to both historical context and discursive form, nevertheless anticipates this study's basic coordinates of "fringe" and "center" in his distinction between extreme and moderate visions of the slave power conspiracy. This distinction is developed early in the first chapter, where Davis considers the conspiracy theory of John Smith Dye, whose 1866 book, *History of the Plots and Crimes of the Great Conspiracy to Overthrow Liberty in America,* is said to represent an instance of "patently abnormal fantasy." Dye's account of the slave power is a story of political assassination that commenced as early as the presidency of Andrew Jackson. Jackson's defiance of Vice President John C. Calhoun is said to have resulted in an assassination attempt that Jackson narrowly escaped. Later presidents who had the temerity to oppose the slave power's designs were not so fortunate. In Dye's account, Presidents William Henry Harrison and John Tyler are said to have been poisoned by agents of the slave power (Harrison for opposing the annexation of Texas and Tyler for opposing slavery in California), and even President James Buchanan's acute illness of 1857 (which, Dye suggests, was also the result of poison) is said to have intimidated him into support for the policies of the slave power. Only those presidents wholly subservient to the slave power—Millard Fillmore and Franklin Pierce—are said to have completed their terms entirely unscathed. Dye clearly falls within the purview of the paranoid style, but what is most interesting for the purposes of my cartographic goal is the contrast Davis establishes between Dye's 1866 vision of the slave power and that of previous antislavery politicians:

We need not dwell on the obviously paranoid qualities of Dye's history of assassination. . . . The important point is that Dye simply fitted more details of personal evil into an explanatory framework that had been popularized by men like William H. Seward, Charles Sumner, and even Lincoln himself. The book can be read as an explicit dramatization of the fairly conventional charge that the Slave Power . . . had slowly poisoned the wellsprings of American life.[22]

To Davis, then, the conspiracy texts of politicians like Lincoln were relatively moderate within the scale of paranoia with which Davis maps the "explanatory framework" common to the slave power conspiracy formation. Despite this nascent sensitivity to the contours of slave power conspiracy discourse, Davis nonetheless makes a number of unproductive overgeneralizations.

For one thing, Davis's continued allegiance to the assumptions of Hofstadter's approach may have hampered his ability to make meaningful distinctions among slave power texts and rhetors. He does not consider the possibility that the slave power conspiracy discourses of paranoid extremists and political moderates represent very different "explanatory frameworks" that are appropriately considered within entirely separate categories. Such an oversight, perhaps, is inevitable when one not interested in unearthing the intricacies of textual form is working on the scale of the discursive formation. While Davis ought not to be criticized for choosing to consider the general "explanatory framework" common to slave power conspiracy texts, it may be said that Davis's account is, on the whole, insensitive to differences among the wide variety of slave power conspiracy rhetors and texts. His approach continues to suggest that we ought to consider the conspiracy discourse of radical abolitionists on the political fringe and that of mainstream politicians seeking to build a national political consensus within the same paranoid style category.

Moreover, Davis exhibits little concern for the particularities of context and the political situatedness of slave power texts. Although his study is narrowly focused on allegations of a slave power conspiracy, his corpus ranges widely from as early as the 1830s to as late as the 1870s, and he fails to make potentially meaningful historical and political distinctions within this period. Consideration of such a broad sweep of history makes it difficult to understand how rhetorical efforts against the slave power engaged particular political situations and audiences. Indeed, the major events shaping the political landscape between 1830 and 1870 readily suggest at least three distinct phases of slave power conspiracy rhetoric. From the 1830s until the Civil War, efforts against the slave power seem to have been the work of abolitionists and antislavery politicians who sought to encourage opposition to the ascendant slave power. During the Civil War, rhetorical texts against the slave power might best be read as wartime propaganda. Finally, following the Civil War, slave power texts were likely closely related to the politics of Reconstruction—serving either to exonerate the North or the average Southerner for war guilt (by narrowly scapegoating the slave power) or to justify vigorous intervention in the South (to destroy the last vestiges of the slave power). Given the vast differences among the political situations, purposes, and audiences conditioning slave power conspiracy discourse during these periods, comparing Lincoln's efforts of the 1850s to Dye's 1866 history of assassinations may be a relatively meaningless endeavor. In order to account for this potential criticism and to ensure that the texts operated within comparable historical contexts, this study will focus on the period from 1830 to 1860 (a time frame commencing with the rise of abolitionist agitation) and especially on the period between 1854 and 1860 (a time frame corresponding to Republican origins and victory).

But discussions of the slave power and the slave power conspiracy began much earlier than 1830, and it is important to recognize this historical backdrop to the present study. Leonard Richards's *The Slave Power: The Free North and Southern Domination, 1780–1860* tells the long story of how the three-fifths clause of the Constitution—which allowed slave states to claim three-fifths of their slave population for the purposes of representation—both empowered slaveholders and created apprehensions of a slave power. Richards introduces his study with precisely the rhetors with whom this study will be concerned—the likes of Abraham Lincoln, Charles Sumner, and other Republicans who helped to arouse Northern fears of a slave power conspiracy. He, too, follows Davis in noting the extent to which charges of a slave power conspiracy were articulated both by prominent politicians and the "lunatic fringe." But his story quickly turns back to the constitutional debates and opposition to the three-fifths clause from principled opponents of slavery as well as Northern aristocrats jealous of growing Southern power. At the constitutional convention, Governeur Morris was the staunchest opponent of the three-fifths clause, and as the new republic grew, many New England Federalists, frustrated with their defeats at the hands of Southern Republicans, would explain their failure in terms of the three-fifths clause and the disproportionate power it granted to Southerners. As he returns to the nineteenth century, Richards's analysis suggests that a number of victories—most notably the Missouri Compromise of 1820—were carried on the basis of a combination of Southern unanimity, the three-fifths clause, and the ability of Southerners to secure the support of sufficient Northerners to carry the day.[23]

Whatever Richards's conclusions about the existence and exploits of the slave power, it is clear that a great number of reformers and politicians in the antebellum North were convinced of the presence of this conspiracy. But these rhetors ought not to be lumped into a single category. Instead, this study aims first to "map" the slave power conspiracy formation against the poles of "fringe" and "center" both as a means to highlight the variety of slave power conspiracy discourse and to develop interpretive strategies to unearth the rhetorical processes that enabled this conspiratorial inter-pretation to thrive at the center of political life, institutions, and ideologies. "Place," for the purposes of this study, corresponds to the social, political, and ideological sites from which slave power discourse was generated, and it is conceptualized in terms of the poles "fringe" and "center." The study understands the "fringe" in much the same way as does Hofstadter, as indi-cating a distance from mainstream social and political life. Persons and groups on the fringe may be said to be on the periphery of social and polit-ical institutions but also on the periphery of the ideas and way of life of the larger community.[24] As such, this locus may indicate ideological rather than sociopolitical marginalization, although the two are undoubtedly re-lated. Persons and groups may find themselves isolated from society pre-cisely because of the ideas they hold (for instance, abolitionists were systematically excluded from political discussions), or they may develop ideas not widely held by the populace due to prior exclusion from main-stream social and political institutions (as is the case with excluded subal-tern groups whose exclusion itself encourages the development of ideological structures distinct from those of the larger society). Correspond-ingly, the "center" may be defined in its opposition to the fringe. To occupy the center of social and political institutions is to participate in and control such institutions, while to be at the center of a community's ideologies means that one embraces the ideas and attitudes that form the basic ideo-logical consensus of a given society. In some respects, then, "place" is a nu-merical indicator. To be on the fringe means to think, live, or act differently than the majority of persons in society, while to be in the center indicates a concord with the majority on these terms at a given time. These poles of fringe and center, of course, are imprecise—representing constructs or ideal types rather than indicating actual empirical correspondence with a given community. With these clarifications in mind, it is appropriate to commence the consideration of the first pole of slave power conspiracy discourse.

Conspiracy Discourse at the Fringe:
William Lloyd Garrison and the Paranoid Style

While it is inappropriate to apply Hofstadter's paranoid style category to all instances of conspiracy discourse, this is not to suggest that Hofstadter's category is never appropriate. On the contrary, the paranoid style seems to remain the best approach for understanding slave power rhetoric on the fringe. After all, Hofstadter's category was developed based almost exclusively on the study of the writings of fringe movements, and the antislavery movement certainly had its fringe. It is predictable, perhaps, that one would choose William Lloyd Garrison and his American Anti-Slavery Society (AASS) as the representatives of the fringe of the antislavery movement. Scholars have long recognized that the extremism of Garrison and his group alienated them from mainstream political audiences, audiences that were later swayed by more politically minded antislavery politicians.[25]

The AASS was preceded by the relatively moderate American Colonization Society, an organization whose goal was to emancipate slaves gradually, and whose membership included a number of slaveholders. The ACS recognized the legitimacy of slavery in its insistence that slaveholders be compensated. Its position that freed slaves must be carried away from the United States to distant locales was consistent with the period's prevailing prejudices regarding the racial inferiority of African Americans. Garrison's abolition movement stood in stark contrast to the principles and policies of the ACS. Beginning in 1831 with the publication of Garrison's *Liberator* and continuing in 1833 with the foundation of the AASS, radical abolitionists advocated immediate emancipation without compensation, sought the full equality of African Americans, and took an uncompromising tone in their denunciations of the evil of the institution of slavery. The AASS hoped to eliminate slavery by a strategy of moral suasion in which they sought to convince Americans—slaveholders and nonslaveholders alike—of the moral bankruptcy of the practice and the need for its abolition. In the decades that followed, Garrison and the AASS pursued their goal by way of the press (especially the *Liberator*), pamphlets, and speaking tours; while they were not successful in persuading large numbers of people, their efforts earned the ire of slaveholders and others convinced of the legitimacy of the institution. As early as the 1830s, angry allies of slavery

both inside and outside the government took a number of steps—the refusal of the abolition petitions, refusal to carry abolition materials through
the U.S. mail, and even the organization of mobs to assault abolitionist
speakers—to silence Garrison and the AASS.[26]

Given the place of the AASS on the fringes of the larger antislavery
movement, this section will use the rhetorical texts of Garrison and the
AASS as a means to flesh out one pole of this study's map of slave power
conspiracy discourse. But it is difficult to characterize a movement so diverse and with such a long history. Several different kinds of rhetorical
texts will serve as evidence. Foremost are the works of William Lloyd Garrison, whose lengthy career in opposition to the slave power can be traced
in an 1852 collection of his writings. While Garrison may be said to function as a kind of "ideal type" representative of the radical extreme of antislavery, his example is perhaps not a sufficient basis for generalization
about the entire abolition movement. Therefore the study will also consider a number of other sources. The speeches of abolitionist Wendell
Phillips will provide an additional portrait of the radical abolitionist vision
of the slave power, one consistent with Garrison's in most respects. In
order to provide as broad a selection as possible of abolitionist thought, the
study also relies upon the 1853 *Proceedings of the AASS*. This document indicates the extent of agreement between Garrison and the larger movement
as well as the continuity of the abolitionist vision of the slave power over
a period of decades. It also confirms the character of the slave power at
the fringe on the eve of the period with which this study is primarily
concerned—1854–60.

Garrison's writings illustrate his vision of the slave power on three basic
levels: the general nature and scope of the slave power, his narrative of the
slave power, and the disposition he hoped to cultivate among readers and
auditors. Garrison left little doubt that he considered the slave power to be
all-powerful: "We are under the absolute dominion of the Slave Power—a
Power, which, like the grave, is never satisfied—and, like the horse leech,
is ever crying, 'Give! Give!' It is ruling us with a rod of iron; and it is constantly lengthening its cords and strengthening its stakes." Not only was
the slave power all-powerful, its influence throughout American society
was pervasive, "entwined around the civil, social, and pecuniary interests
of the republic . . . religious sects and political parties are banded together
for its safety from internal revolt and external opposition . . . the people,
awed by its power and corrupted by its influence, are basely bending their
knees at its footstool." The slave power's control of political and religious

institutions, in particular, meant that its rule was perpetuated by both the "profligate demagogues" of the major political parties and the "designing priests" of the mainline denominations. Control of religious and political leaders provided the slave power with a powerful propaganda machine capable of deflecting attention away from the evil of slavery and justifying efforts to expand the peculiar institution.[27]

But control of mainstream political and religious institutions was not enough. In addition to a vast propaganda machine capable of swaying public opinion, Garrison's slave power also controlled the legal and political apparatus, which enabled it to stifle any dissenting opinions. Garrison cites the litany of measures directed against the abolitionists by national and state government, and by slave power organized mobs:

> We are denied the right of locomotion, freedom of speech, right of petition, the liberty of the press, the right to peaceably assemble together . . . in fifteen states of the Union. If we venture South . . . we do so at the peril of our lives. If we would escape torture and death, on visiting any of the Slave states, we must stifle our conscientious convictions . . . and do homage to the slave-holding power—or run the risk of a cruel martyrdom! These are appalling and undeniable facts.[28]

In terms of the character and scope of the conspiracy, Garrison's slave power rhetoric is in accord with the paranoid style.

Garrison was not alone in considering the slave power in this manner. Other abolitionists echoed his imagery of sinister evil and tremendous power. Several speakers at the 1853 AASS convention expressed the evil of the slave power in terms of demonic imagery. Joseph Barker warned that all ought to be "on their guard against the infinite wiles by which emissaries of the Slave Power will seek to entrap their comparatively unthinking and unprepared souls." Charles Burleigh echoed these sentiments, portraying the slave power's oppressive system as "the most detestable system of villainy that ever yet emerged from the bottomless pit of perdition, to find a dwelling-place on God's green earth," and alluding to the character of slaveholders in terms of "the avarice of Mammon, and the lust of Belial, and the blood-thirstiness of Moloch." Wendell Phillips characterized the slave power as representing "[one] hundred thousand sagacious, intelligent men, with two thousand millions of dollars" and insisted that this immense wealth made "such a power . . . almost omnipotent." Phillips spoke not only of the power of slaveholders, however, but resorted to serpent imagery to describe the slave power as a force coiled around the

Constitution itself. Many speakers at the 1853 AASS convention also con-
curred as to the immense control the slave power had achieved over the
government and public opinion, and they did so with the lurid and exaggerated imagery we have come to expect from the paranoid style. Joseph
Barker spoke of the political influence of the slave power as "one mass of
moral putridity" that was generating "a malaria sufficient to spread over
the whole land" and of the absolute control that the slave power had
achieved over both political parties as well as the national government.
The result, according to Henry White, was detestable: "I maintain that
there is not, on this globe, a government so steeped in blood, so unjust, so
horribly tyrannical, so destitute of mercy, so utterly malignant, as the government of the United States." But as in Garrison's account, it was not just
the slave powers' control over political institutions that enthroned the
slave power but its mastery over public opinion North as well as South.
This mastery was achieved, according to a number of AASS speakers, by a
total control of the instruments of socialization—church and state, schools
and colleges, and even literature.[29] In sum, Garrison's texts, as well as
those of his fellow abolitionists, reveal a slave power conspiracy that fits
comfortably within the paranoid style category. To use Hofstadter's words,
abolitionists' "central image is that of a vast and sinister conspiracy, a gigantic and yet subtle machinery of influence set in motion to undermine
and destroy a way of life."[30] Not only is the conspiracy portrayed as excep-
tionally powerful and the conspiratorial enemy as exceedingly evil, but we
also find the exaggerated and lurid imagery that the paranoid style suggests
will characterize representations of the conspiratorial enemy.

The abolitionists' slave power conspiracy theory was similar to most
other conspiracy theories in that it relied upon historical narratives in
order to illustrate the presence and influence of the malign conspiracy. Indeed, a wide spectrum of critics, operating from within and without the
paranoid style paradigm, have attested to the importance of narrative to
understanding conspiracy discourse generally. In particular, Zarefsky has
noted the essential role of narrative in the mainstreamed slave power conspiracy arguments of the Lincoln-Douglas debates: "[these conspiracy argu-
ments] tell a story that is vivid and plausible. Even though there are
lacunae in the supporting acts and documents, these are woven together
into a believable narrative. Conspiracy arguments depend on the inventional genius of the arguer in perceiving patterns of experience." As this
study will illustrate, in the case of most efforts against the slave power, the
conspiracy is identified by the mark it left on American political history. To

establish the existence of that which was secret, rhetors needed only to point toward what they believed to be the increasingly proslavery policies of the government. In this respect, historical narratives were one of the primary means by which rhetors were able to make the existence of a slave power conspiracy seem plausible to readers and audiences.[31]

All narratives consist largely of events, and Garrison's narratives of conspiracy are no exception. Within a given story, of course, some events are more important than others, a concept clarified in Roland Barthes's structural approach to narrative. For Barthes, the moments of choice in a story that "inseminate the narrative with an element that will later come to maturity" are known as "cardinal functions."[32] Within the historical narratives with which this study is concerned, the cardinal functions will correspond to the prominent slavery controversies and other important events in American political history—the Revolution, the Constitution, the Missouri Compromise, Texas annexation, the Nebraska bill, bleeding Kansas, Dred Scott, etc. Within many slave power conspiracy narratives, each of these events constitutes a moment in the consolidation and growth of the slave power. But in most narratives of conspiracy, one particular event will serve as the key cardinal function of the conspiracy narrative— the point at which the slave power initially gained ascendancy and was able to fully control subsequent events.

The first cardinal function in Garrison's narrative of U.S. political history is the Revolution, which appears as an important precursor to the slave power's domination. But the Constitution was the key cardinal function of the conspiracy narrative. Garrison describes the Constitution as "a covenant with death, and an agreement with hell," that, far from being antislavery, has "consigned to chains and infamy an inoffensive and helpless race," and he points out that measures "related to the prosecution of the foreign slave trade for twenty years, to the allowance of a slave representation in Congress, to the hunting of fugitive slaves, and to the suppression of domestic insurrections" were "for the special benefit of the slave States."[33] Criticizing political antislavery men who sought to use the Constitution against slavery, Garrison insists that American homage to its past has been merely a cloak for complicity in the slave power conspiracy, and he states:

> Let us confess the sin of our fathers, and our own sin as a people, in conspiring for the degradation and enslavement of the colored race among us. Let us be honest with the facts of history, and acknowledge the compromises that were made to secure the adoption of the Constitution, and the consequent establishment of the Union.[34]

As the key cardinal function of conspiracy within Garrison's narrative, the Constitution was productive of other cardinal functions of conspiracy—that is, policies and programs designed to serve the interests of slavery and the slave power:

> For more than two centuries, slavery has polluted the American soil. It has grown with the growth and strengthened with the strength of the republic. . . . From the adoption of the American Constitution, it has declared war and peace, instituted and destroyed national banks and tariffs, controlled the army and navy, prescribed the policy of government, ruled both houses of Congress, occupied the Presidential chair, governed the political parties, distributed offices of trust and emolument among its worshippers, fettered Northern industry and enterprise, and trampled liberty of speech and conscience in the dust.[35]

Again, Garrison's narrative of American political history is consistent with Hofstadter's paranoid style, in which a "'vast' or 'gigantic' conspiracy" is "the motive force in historical events," and "[h]istory is conspiracy, set in motion by demonic forces of almost transcendental power."[36]

The structural approach to narrative has the advantage both of describing Garrison's narrative of conspiracy and enabling formal comparison with the slave power narratives of later Republican politicians; but narratives can also be described productively in terms of "plot" as well as structure. The concept of emplotment itself has a long history, but this study follows the work of Hayden White, whose *Metahistory: The Historical Imagination in Nineteenth-Century Europe* suggests that a narrative's mode of emplotment—be it romantic, comic, tragic, or satirical—encompasses the "'meaning' of a story by identifying what kind of a story that it is."[37] This study will be concerned especially with the comic and tragic modes of emplotment. Both of these plot types have long and complex conceptual pedigrees, but for present purposes it will suffice to indicate the driving force and mode of resolution for each. Comic plots are driven by misunderstanding and error and are resolved when participants learn the truth and overcome their misperceptions. Insofar as this progression holds out hope for human improvement, comic plots are relatively optimistic. Tragic plots, on the other hand, are driven by a tragic flaw or condition and are resolved in a climactic tragic event that leaves little room for optimism regarding human agency. Given that Garrison's narrative of political history is driven by the slaveholding character of the Constitution and proceeds along an increasingly pessimistic trajectory emphasizing the apparently unassailable dominance of the slave power, Garrison's narrative of political history is best described as tragic.

Explanation by emplotment is usually considered a means to describe a narrative's formal characteristics within a text, but some scholars conceptualize emplotment in terms of the possibilities a given plot offers for audience enactment. Lucaites and Condit express this notion in their "functional" approach to narrative. Within this scheme, rhetorical narratives are functional in the sense that their ultimate goal is persuasion and the wielding of power. Insofar as rhetorical narratives function to move audiences to certain types of actions, then "the rhetorical narrative is functionally constrained to stop short of the formal stage of plot 'resolution' by virtue of its purpose to encourage audience enactment. This may even be to say that there really is no 'plot,' in any traditional sense, in a rhetorical narrative."[38] The nexus between plot and audience enactment is also explored by Stephen O'Leary. O'Leary's study of apocalyptic rhetoric finds that the form of emplotment significantly conditions the possibilities of audience action. Comic emplotments (or frames) construct a flawed world, but one in which human action and human agency are capable of making a difference, and comic narratives encourage action in this respect. Tragic emplotments (or frames), on the other hand, present a world driven by forces or conditions against which human action is capable of achieving little, correspondingly discouraging action.[39] This relationship between narrative emplotment and the possibilities for action are of profound importance for understanding the kind of actions associated with Garrison's efforts against the slave power conspiracy. Paradoxically, the tragic character of Garrison's narrative encouraged two apparently contradictory yet related avenues for action against the slave power: the first, an apocalyptic crusade; the second, withdrawal.

Hofstadter observed that "a fundamental paradox of the paranoid style is the imitation of the enemy." The only way to defeat a conspiracy is to adopt its strategies and tactics.[40] This observation suggests what may be an important characteristic of conspiracy rhetoric—the proportionality of the response. If the conspiracy is weak and banal, simple measures are sufficient to address it. But when the conspiracy assumes the monstrous proportions of Garrison's slave power conspiracy, the reaction must be equally comprehensive. Garrison's slave power rhetoric may be said to illustrate this principle of proportionality, for he suggests that the opponents of slavery and the slave power ought to engage in an all-out crusade against slavery. Garrison writes: "Put on the whole armor of God; so shall you be invulnerable and invincible; so shall no weapon against you prosper. The war admits of no parley. No flag of truce will be sent by or received by you. . . . As Samuel hewed Agog in pieces, so, with the battle-axe of Truth, you must cleave Slavery to the ground, and give its carcass to the fowls of the air." In order to defeat the slave power, Garrison was willing to pay a huge price:

> Slavery must be overthrown. . . . No matter, though, to effect it, every party should be torn by dissensions, every sect dashed into fragments, the national compact dissolved, the land filled with the horrors of a civil and a servile war—still, slavery must be buried in the grave of infamy, beyond the possibility of a resurrection. . . . let the State perish. . . . let the Church fall. . . . let the American Union be consumed by a living thunderbolt. . . . let the Republic sink beneath the waves of oblivion. . . . Against this declaration, none but traitors and tyrants will raise an outcry. It is the mandate of Heaven, and the voice of God.[41]

Speaking with such divine sanction, Garrison asks his followers to fight the slave power—to prevent its continued "kindling [of] the flames of hell throughout our borders." Other abolitionists also spoke in terms of a holy war against slavery and the extent to which such action had divine sanction. Charles Burleigh insisted that an abolitionist "is worshipping God in every act which he does to promote this cause. He is giving expression to his love for justice, when he makes war against this iniquity of the Slave Power."[42] Once again, Garrison and his fellow abolitionists seem to fit precisely within the paranoid style. For them, "what is felt to be needed to defeat it is not the usual methods of political give and take, but an all out crusade. The paranoid spokesman sees the fate of this conspiracy in apocalyptic terms—he traffics in the birth and death of whole worlds, whole political orders, whole systems of human value."[43]

Garrison's all-out crusade was unlike what one might expect, however. It was distinguished, at least in the early stages of the movement, by its nonviolent character. For most of his abolitionist career, Garrison was an advocate of "nonresistance" and pacifism and an uncompromising opponent of violence. Some historians have questioned the veracity of Garrison's pacifism. He was, after all, on good terms with violent abolitionists, and as the above passages suggest, his call for a nonviolent crusade often was expressed in the figural language of violence, revolution, and upheaval. Whatever his actual position on the matter, by the 1850s many abolitionists had abandoned their faith in the efficacy of nonviolent means or at least had come to accept that violence might be necessary to eliminate slavery. Despite these defections, however, Garrison would not publicly approve of violent means until after John Brown's raid on Harper's Ferry.[44]

This shift from pacifism to violence in the abolition movement was associated with an increasingly tragic narrative of American history and an associated changing conception of the millennium and the eschatological significance of American history. Stephen O'Leary's study of millennialism among nineteenth-century reformers identifies two kinds of millennialism, each associated with a distinct plot type or frame. Postmillennial eschatology sees the present as a time in which the kingdom of God was being built on Earth to prepare for the second coming. Premillennial eschatology, on the other hand, assumed a perspective in which a final apocalyptic battle was to be preceded by a reign of the Antichrist on Earth. O'Leary finds that this premillennial perspective corresponds to a tragic frame, while the postmillennial corresponds to a comic frame.[45] According to O'Leary, the early stages of the abolition movement are characterized by a comic postmillennialism in which reformers made comic assumptions about evil in the world—in particular, that it was the result of error and therefore capable of elimination by the educative capacities of moral suasion. When these efforts met with years of stubborn opposition and suppression by the powerful political and economic interests supporting slavery, however, many within the movement came to adopt a tragic premillennial eschatology that viewed the slave power as an all-powerful evil that would grow unabated until the coming of the end times. Under this set of eschatological assumptions, moral suasion no longer seemed capable of ameliorating evil in the world, leading the AASS to abandon this strategy in favor of more radical solutions (even as the newly formed American and Foreign Anti-Slavery Society [AFASS] continued its comic efforts at moral suasion in the form of the Liberty Party).[46]

One expression of this radicalism was, by the 1850s, an increasing acceptance of violent solutions to ending slavery. As early as the 1853 AASS convention, Joseph Barker could freely express a cavalier agnosticism regarding the manner of slavery's demise: "our only choice is allowing it to be extinguished by the operation of public reprobation against it, or allowing it to be extinguished in blood. But, whether it expire in blood or in quietness and peace, our duty is clear, to labor for its speedy extinction." John Brown's series of murders in Kansas and his 1859 raid on Harper's Ferry eventually forced the larger movement to directly reconsider the role of violence in its crusade. Wendell Phillips's speech of November 1, 1859, "Harper's Ferry," identifies Brown as a modern-day "Cromwellian" and unashamedly credits him with having both "redeemed the long infamy of sixty years of subservience" and effected a fundamental transformation of the abolition movement: "I think the lesson of the hour is insurrection. Insurrection of thought always precedes insurrection of arms. The last twenty years have been an insurrection of thought. We seem to be entering on a new phase of this great American struggle." Phillips stops short of directly advocating violence, insisting on his preference for "types" over "bullets" as an instrument of struggle. This preference is qualified, however, by a preference for "rifles" over "fetters."[47] The relationship between tragic radicalism and violent means, of course, reflects a logic of proportionality—tragic narratives of all-powerful conspiracies represent threats whose magnitude requires recourse even to violence.

Other abolitionists, like Garrison, resisted such an escalation, opting instead to retreat temporarily in the face of a superior foe. Holding to his pacifism long after many other abolitionists, Garrison responded to the tragic logic of the premillennial eschatology with a call to drop out of a society thoroughly corrupted by slavery: "Let us, who profess to abhor slavery, and who claim to be freemen indeed, dissolve the bands that connect us with the Slave Power, religiously and politically." Tragic resignation to the reality that evil would continue to grow unabated until the time that God chose to intervene in the world and end it encouraged many antislavery reformers to withdraw from the corrupt and sinful public world of the Antichrist in order to await the end times for the resolution of the problem of evil. According to James Darsey, such a "withdrawal from contaminated institutions" not only allowed the maintenance of purity but also was a reaffirmation of group identity enabled by the logic of the slave power conspiracy: "The conspiracy theme . . . is a vehicle for signification. God, or some other absolute value standing in His place, is implied in the notion that there are ideals to which the conspiracy can be opposed." In sum, while the logic of the tragic narrative of the slave power could encourage a holy war or all-out crusade, it could also be considered in the terms of its epideictic function—encouraging withdrawal from society and a corresponding reaffirmation of group identity.[48]

That Garrison's tragic narratives of an American history driven wholly by the unstoppable slave power encouraged withdrawal from political and social life may help to illustrate why the paranoid style has largely been the strategy of those on the margins of politics and society. Mark Fenster provides a partial answer, suggesting that "conspiracy theory" is a "disabling" theory of power that tends to encourage adherents to amass evidence rather than build the movements and coalitions that make for effective political engagement. But the case of Garrison clearly illustrates that it is not simply the concern to amass evidence that makes the paranoid style an ineffective tool for political engagement. The paranoid style discourages political action, in part, because the tragic narratives characteristic of the paranoid style leave little room for conventional political remedies. Rather, tragic narratives of conspiracy seem to invite a pessimism encouraging desperate and apolitical forms of action such as violence (proportional to the vast scope and power of the conspiracy) or resigned inaction and withdrawal from political life. Equally important, the paranoid style's tendency toward totalizing conspiracies eliminates most potential political allies and coalition partners. Coalition partners, even if not active agents of the conspiracy, are likely compromised in some way. After all, within the paranoid perspective, the conspiracy is virtually everywhere—how could one trust outsiders enough to ally with them? For this reason, Garrison viewed the efforts of antislavery politicians as foolhardy and immoral. He knew they could succeed only if they were willing to accept coalition partners who were (in his mind) tainted by the odium of slavery.[49]

At this point it should be evident how consideration of Garrison's version of the slave power conspiracy—and of those of his fellow abolitionists—has contributed to this study's goals. First, Garrison's slave power conspiracy has provided an essential point on the map of slave power conspiracy discourse. Garrison represents the extreme abolition version of the slave power conspiracy—a version that seems to have much in common with the themes and images of Hofstadter's paranoid style. Garrison posited a vast and sinister slave power that had been the motive force in American history, and he advocated an all-out crusade—or withdrawal—as the appropriate response. But precisely because Garrison exemplifies the political fringe of the antislavery movement, he also provides one essential coordinate against which one might begin to think about the characteristics of the slave power conspiracy at the center of the political mainstream. For Garrison, the pervasive influence of the slave power in American history was indicated by his choice of the Constitution as the key cardinal function of his conspiracy narrative. One might expect that narratives of the slave power conspiracy at the center of the political mainstream would give it a more limited role—one that began more recently. One might expect later events—such as the Missouri Compromise of 1820, the gag rule and efforts against the abolition petitions in the late 1830s, the annexation of Texas in 1844, or the Kansas-Nebraska Act of

1854—to serve as the key cardinal functions conspiracy narratives at the center of the mainstream. In addition to these structural differences—though also corresponding to them—one might also expect slave power conspiracy narratives at the center of the mainstream to be emplotted comically rather than tragically. These comic emplotments, along with shorter conspiracy narratives, encourage more effectual efforts against the slave power.[50] Finally, a slave power conspiracy of more limited scope and duration might encourage opponents to be more willing to build the sort of coalitions that make for effective political engagement. A less pervasive slave power means that there are more potential allies to enlist against it.

Conspiracy Discourse at the Center:
Antislavery Politicians

That the slave power conspiracy would become a prominent theme or claim at the center of American institutions and ideologies (firmly within the political mainstream) is widely acknowledged. As Eric Foner has noted, the slave power conspiracy was a primary component of antebellum Republican Party ideology, and within the logic of this party ideology, the existence of the conspiracy was used to show the necessity of political organization and action. Unlike the politically ineffectual paranoid style, Republican conspiratorial interpretations were instrumental in building the political coalitions and constituencies necessary for the emerging party. Given these readily apparent differences, a few scholars—especially Creps and Zarefsky—have suggested the possibility that such "mainstream" conspiracy rhetoric is distinguishable from the paranoid style.[51]

Since radical abolitionists were consigned to the fringe, the goal of considering slave power conspiracy rhetoric in the political mainstream or center of political discourse will favor consideration of antislavery politicians. Abolitionists took the moral high ground—emphasizing the suffering of slaves, the need for total and immediate emancipation, and the equality of African Americans—and practiced a relatively "pure" rhetoric that played a role in consigning them to the fringe of society and politics. Antislavery politicians, on the other hand, were more pragmatic. This pragmatic orientation encouraged them to aim at the more limited goal of preventing slavery's expansion and to emphasize the threat posed by the slave power to Northern whites rather than the plight of slaves. Because they sought relatively practical goals—electoral victory and influence over government policy—their rhetoric aimed not at reforming their audiences but accommodating their beliefs and prejudices.[52] In this respect, it was politicians, not abolitionists, whose rhetorical efforts were conditioned by the need to occupy the center of American political institutions and ideologies.

As Richards's account has indicated, fears of the slave power had populated American political discourse since the time of the Constitution, but politicians began engaging in slave power conspiracy rhetoric in earnest as early as the 1830s, as fear of the rising abolition movement encouraged Southerners and their allies to take steps—like the gag rule and refusal of abolition petitions—to prevent continued agitation. But these steps to restrain radical abolitionists encouraged a number of politicians to suspect larger conspiratorial designs. In the U.S. Senate, Thomas Morris of Ohio was one of the first Democrats to claim that a slave power threatened American institutions. Morris claimed that Congress's refusal to consider citizens' petitions was "something new . . . one of the devices of the slave power." This new power was said to have forged an alliance with the Democrats' old enemy: "the slave power of the South and banking power of the North . . . are now uniting to rule this country. The cotton bale and bank note have formed an alliance. . . . both looking to the same object— to live on the unrequited labor of others." This alliance of aristocrats, motivated by "love of gain and arbitrary power," allegedly sought to reduce Northern laborers to the status of slaves by making each of their representatives a "slave to party." In revealing this alliance, Morris did not seek to destroy the Democrats. Rather, he proposed the present as the time for Democrats to eliminate the conspiracy before it was too late: "the slave power and the bank power are thus to unite in order to break down the present Administration. . . . The aristocracy of the North, who, by the power of a corrupt banking system, and the aristocracy of the South, by the power of the slave system, both fattening on the labor of others, are now about to unite in order to make the reign of each perpetual."[53] According to Morris, timely action could still prevent the ascendance of the slave power.

In the House of Representatives, John Quincy Adams provided one of the earliest expressions of a slave power conspiracy position in Whig terms. Responding to the same abolition petition controversy that had inflamed Morris, Adams portrayed the measure as one part of a "system of oppression" designed to silence opposition to the slave power and conceal its plot to add Texas to the Union. Slaveholders, Adams insisted, had utilized the "submissive *party discipline* of the North" in order to suppress abolition petitions. In addition, slaveholders had sought to suppress the resolutions of Northern state legislatures against Texas annexation—a measure designed to "strengthen the slave-holding interest and perpetuate the *blessing* of the 'peculiar institution.'" In sum, Adams sought to reveal the "torturous and double-dealing system of measures and policy, to fortify, sustain, and perpetuate the institution of slavery and the ascendancy of the slaveholding interest over that of freedom in this Union" in order that timely political action might prevent the consummation of the slave power conspiracy's latest plot.[54]

Several years later the Texas annexation controversy inspired further denunciations of the slave power by a few Democrats and a growing number of Whigs. According to Democrat Thomas Hart Benton, the timing of the proposal to annex Texas was part of a plot to foil Martin Van Buren's nomination for president and consolidate Southern control of the Democratic Party. Benton claimed that President Tyler, Texas leaders, and corrupt politicians had conspired not only to bring another slave state (or states) into the Union but also had timed the proposal precisely to upset Van Buren's nomination at the Baltimore convention. In the next session some Northern Democrats, incensed by the Southern defeat of Van Buren at the Baltimore convention, continued to oppose annexation on the grounds that it was part of a Southern plot to expand slavery and therefore Southerners' political power. Jacob Brinkerhoff of Ohio insisted that annexation was a "southern question. . . . with a direct view to strengthen her institutions, increase her power, extend her influence, and swell her aggrandizement." Brinkerhoff complained of the increasing marginalization of Northern Democrats within the party, indicating that Southerners thought "some of us [Northern Democrats] might have . . . been wanting in the due degree of servility, had we not been recalled by the sound of the lash! Some of us might have forgotten the late sacrifice of one of the wisest and purest of republican statesmen, and been wanting in the requisite tameness." A handful of other Northern Democrats made similar arguments—condemning annexation as part of a slave power conspiracy to consolidate Southern control of the Democratic Party and the national government.[55]

While Democratic opponents of annexation were a small minority within their party, many more Whigs—especially those from the North—denounced Texas annexation as part of a slave power conspiracy. In 1844 Joshua Giddings of Ohio denounced the move as motivated by a desire on the part of Southerners to "extend and perpetuate slavery" and by way of the three-fifths clause of the Constitution to expand Southern power in the national government. In the next session, when the defeated annexation treaty was reintroduced as a bill, Giddings portrayed annexation as another in a long line of government actions designed to expand and protect slavery. Giddings condemned the slaveholders who had "for twenty-five years perverted the powers of the government to the unconditional support of slavery, and held almost the entire North in servile silence in regard to their own rights in respect to that institution" and hoped that "the practice of cowardly cringing before the supercilious frown of southern taskmasters, is not much longer to characterize the course of Northern representatives on this floor." Other Whigs, such as Jacob Miller, pointed to the vast array of influences in favor of annexation. The president, president-elect, cabinet, land-jobbers, politicians, and even Andrew Jackson himself favored the measure. Assisting this combination for annexation was their total control of executive patronage and their ability to manipulate public opinion through party presses. Miller also portrayed Texas annexation as but the first step toward a further expansion of slavery: "Our slaves, I have no doubt, will pass into Mexico as they have passed into Texas; but they will go in company with their masters, the Anglo-American race, forming new slave States, hereafter to be admitted into the Union under the precedent we are now about to establish." Still other Whigs pointed out that the proposal to annex Texas only confirmed John Quincy Adams's earlier predictions regarding a Andrew Jackson–Samuel Houston conspiracy.[56]

In the 1830s and 1840s the need of the major parties to retain the transsectional character of their organizations made the slavery issue one to be avoided. Correspondingly, those politicians expressing strong antislavery views were suspect.[57] For this reason, politicians like Morris, Adams, Giddings, and Brinkerhoff—though much closer to the center of American political institutions and ideologies than the likes of Garrison—remained somewhat marginalized from the mainstream of their parties. Nevertheless, these early political efforts against the slave power provide important insights into the kinds of contexts and interpretive strategies that are most appropriate to reading the texts generated at the center of the antislavery movement. Indeed, these cases suggest at least three substantial differences between abolitionists at the fringe and more mainstream politicians, differences that further flesh out the other pole of the study's map and hence provide guidance in the task of interpreting the texts of Chase, Sumner, and Lincoln.

Traditional Conspiratorial Enemies: Aristocrats and Demagogues

One characteristic distinguishing the conspirators inhabiting Whig and Democratic narratives is their banality. Far from the demonic and all-powerful shapers of American political history within the paranoid style, they were but a recently empowered political faction motivated solely by desire for power and enabled by conventional political means. This difference in the character of the conspiratorial enemy reflects a fundamental distinction between the fringe and the center on the level of intertextuality. From an intertextual perspective, "the context of a text comes from, or is constructed from, other texts. . . . Intertextuality can refer to one text drawing upon one or more other texts as pre-text(s), or it can show how one text is referred to by others as their pre-text." This approach has the advantage of recognizing the text as always in dialogue with other texts (or authors with other authors, depending on one's prejudices) and at least rudimentarily reconstructing this dialogue.[58] The conspiracy literature is of two minds on issues of intertextuality. For Hofstadter, intertextuality is not an issue—the paranoid style recurs in virtually identical form almost spontaneously as deranged minds respond to increasing social conflicts about values by generating conspiratorial interpretations. Davis also postulates that different groups conceive of their conspiratorial enemies in remarkably similar ways due to the common tension, needs, and fears. But he also speculates that some such commonalities are the result of much more "direct continuities between various movements of counter-subversion." Both Jacksonian Democrats and later antislavery forces are said to have drawn upon the rhetoric and imagery of the anti-Masonic movement, and antislavery opponents of the slave power are said to have drawn upon the imagery not only of anti-Masonry but of Jacksonian and nativist conspiracy discourse as well.[59] What Davis has not considered seriously enough is the possibility that slave power conspiracy rhetors drew upon a much broader and deeper intertextual network that provided much less fantastic conspiratorial enemies than one would expect from the paranoid style.

Bernard Bailyn, Gordon Wood, and others have noted the lengthy tradition of conspiratorial interpretations within the history of Anglo-American political discourse, but it is also possible to be even more specific and extract from the American tradition of political discourse a typical type of conspiratorial enemy bedeviling the nineteenth-century political imagination—political actors who were able to acquire a disproportionate share of political power. These more pedestrian conspirators shared little with the demonic and almost omnipotent villains portrayed by conspiracy theories in the paranoid style. A brief survey of mainstream American political discourse, in fact, reveals two distinct kinds of villains about which

vigilant Americans sought to warn their compatriots: aristocrats and demagogues. Aristocrats—conceived of as "moneyed men" and "stockjobbers"—
were the familiar conspiratorial enemy of the English "Country" Party as
well as American revolutionaries, Jeffersonian Republicans, and Jacksonian Democrats. Demagogues, too, have been a familiar conspiratorial
enemy of republics. Beginning with American Federalists, Catiline's legacy
came to symbolize the constant danger that demagogic conspiracies posed
to republics. The neo-Catilinarian strain of conspiracy argument associated
with the Federalist Party recurred in polemics of later Whigs.[60]

Within the political discourse of Federalists and Republicans and Whigs
and Democrats, there is a long tradition of relatively ordinary conspiratorial enemies. Some contemporaneous rhetors, to be sure, warned of the
danger of global Masonic or papal conspiracies; but of the alleged conspirators populating American political rhetoric, aristocrats and demagogues—
in all their banality—were by far the more numerous. For this reason, it is
a mistake to understand conspiracy discourse at the center primarily in
terms of the intertextual networks of anti-Masonism or nativism. The
nineteenth century, after all, was the age of filiopiety, and while abolitionists such as Garrison discarded the heroes, documents, and texts of the
American past as the detritus of the slave power, most other political actors
were concerned to articulate their appeals in the authoritative terms of the
Anglo-American political tradition.[61] Indeed, we would expect that rhetors
seeking the assent of the largest possible audience would situate their conspiracy rhetoric in the terms of the revered texts and figures of the American political tradition. In this respect, the intertextual network of the
American political tradition is a much more promising context within
which to read slave power conspiracy texts at the center of the mainstream
than are the intertexts associated with the paranoid style.

Narratives at the Center: Functions and Plots

Related both to their place closer to the center and to the nature of the
conspiratorial enemy within their intertextual network or tradition, the
texts of the earliest antislavery politicians contain slave power narratives
that are already distinct from those of the abolitionist fringe and which
therefore provide guidance into what one might expect of conspiracy narratives at the center of the mainstream. First, these antislavery politicians
posited very recent cardinal functions of conspiracy. Unlike radical abolitionists, whose key cardinal function of conspiracy was the Constitution,
antislavery Whigs and Democrats positioned their present as the key

cardinal function of conspiracy. Morris and Adams told tales of a conspiratorial plot whose machinations, though ongoing, were only now (in their present) coming to fruition. Similarly, later opponents of Texas annexation found the key cardinal function of conspiracy in their present or in the very recent past. Each told the tale of a conspiracy whose grip on American political institutions was not yet complete. Second, in part due to the relatively banal character of the conspirators, as well as the very recent nature of their rise, Whig and Democratic narratives of conspiracy lent themselves to comic resolution. Politicians wielding the slave power conspiracy rhetoric used it in a deliberative capacity in the attempt to move citizens and fellow legislators toward timely political action against the slave power. Under such circumstances, extreme measures were not necessary. The ordinary means of politics—persuasion, citizen mobilization, and coalition building—were the preferred methods of these Whigs and Democrats.

Civic Republicanism and Conspiracy

The tale of impending conspiracy told by antislavery Whigs and Democrats, as well as their forebears among the Federalists and Republicans, provides an important context for the efforts of Chase, Sumner, and Lincoln. Similarities within this tradition also suggest that these diverse figures nonetheless shared a foundational civic republican ideology whose assumptions encouraged the first generations of Americans to think about political life in the terms of conspiracy. Ideology may be understood in a number of different ways, but this study understands ideology generally as a symbolically mediated set of integrated assumptions, beliefs, values, feelings, and attitudes by which humans make their world meaningful.[62]

In the first century of the American republic, civic republican ideology provided an important set of assumptions that rendered the political world meaningful. Within the republican view of politics, the state is conceived as the embodiment of a political community and defined by its capacity to secure liberty for its citizens and to ensure the public good. But civic republicanism views the republic—along with the liberties it enables and maintains—as fundamentally fragile and finite, continually threatened by conspiracies on the part of ambitious individuals as well as self-interested factions.[63] Within this ideological framework, conspiracy was the outward manifestation of the more basic human desire for power and hence the major contributing factor to the fragility of republics. In response to this perceived vulnerability, republican ideology as received in the United States encouraged an eternal vigilance against the dangers of concentrated power and conspiracies against political liberty and the state. Within a civic republican worldview, then, conspiracy discourse was the purview of the vigilant and virtuous citizen and politician rather than the crackpot or lunatic.[64]

Social and Political Contexts: Political Parties and the Social Logic of Text

The brief review of the efforts of early antislavery politicians against the slave power telegraphs a number of expectations about the slave power conspiracy at the center of the political mainstream. Antislavery Whigs and Democrats described relatively banal conspiratorial enemies and told stories with very recent cardinal functions of conspiracy, whose comic plots suggested the appropriateness of political action. Each of these insights will loom large as the study progresses to consider the slave power conspiracy at the center of the mainstream. But these texts and rhetors also help to illustrate the importance of attending to what historian Gabrielle Spiegel calls the "social logic of the text." Attention to the text's social logic, for Spiegel, involves not only intertext but the text's location within a network of social relationships.[65] This chapter has already considered the social logic of the abolition movement, but it is also necessary to consider the partisan social logic of mainstream antislavery politicians as well as the manner in which the development of mass political parties in the nineteenth century provided a social logic within which conspiracy discourse thrived.

In general, political parties may be said to have been generative of conspiracy discourse in at least two respects. First, mass political parties were inconsistent with republican ideology's assumption regarding the superiority of the public good over any particular good. Within this understanding of politics, parties were naturally suspect because they represented only a part of the people—a faction—that was likely to look to its own good in preference to the good of the whole. The "antipartyism" fostered by republican ideology suggested, in fact, that political parties were themselves conspiracies against the public good. Several scholars confirm the nexus between conspiracy and the dual republican emphases on the desirability of unanimity and the danger of faction.[66] As one might imagine, this ideological predilection set the stage for a conflict between emerging political institutions and older ideological assumptions, a conflict that was generative of a great deal of conspiracy discourse within the political mainstream of the nineteenth century.

But political parties not only inspired condemnation as conspiracies, they themselves utilized conspiracy discourse in order to overcome

antipartyism and achieve their organizational and electoral goals. Faced
with the ideological constraints posed by republican antipartyism, new parties relied upon conspiratorial interpretations of politics as a means to gain
legitimacy. Partisan conspiracy interpretations directed against the governing coalition functioned to mitigate the constraint posed by antipartyism,
for the logic of the opposition conspiracy claim at once marginalized those
in power as part of a conspiracy against the public good and placed the opposition party in a position to claim the mantle of the public good for itself.
In this respect, political parties justified on the basis of their opposition to a
conspiracy were in a position to nullify, to some extent, the widespread
suspicion of political parties as themselves factions or dangerous conspiracies. The activities of political parties within an ideological climate of antipartyism, then, generated conspiracy discourse in two respects. The
development of a political party led its opponents in power to label it a
conspiracy, even as the new party developed its own conspiratorial interpretations of politics.[67]

In addition to the legitimating function that conspiracy discourse served
for new political parties, it also served more general institution-building and
electioneering functions. Political scientists have long recognized the importance of rhetorical discourse to political parties, leading Joel Silbey to refer
to rhetoric as an essential "weapon of party warfare" in the antebellum period. Rhetoric was a means by which politicians could achieve two related
goals essential to the success of political parties and their candidates: the reinforcement of established partisan identities and loyalties and the mobilization and conversion of new party members. Rhetorical appeals were
especially important to the Republican Party in the 1850s, for it lacked the
resources—be they patronage, established organizations, or established
voter loyalty—of the existing parties. But antebellum political parties relied
upon a specific kind of rhetorical appeal, utilizing the rhetoric of conspiracy
as a means to create a politically compelling ideology capable of mobilizing
the electorate. Party mobilization was achieved by way of providing common enemies against which citizens might organize. William Chambers describes this important ideological function: "the party in the full sense
entails a distinguishable set of perspectives, or ideology, with emotional
overtones . . . beliefs develop into faiths, identifications emerge as loyalties,
ideas of right and wrong become moral commitments." Chambers also
notes the oppositional nature of party ideologies: "Party outlooks are drawn
in terms of 'we' and 'they'—our rightness and their wrongness, the good-
ness of having our leaders in office and the danger of leaving theirs, the

'truth' of our doctrine and the 'error' of theirs." Indeed, much partisan political rhetoric involved repeated identifications and denunciations of the
common enemy that helped to construct partisan identity and identification. Not surprisingly, conspiracies of various sorts provided the common
enemy for almost all antebellum political parties. The Republican Party was
no exception. Its advocates used the slave power conspiracy as a way to
show the necessity of political organization against the slave power.[68]

The emerging Republican Party, however, did not arise within a political
vacuum, and its version of the slave power conspiracy needed to be expressed in the terms of the Whig and Democratic ideologies of the constituents it hoped to convert. The early antislavery politicians each
constructed a slave power consistent with the traditional enemies of their
respective party ideologies. Whigs like Adams and Giddings, consistent
with a party ideology that echoed the Federalist emphasis on the danger of
demagogic conspiracies, portrayed the slave power in the terms of demagoguery, party machines, and mass deception. Democrats Morse and
Brinkerhoff, on the other hand, operated with a party ideology that retained the Jeffersonian Republican suspicion of plotting aristocrats, and
their Democratized slave power was an aristocratic faction allying itself
with the ever dangerous moneyed power. Even as early as the 1830s and
1840s, then, the slave power conspiracy of antislavery politicians assumed
a variety of forms that varied according to the conditioning of particular
partisan ideologies.[69] Insofar as the Republican Party of the 1850s emerged
from the decaying Whig-Democratic party system, it needed to draw converts from the ranks of both of these parties. Given this dynamic, the partisan social logic of Republican slave power texts suggests the importance
of considering the manner in which later Republicans sought to appropriate Whig and Democratic ideologies. One might, in other words, read the
structure of Whig and Democratic ideologies within particular Republican
texts against the slave power conspiracy.[70]

Seeking the Center of the Mainstream: Republican Politicians of the 1850s

Garrison and the AASS, whose rhetorical texts are best understood within
the terms of the paranoid style, occupy one pole—the fringe—of this
study's map of the slave power conspiracy formation. The rhetorical efforts
of early antislavery Whigs and Democrats provide guidance as to a number
of contexts and rhetorical strategies that are essential to understanding the
map's other pole—the center. But while Morse, Adams, Brinkerhoff, and

Giddings did their best to alert their constituents to the danger posed by the slave power, charges of a slave power conspiracy were relatively sporadic among mainstream politicians in the 1830s and 1840s. Historians have noted that charges of the existence of a slave power conspiracy did not become plausible to most audiences until the late 1850s. As political events unfolded, the repeal of the Missouri Compromise in 1854, events in Kansas in 1855–56, and the 1857 Dred Scott decision "suggested a degree of Southern unity, premeditation, and control which was hardly credible in earlier years" that "led many northerners to finally accept as a fact the existence of an aggressive Slave Power."[71] In accordance with these observations and the goal of comprehending the conspiracy texts closest to the center of the political mainstream, this study focuses narrowly on slave power conspiracy texts of Republican Party politicians produced between 1854 and the Civil War. Selecting among Republican politicians of this period for their conformity to the mainstream is a relatively simple matter. Political parties nominate presidential candidates on the basis of their "availability," their presumed acceptability to the average voter. This suggests that Salmon P. Chase, Charles Sumner, and Abraham Lincoln—each a serious contender for the 1860 Republican presidential nomination—provide the best cases for examining slave power texts in the mainstream.[72] Fortunately, these rhetors' most prominent efforts against the slave power correspond nicely to the major events of the late 1850s that made the slave power conspiracy seem plausible to Northern audiences. Chase is best known for his anti-Nebraska *Appeal of the Independent Democrats* (1854); Sumner for "The Crime Against Kansas" (1856), his response to "bleeding Kansas"; and Lincoln for his "House Divided" speech (1858), which dealt primarily with the consequences of the Dred Scott decision.

The remaining chapters are organized both around the chronology of the Republican narrative of the slave power conspiracy and the efforts of its most prominent mainstream politicians. The second chapter considers two texts of party organizer Salmon P. Chase in order better to understand conspiracy discourse within a partisan social logic as well as to illustrate the diachronic development of his conspiracy position. In the 1840s, Chase was instrumental in organizing the Liberty Party—the first antislavery political party—and his 1845 *Address of the Southern and Western Liberty Convention* is a major landmark in the political antislavery movement as well as slave power conspiracy rhetoric. The chapter then moves to a consideration of Chase's 1854 *Appeal of the Independent Democrats*—a key text that is credited with fueling the anti-Nebraska movement that would eventually evolve into the Republican Party. Because Chase was a party builder and leader, his texts are the ideal cases with which to consider the interpretive possibilities of partisan rhetoric, civic republican ideology, and the role of conspiracy narratives in party mobilization. Chapter 3 turns to Charles Sumner and another landmark text in Republican slave power conspiracy rhetoric—the 1856 "Crime Against Kansas." This philippic dramatized the violent events in Kansas as part of a slave power conspiracy and earned Sumner a vicious caning on the floor of the Senate—forever linking "bleeding Kansas" and "bleeding Sumner" in the Republican mythology of the slave power. This chapter continues the concern with the narrative complexities of conspiracy texts and the interpretive possibilities of civic republicanism and introduces the oratorical tradition of conspiracy as a mode of understanding Sumner's conspiracy rhetoric. The fourth chapter turns to Abraham Lincoln and one of the best-known slave power conspiracy texts—his "House Divided" speech of 1858. Here Lincoln implicated Stephen Douglas as part of a well-coordinated conspiracy to nationalize slavery. The chapter continues the trajectory of the study, utilizing narrative theory and partisan contexts in order to deepen our understanding of this text. In addition, the chapter introduces new issues—in particular, the logical dimension of conspiracy rhetoric and the importance of considering the political culture in which conspiracy rhetoric occurs. Chapter 4 concludes with a consideration of the reception context of the speech in terms of the assumptions of civic republicanism and liberal pluralism. This book is constructed so that each chapter, to a certain degree, stands by itself. Each provides a case study that interprets the conspiracy texts within their original contexts and examines the larger issue of the role of conspiracy rhetoric within the rhetor's political career. Chapters 2–4, in this respect, contribute primarily toward one of this study's main goals—marshaling a variety of interpretive strategies that enable further understanding of the rhetorical strategies that help to make a conspiratorial interpretation persuasive and hence successful. Chapter 5 returns to the issue of mapping slave power conspiracy rhetoric, synthesizing the findings of the earlier chapters into a basic map of the slave power conspiracy formation in order to better account for how "place"—at the fringe or center of American political institutions and ideologies—conditions conspiracy rhetoric. The concluding chapter also explores the broader ramifications of the study's findings and points toward future avenues of research.

2

The Slave Power According to Salmon P. Chase: Entering the Mainstream of Partisan Rhetoric, 1845–1854

It is hoped . . . by the influence of a Federal Government controlled by the slave power, to extinguish freedom and establish slavery in the States and Territories of the Pacific, and thus permanently subjugate the whole country to the yoke of a slaveholding despotism. Shall a plot against humanity and democracy, so monstrous, and so dangerous to the interests of liberty throughout the world, be permitted to succeed?

—Salmon P. Chase, *Appeal of the Independent Democrats*

The rhetorical texts of Salmon P. Chase are an ideal place to begin a consideration of slave power conspiracy discourse in the political mainstream, for Chase has been credited with fundamentally altering the nature of the antislavery movement: "The American anti-slavery movement, which began as a moral crusade, eventually found that it would have to turn to politics to achieve its goals. . . . No anti-slavery leader was more responsible for the success of this transformation, and none did more to formulate an anti-slavery program in political terms than Salmon P. Chase of Ohio." Crucial to this transformation was Chase's development of "the idea that southern slaveholders, organized politically as a Slave Power, were conspiring to dominate the national government, reverse the policy of the founding fathers, and make slavery the ruling interest of the republic."[1]

Given Chase's pivotal role in the politicization of antislavery and popular-
ization of the slave power conspiracy, there seems good reason to believe
that reading his texts will illuminate the character of that species of slave
power conspiracy discourse that eventually came to partake of authoritative American ideologies and occupy the center of American political institutions and political discourse.

Salmon P. Chase was first and foremost a party politician, and contemporaries recognized that some of his most and least desirable traits
stemmed from this role. Many of his contemporaries distrusted Chase, considering him an opportunist who was more concerned with furthering his
own ambition than the antislavery cause. But few contemporaries disputed
his abilities as a party organizer and propagandist.[2] Chase spent the balance
of his political career in the 1840s and 1850s attempting to organize an
antislavery political party. Since Chase's efforts were focused around issues
of party and partisanship, this chapter will be especially concerned with
unlocking the partisan social logic conditioning his rhetorical texts. Because Chase's antislavery efforts spanned two decades, a wide selection of
texts is available. This chapter will be concerned primarily with two Chase
texts. The first, the *Address of the Southern and Western Liberty Convention* of
the Liberty Party, was prepared in 1845 at a time when Chase was working
diligently to expand the party's base in order to create an antislavery coalition composed of Liberty partisans as well as antislavery Whigs and Democrats. This was one of Chase's first efforts to mainstream his
marginalized Liberty Party through the use of slave power conspiracy rhetoric. In addition to this important text, this chapter will also consider
Chase's most famous text, the *Appeal of the Independent Democrats*, a document produced in 1854 in opposition to Stephen Douglas's Nebraska bill.
This text's importance to this study is underscored by its wide distribution
to mainstream audiences and the weighty influence assigned to it by contemporaries and historians.[3]

Chase's relatively lengthy antislavery career provides not only a rich selection of slave power texts, it also lends itself to a diachronic survey of the
evolution of Chase's practice of slave power conspiracy rhetoric as he
sought to realign the party system around the issue of slavery over the
course of two decades. In the early 1840s Chase's Liberty Party was a tiny
minority consigned to the fringes of the political system, but by 1854
Chase's *Appeal of the Independent Democrats* would reach a nationwide audience and help to place antislavery and the slave power conspiracy in the
mainstream of Northern politics. As such, the diachronic study of Chase's

evolving conspiratorial interpretations affords the opportunity to examine the manner in which his own conspiracy position changed as he and his cause moved from the periphery to the center of American political life.

The Liberty Party and the Address of the Southern and Western Convention

Chase and the Liberty Party

Prior to 1841, Salmon P. Chase was a devout Whig both in sensibility and in affiliation. This sensibility was initially cultivated by his years spent in Washington, D.C., living under the patronage of William Wirt. Soon after Jackson's election to the presidency in 1828, Chase moved to Cincinnati. Here his distaste for the Democrats and his fear of Democratic inroads in Ohio led him to join the other young professionals of that city in supporting what was then the National Republican Party, or anti-Jackson coalition (soon to be the Whig Party). But Chase would not fare well with the Whig Party. His growing antislavery opinions—kindled by his experiences with anti-abolitionist mobs and fugitive slave cases—made him an unacceptable radical to most conservative Whigs. Chase recognized that he would have no future with the Whigs of Ohio.[4]

Chase also recognized that antislavery had no future with either of the major political parties. He wrote in 1840 that "when I witness the complete subservience which both parties have manifested to the South upon the great, and, in my judgment, *vital* question of slavery, I feel almost inclined to withdraw from the contest in despair. . . . [a]lthough I am not willing to take part in the third party movement, regarding it . . . premature." Chase's resistance to a third party would eventually dissolve in the fall of 1841 when he joined the Liberty Party—the first political party organized in opposition to slavery. He played a variety of important roles in the continuing efforts of the Liberty Party, but his most important contribution to the antislavery movement was the rhetorical legacy he would bequeath to a later, much more successful, antislavery party. The moderate antislavery position Chase developed to assist the Liberty Party would eventually become the mainstay of the Republican persuasion of the 1850s. Central to Chase's position was a clear-cut distinction between antislavery and abolition: "While abolition is not properly speaking a political object, antislavery is. Antislavery, I understand to be hostility to slavery as a power antagonistic to free labor, [one that] aims at the complete deliverance of the Government

of the Nation from all connection with & all responsibility for slavery."
Chase's strategy of political action through the Liberty Party was said to
present "a glorious opportunity to restore the government to its original
principles" by way of "the deliverance of the country . . . from the control
of the slaveholding policy and the slave power."[5] But these political goals,
he suggested, were attainable only with the proper strategy:

> A skillful general will not . . . engage his forces in a promiscuous struggle,
> nor attack, indiscriminately, all the positions of the enemy. We must imitate
> this prudence, and direct our main efforts against those positions of the
> Slave Power which are most exposed. Our first and chief effort should be di-
> rected to the denationalization of slavery—to the absolute and complete di-
> vorce of the General Government from all connection with the Slave
> System.[6]

This strategy was a narrow one that involved directing "all the energies of
our political action against the unconstitutional encroachments of the
Slave Power." In sum, Chase sought to build the Liberty Party into a viable
political organization by opposing the slave power rather than slavery
itself.[7]

This account of Chase is consistent with the conventional wisdom that
he was a pragmatic politician set on reconfiguring antislavery politics. But
it is a mistake to take this conventional wisdom too far—portraying Chase's
Ohio Liberty Party rank and file as similarly minded pragmatic westerners.[8]
In fact, Chase led a party whose rank and file were frequently at odds with
his leadership in many respects. Understanding precisely how and why
Chase and his party differed is an important step toward gaining a fuller
understanding of Chase's role in the party as well as the *Address of the Southern and Western Liberty Convention.*

The Liberty Party originated in the secession of the AFASS from Garrison's more radical AASS. While members of the AFASS disagreed with the
Garrisonians on many issues (particularly the viability of political action
and the status of women in the organization), they shared a fundamental
belief in the equality of the races and a profoundly eschatological understanding of the movement's role within American history.[9] Like the Garrisonians, many Liberty men saw the slavery issue as part of a millennial
struggle between the forces of good and evil. But Liberty men retained a
postmillennial view, even as the AASS moved toward a more pessimistic
premillennial view, a difference that is clearly reflected in their respective
narratives of the slave power and antislavery.

Garrisonians and Liberty men agreed that the slave power had taken control of the Republic early in the new nation's existence. Garrisonians identified the events of 1787–89 as the key cardinal function of their conspiracy narrative, calling the founding document crafted and ratified during these years " . . . a covenant with death, and an agreement with hell." But Liberty partisans like William Goodell thought the Republic's first principles were sound and that its founding moments, the Revolution and Constitution, were great and worthy endeavors undertaken in terms of a highly Christian understanding of liberty. According to the Liberty account, the slave power had been able to gain control because the Christian basis of the Republic was eroded by the atheistic influence of the French Revolution on the eventually victorious Jeffersonian Republican Party. Goodell's Liberty narrative, in sum, took the form of a jeremiad. The American people—once chosen of God—had become backsliders whose lack of faith and commitment to their holy mission had enabled the slave power to gain ascendancy. His Liberty narrative from the 1790s onward was one both of backsliding, the corresponding corruption of religious and political institutions by the slave power, and a string of seemingly endless policy victories for slavery and the South.[10]

Liberty partisans did not adopt a tragic perspective encouraging them to shrink from the awesome challenge posed by fifty years of slave power dominance, however, for their postmillennial eschatology led them to believe that their own struggles were part of a divine plan in which the Second Coming was preceded by a comprehensive reform of all religious and political institutions and the political system was repurified by Christianity in preparation for the eventual establishment of the government of God on Earth. Because of their commitment to the reform of earthly institutions, Liberty members viewed a politicized form of moral suasion as the best means to bring about the party's goals. Such an eschatologically motivated approach to politics, however, meant that religious-minded Liberty partisans often ignored the tactics and organization of conventional parties. Organizationally, the Liberty Party usually relied on the church as the basic unit, and this church-centered organization overlay an unwillingness on the part of many Liberty men to engage in conventional political tactics. Many were more concerned with moral purity, that the party not be associated with the slavery parties in any way, than with coalition building and electoral victory. An emphasis on morality entailed the rejection of compromises, alliances, and the pluralistic perspective that could make their party a "big tent" congenial to many coalition partners. For them, the party was little more than an instrument of God, one enabling them to bring their message of reform to a wider audience and therefore to hasten the coming of the millennium.[11]

This "perfectionist" reform impulse of the Liberty Party's rank and file stands in contrast to the disposition of the "nonperfectionist" leaders like Chase. Indeed, the party was quickly beset by a division between politically minded "coalitionists," who saw it as a first step toward a larger political antislavery movement, and religiously minded "universal reformers." Chase represented the coalitionists, and he worked to forge an alliance with antislavery Whigs and Democrats. In Ohio, the schism between universal reformers and coalitionists was further aggravated by a stark regional and organizational dichotomy. Party leaders Chase and Gamaliel Bailey operated out of Cincinnati—a region virtually devoid of Liberty Party supporters—and controlled the party machinery, in particular the state party press, the *Philanthropist,* and the state convention apparatus. While Chase and Bailey ran the Liberty Party from Cincinnati, however, the bulk of Liberty support came from the "universal reform" constituencies of the Western Reserve.[12] In sum, while the Liberty Party rank and file were politically oriented and pragmatic relative to radical Garrisonians, in Ohio, at least, they retained several attitudes that distanced them from Chase and the coalitionist wing. The bulk of Liberty voters in Ohio continued to view the antislavery effort in primarily religious terms. Obviously, maintaining the loyalty of this component of the Liberty Party—the vast majority in Ohio—would complicate Chase's task of reaching out to the moderate antislavery elements of the Whig and Democratic parties. If Chase was to bring the Liberty Party into the mainstream, he would do it despite the wishes of many Liberty partisans.

Coalition Potential:
The Whig and Democratic Parties

Chase's strategy of converting Whigs and Democrats to the Liberty Party required that he acknowledge Democratic and Whig ideologies and policy programs. As noted, party ideologies almost invariably were constructed in opposition to some sort of conspiratorial enemy whose machinations required remedial efforts. Democratic ideology justified the existence of the party in terms of its opposition to an ongoing aristocratic conspiracy, and on this basis Democrats constructed both their political organization and policy program. Democrats insisted that because American aristocrats were ever united by the bond of self-interest, the diffuse sentiment of the majority must be equally well organized, and they utilized the tools of New York's Albany Regency machine—legislative caucuses, party newspapers, and strategic use of patronage to reward loyal political allies—to effect this unity. As a national organization, the party was comprised of a pyramid structure of conventions and committees beginning at the local level and ascending to the state and national levels. Because each convention nominated only one candidate for each office, these institutions ensured that the votes of party members were united behind approved candidates. Democrats also sponsored several national newspapers and other publications—such as pamphlets, periodicals, and franked speeches—that assisted in disseminating the appropriate information to the electorate. Finally, control of patronage helped to discipline the party at all levels.[13] United by such means, the Democratic Party proposed a coherent policy program designed to safeguard society from American aristocrats. Democrats opposed all policies thought to benefit aristocrats at the expense of the rest of society—in particular, the national bank, internal improvements, and exclusive corporate charters. Because of their concern with the maintenance of states' rights and the restriction of federal power, Democrats also insisted on the strict construction of the Constitution. The government was continually vulnerable to control by the wealthy classes, the Democratic argument went. This meant that to interpret the founding document loosely had the consequence of permitting a degree of government power enabling the passage of a string of policies partial to the interests of the aristocrats. Although this disposition within Democratic ideology had largely negative policy implications (proscribing much potential governmental policy), the Democratic emphasis on equality meant that the party looked favorably on territorial expansion, insofar as such expansion provided an opportunity for increasing concentrations of wealth in older states to be offset by new states consisting of relatively equal societies of independent landholders.[14]

The Whig Party was a heterogeneous coalition united primarily by its steadfast opposition to the Democrats. Where the Democrats saw themselves as permanent popular-based opposition to a standing aristocratic conspiracy, Whigs justified their party in an opposition to conspiracies enabled by executive tyranny (personified by Andrew Jackson), demagogues, and party bosses and their corrupt party machines.[15] Whigs adhered to the standard antiparty position that parties, because organized to pursue particular interests, threatened the very goal of republican government—the disinterested pursuit of the public good. To Whigs, the well-organized

Democrats appeared as a disciplined phalanx relentlessly pursuing their agenda at the expense of the rest of society. Whigs feared that such discipline threatened political independence in two respects. Not only did the convention system put the choice of candidates in the hands of a small group of party leaders and their representatives, but dissent from the party line risked punishment in the form of the withdrawal of patronage. In contrast to Democrats, Whigs portrayed themselves as independent statesmen exercising their refined judgment for the common good and claimed that only their brand of responsible leadership was capable of preserving and building upon the legacy of the founders. Whigs sought to build upon the founders' achievement by creating the social and economic conditions conducive to both material and moral progress. Such progress, they maintained, was best achieved by an active and paternalistic national government that promoted policies like a national bank, internal improvements, and the tariff. Finally, Whigs thought that their goals of preserving the founders' legacy and nurturing the development of an organic society were threatened by too rapid an expansion westward. Whigs pointed to Rome and Russia to illustrate the ultimately discordant and despotic results of rapid imperial expansion.[16]

Together, Whigs and Democrats comprised a competitive two-party system—one in which only candidates of the major parties had a realistic chance of winning elections. But maintaining this monopoly on elections and offices required Whigs and Democrats, despite their differences, to share an opposition to the entry of the slavery issue into electoral politics. As trans-sectional organizations, the parties could be maintained only if the slavery issue was off-limits. The Whig-Democratic party system's conservatism regarding slavery is manifest in the "federal consensus" narrative of American history, which postulated that the North and South—from the beginning in 1787—were (and ought to be) equal partners in an ongoing series of compromises (especially territorial) that served to preserve the Union.[17] Though both parties punished those expressing overtly sectional views on the slavery issue, by 1845 noticeable antislavery factions in both parties gave Chase reason for hope. At least a few Whig and Democratic leaders had seen Congress's refusal to receive the abolition petitions as part of a slave power conspiracy. With the controversy over the annexation of Texas in 1844 and 1845, however, the slave power conspiracy became increasingly plausible to some Northern Whig and Democratic politicians. In response to these developments, Chase hoped to craft Liberty Party rhetoric in such a way that it might resonate less with the universal reform constituencies and more with the increasing unease with the slave power expressed by growing numbers of Whig and Democratic politicians.

The Social Logic of the Liberty Party

Like the major parties, the Liberty Party relied upon rhetoric—the essential "weapon of party warfare"—to reinforce established partisan identities and to mobilize new support within the electorate. And like the major parties, the Liberty Party relied on conspiracy rhetoric in order to serve these functions. These rhetorical appeals were especially important to an externally mobilized party (a party established by leaders outside of positions of power in the regime) such as the Liberty Party, for while the Whigs and Democrats could rely on rhetoric as well as material resources—patronage, established organizations, established voter loyalty—to gain support, the Liberty Party would stand or fall based on the effectiveness of its rhetorical appeals alone.[18]

Those within the party, however, disagreed as to the most appropriate rhetorical strategies. The universal reform contingent within the party preferred a strategy of moral and religious appeals consistent with what has been called an "ideological style" of party competition. Under the ideological style, a party seeks to capture a portion of the electorate by offering clearly defined and highly principled policy positions. Chase and the coalitionists within the Liberty Party, on the other hand, adopted a "coalitional style" that utilized relatively noncontroversial and nondivisive issues in order to build as broad a coalition as possible. This vast difference in strategy and style between reformers and coalitionists highlights what is perhaps the most significant complication Chase faced as a leader of the Liberty Party—the tension between the inside and the outside. How might Chase broaden the appeal of his antislavery party? How might he bring it into the political mainstream without diluting his message to the point that his existing constituency of universal reformers became disgusted and disillusioned? The tension between inside and outside of a political party is a function of multiple audiences and hence may be expressed in many ways.[19] But for the purposes of Chase's *Address*, the tension between inside and outside might best be expressed in the terms of the problem of ideological innovation.

Party ideologies have their origins in the rhetoric of party leaders. While leaders of established parties use rhetoric and ideology in order to "stimulate the faithful" and "convert the wayward," leaders of emerging parties have the unique opportunity to give ideological shape to a new—and as yet unformed—political institution.[20] But party leaders have never been entirely free to shape party ideologies. According to John Gerring (speaking of party leaders generally), they "formulated, disseminated, and executed" partisan ideologies in accordance with the ideological beliefs of their constituents—both existing and prospective. Gerring, however, emphasizes the possibility of ideological innovation within these constraints:

> Party constituencies should be thought of as a constraint, not a deciding factor, in the creation and re-creation of party ideology. . . . Party constituencies represented obstacles to be negotiated—either placated or persuaded. . . . [L]eaders were forced to choose among competing views and competing constituencies. This power of choice meant that, on many issues, leaders would play a decisive role in shaping the party's agenda.[21]

Chase's decisive role in shaping Liberty Party ideology has long been recognized, and one goal of this chapter is to trace how the tension between the outside and inside of the Liberty Party conditioned the process of ideological innovation within the *Address of the Southern and Western Convention*.

Reading the Address: Introduction and Textual Overview

More than two thousand delegates—coming from all midwestern states and territories as well as Virginia, Pennsylvania, Kentucky, Rhode Island, New York, and Massachusetts—attended the Southern and Western Liberty Convention in Cincinnati on June 11 and 12, 1845. By 1845 the partisan convention—the "most conspicuous feature" of the second party system's elaborate organizational structure—had only recently replaced the legislative caucus as the arbiter of party platforms, ideologies, and candidates. While the legislative caucus was an elite-centered form of decision-making consistent with the character of the first (Federalist-Republican) party system, the increasingly participatory political culture of the second (Whig-Democratic) party system needed an institution consistent with its assumptions. Party conventions fit this need, for they were both public and democratic in appearance. Attended by delegates who were themselves elected from state and local party organizations, they were ostensibly decision-making bodies.[22]

Chase played a key role in organizing the 1845 Liberty convention, and his authorship of the *Address* is clearly indicated in the notes attached to the printed version. By 1845 Chase's associates are said to have become dependent on his skill at writing such statements, as well as party platforms. But the text of the *Address* as printed was itself a product of the convention process. At the behest of members of the committee responsible for issuing an address representative of the convention and party, Chase made further revisions in the document. In this respect, Chase's authorship of the *Address* was heavily conditioned by the institutional requirements of party conventions as well as by the needs of his audiences—both inside and outside the convention. As Chase himself wrote in a letter to Quintus Atkins, "in preparing an address or public document my aim is not to give all my own views, but to present those which the party generally hold & in which I as an individual concur: and in writing the Address of the Convention my aim was to prepare a document which should exhibit the general conclusion of Liberty men." While Chase undoubtedly sought to leave his own mark on the *Address*, this passage is a valuable reminder of the generic conventions surrounding such texts. Within the generic conventions of party conventions, the text asks to be read not as the work of Chase but as representative of the whole Liberty Party. At the same time, we ought to be mindful of Chase's presence within the text as a third-party leader who worked to innovate a party ideology within the bounds of what his constituents would accept.[23]

The text of the *Address* is short—only about fifteen pages long—and generously supplied with detailed footnotes providing evidence for its historical and other claims. Its organization is partially signaled by way of section headings. Functionally, thematically, and topically, however, the *Address* may be divided into several larger sections. Following a brief one-paragraph introduction are the "founding narrative," "conspiracy narrative," "partisan choice," and "targeted audience" sections. On a more general level, the *Address* exhibits a temporal organization. The first section deals with the past, using the founders as an anchor for the first principles of the Liberty Party. The second section uses the slave power as a device to move the text toward an orientation of the problems of the degenerate present. The final two sections pertain to the parties and audiences of the present, and the conclusion gestures toward the need for timely political action in order to secure the future of the Republic.

Reading the Address from Past to Present

The introduction to the *Address of the Southern and Western Liberty Convention* is short and sufficiently important to quote in its entirety:

> Having assembled in Convention as friends of Constitutional Liberty, who believe the practice of slaveholding to be inconsistent with the fundamental principles of Republicanism, of Religion, and of Humanity, we think it our

duty to declare, frankly to you, our fellow citizens, the views which we
hold, the principles by which we are governed, and the objects which we
desire, by your cooperation, to accomplish. We ask and expect from you a
candid and respectful hearing. We are not a band of fanatics, as some fool-
ishly imagine, and others slanderously assert, bent on overthrowing all Government and all Religion. We are citizens of the United States, having our
homes in the West and the Southwest, some in the Slave states, and some in
the Free, bound to our country by the most endearing ties and the most
solemn obligations, filled with the most ardent desires for her prosperity and
glory, and resolved, so far as in us lies, to carry forward and perfect the great
work of individual, social, and civil elevation which our fathers nobly
began.[24]

Consistent with generic expectations, the text asks to be read as encompassing the opinions of the entire convention, and the fundamental
principles—of republicanism, religion, and humanity—on which the convention opposes slavery leave grounds for both political and religious motivations. The "we" of the convention is constructed in such a way that
distances the Liberty Party from radical abolitionists, conceiving of the
party as composed of vigilant and filiopietistic citizens intent on sustaining
their fathers' republic rather than fanatics bent on its destruction.

   In the filiopietistic atmosphere of nineteenth-century political discourse,
Garrison's radical critique of the Republic's foundations was impolitic.
Chase recognized that appropriation of the set of critical consensual symbols revolving around the founders was essential for the Liberty Party's
success. Consistent with this need, the first several pages of the text develop the Liberty Party's understanding of the founding as an antislavery
event. The text's portrait of the Revolution as "a necessary battle . . . between the Aristocratic and Democratic principle" is one of the first of many
implicit gestures toward Democratic ideology, which justified the existence
of the party in terms of its opposition to an ongoing aristocratic conspiracy.
But the primary purpose of this founding section is to provide a necessary
antidote to the prevailing portrait of the "American government as the
guardian of slavery." Within the *Address*, Chase and the Liberty Party seek
to redeem the founders from such libels by way of trying to prove that
"from the assembling of the First Congress in 1774, until its final organization under the existing constitution in 1789, the American Government
was antislavery in its character and policy."[25] This basic thesis is elaborated
in both narrative and testimonial manners.

The symbolic appropriation of the founders is initially grounded by way of a narrative representation encompassing the acts of the government from 1774 to 1789 under the headings "First Congress," "Declaration of Independence," "Ordinance of 1787," and "The Constitution." The First Congress's alleged antislavery sentiments are exemplified in the Non-Importation, Non-Consumption, and Non-Exportation Agreement under which the Revolutionary government forsook all involvement in the slave trade. This act is positioned as "a deliberate national vow and covenant against all traffic in human beings," one that was "so understood by the people at large," both North and South. The next governmental act in the founding narrative is the Declaration of Independence, said to express *the* first principle of the Republic: "the inalienable RIGHT of every man to life, liberty, and the pursuit of happiness, solemnly proclaimed AS THE BASIS OF A NATIONAL POLITICAL FAITH." The next act, the Ordinance of 1787's prohibition of slavery, is said to represent a "clear, unqualified, decisive action in fulfillment of the solemn pledge given in 1774, reiterated in 1776, and in pursuance of the settled national policy of restricting slavery to the original states." The *Address*'s moderate voice, while imitating the founders' antislavery principles, also imitates their prudence—pledging to follow the practice of leaving the peculiar institution within the exclusive jurisdiction of the states.[26] This move seems designed to appease slaveholders, but it also represents an appropriation of the limited government and states' rights strain of Democratic ideology. Chase's position was presented as one that would limit the power of the national government, consigning ultimate authority over slavery solely to the states.

The Constitution, insofar as it was thought to protect slavery and was perceived by many—including radical Garrisonians *and* advocates of slavery—as a proslavery document, posed a potential problem for the Liberty Party's founding narrative. The text of the *Address* approaches this dilemma in several ways, but the primary move making for an antislavery Constitution is to read it against the previous narrative points: "it seems clear, that neither the framers of the Constitution, nor the people who adopted it, intended to violate the pledges given in the covenant of 1774, in the declaration of 1776, in the Ordinance of 1787." The plausibility of an antislavery Constitution is suggested not only by reading it against its immediate political past but also by observing that the Ordinance of 1787 and Constitution were contemporary acts that ought to be consistent with one another. The "acts" portion of the founding narrative concludes: "We have thus proved, from the Public Acts of the Nation, that, up to the time of the adoption of the Constitution, the people of the United States were an anti-slavery people; that the sanction of the national government was never given, and never intended to be given, to slaveholding."[27] By positioning the Constitution as an antislavery document, Chase not only rescued this authoritative symbol from the slave power, he also contributed further to his goal of couching his position in the limited government and states' rights strain of Democratic ideology.

The antislavery narrative of the founders' acts is reinforced by way of an account of the "Sentiments of Distinguished Men of the Revolutionary Period." Here the "recorded opinions of the Patriots and Sages of the Revolutionary Era" relating to the odiousness of slavery and the expectation or wish that it be gradually abolished are reproduced. These opinions are not temporally arranged. The text jumps from 1781 to 1832 and reproduces opinions from letters, speeches, and other works. Two criteria, however, seem to govern the selection of particular founding figures. First, the heading begins with the prominent Southerners and preeminent founders Jefferson and Washington. Second, of the other eleven figures, nine are also Southerners. This selection emphasizes the extent to which the Southerners of 1845 significantly deviate from their Revolutionary counterparts on matters of slavery.[28]

This radical divergence of the principles and policy between the founding past and the present, however, leaves readers confronted with a puzzle: what accounts for the shift in national policy and rhetoric? If Chase's Liberty Party account of the founding period is correct, how is it possible to explain the vast chasm between the antislavery past, in which the founders hoped slavery would gradually disappear, and the proslavery present, in which slavery continues to expand westward? The "conspiracy narrative" section both provides an explanation for the difference between past and present slavery policy and serves as a device that moves the text of the *Address* to an orientation in the present. Before introducing the slave power, however, a counterfactual history further exacerbates the apparent divergence of past and present policy: "Let us pause here. Let us reflect what would have been the condition of the country had the original policy of the nation been steadily pursued, and contrast what could have been with what is." To follow the trajectory established by the founding narrative, Chase's text suggests, would lead to a very different present:

> had the original policy and original principles of the Government been adhered to, this expectation would have been realized. The example and influence of the General Government would have been on the side of

freedom. . . . Amid the rejoicings of all the free, and the congratulations of all the friends of freedom, the last fetter would, ere now, have been stricken from the last slave, and the principles and institutions of liberty would have pervaded the entire land. [29]

With this counterfactual history, the *Address*'s narrative seems even less coherent, as the gulf between the antislavery past and the proslavery present appears to widen.

Only following the counterfactual history, under the heading "Actual Results," is the slave power introduced as a device that bridges the gulf the *Address* has so far established between the past and present. According to Chase's Liberty Party narrative, once the danger to freedoms had passed, Americans grew increasingly insensible to the rights won in the Revolution. This flagging of vigilance and growing insensibility to rights, rather than the spiritual backsliding of Goodell's account, are said to have "prepared the way for the political slave power," a power that "has virtually established in this country an aristocracy of slaveholders."[30] Even the Democratic Party, whose ideology positioned it as a bulwark against all aristocracies, is said to have succumbed to the slave power: "The nation has always been divided into parties, and the slaveholders, by making the protection and advancement of their peculiar interests the price of their political support, have generally succeeded in controlling all." With its political influence secured by common interest, the three-fifths clause, and control of both parties, Chase writes, the slave power

> has upheld slavery in the District of Columbia and in the Territories in spite of the Constitution: it has added to the Union six slave States created out of national Territories: it has usurped control of our foreign negotiation, and domestic legislation: it has dictated the choice of high officers of our Government at home, and our national representatives abroad: it has filled every department of executive and judicial administration with its friends and satellites: it has detained in slavery multitudes who are constitutionally entitled to their freedom: it has waged unrelenting war on the most sacred rights of the free, stifling the freedom of speeches and debate, setting at naught the right of petition, and denying in the slave States those immunities to the citizens of the free, which the Constitution guaranties: and, finally, it has dictated the acquisition of an immense foreign territory, not for the laudable purpose of extending the blessings of freedom, but with the bad design of diffusing the curse of slavery, and thereby consolidating and perpetuating its own ascendancy.[31]

This lengthy list of slave power actions, though not presented in narrative form and only implicitly corresponding to particular events (specifically, the refusal of the abolition petitions, the gag rule, and Texas annexation), completes the *Address*'s Liberty Party narrative of founding and conspiracy. Unlike many other rhetors against the slave power who explicitly prove the existence of the slave power solely by way of a narrative representation of its acts through the general government, the *Address* provides only a compressed summary of the slave power's extensive influence. Nevertheless, this account functions to resolve the founding narrative's incompatibility with the policy and rhetoric of the mid-1840s. Commencement of the operation of the government is the key cardinal function in the conspiracy narrative, and this point accounts for the derailment of the trajectory established by the founders. Consequently, it is precisely the difference between the founders and the present that testifies to the control of the general government by the slave power.

The account of the slave power shifts the *Address*'s temporal orientation to the present, the moment at which the Liberty Party presents voters with an opportunity to restore the Republic. Accordingly, the "partisan choice" section commences with a statement of the party's goals and plans under the headings "What We Mean To Do" and "How We Mean To Do It." The "What" of the Liberty Party expresses the conventional wisdom that party identities are constructed against a conspiratorial enemy:

> Against this influence, against these infractions of the Constitution, against these departures from the national policy originally adopted, against these violations of the national faith originally pledged, we solemnly protest. Nor do we propose only to protest. We recognize the obligations which rest upon us as descendants of the men of the revolution, as inheritors of the institutions which they established, as partakers of the blessings which they so dearly purchased, to carry forward and perfect their work. We mean to do it, wisely and prudently, but with energy and decision. We have the example of our fathers on our side. It is our duty, and our purpose, to rescue the Government from the control of the slaveholders.[32]

Turning to the "How" of the Liberty Party, the text advances the policy of denationalization, involving the repeal of "all legislation, and discontinuing all action, in favor of slavery, at home and abroad." In practice, this meant abolishing slavery in the District of Columbia and prohibiting it in all U.S. jurisdictions, including the territories. Following the summary of the Liberty Party's goals and agenda, the section concludes with an invitation to readers: "Such, fellow citizens, are our views, principles, and objects. We invite your cooperation in the great work of delivering our beloved country from the evils of slavery." In sum, the *Address* suggests nothing less than a realignment of American politics from cleavages surrounding economic policy to the issue of slavery, the "paramount moral and political question of the day." Insofar as the slavery issue is paramount, "[i]t follows, as a necessary consequence, that we cannot yield our political support to any party which does not take our ground on this question."[33]

Addressing Present Partisan Identities and Ideologies

Under the heading "The Different Parties," the *Appeal*'s text moves to a simultaneous critique and appropriation of Democratic and Whig ideologies with the goal of bringing antislavery members of these major parties into the Liberty fold. But this is an extremely difficult task. Partisan identities and loyalties, once formed, are said to be quite durable, and both Whigs and Democrats were reluctant to desert their parties. Party leaders were particularly reluctant to abandon the organizations that were their basis of power and influence. Chase, as a converted Whig, recognized the intractability of established partisan identities.[34] This conversion experience, however, may also have enabled him to recognize that it can be less difficult to desert a party if one can justify doing so on the basis of loyalty to its most basic principles.

The *Address*'s narrative of the slave power, insofar as it represented each of the major parties as tools of the slave power conspiracy, had already begun the process of undermining existing partisan loyalties. But the text quickly moves to a much more pointed critique of the Democratic and Whig parties. The Democratic Party is considered first in terms of its claims to be guided by such liberal principles and mottoes as "equal and exact justice to all men"; "equal rights for all men"; "inflexible opposition to oppression." The *Address* finds these "maxims of true Democracy" to be laudable yet hopelessly tainted by the influence of the slave power:

> when we compare the maxims of the so-called Democratic party with its acts, its hypocrisy is plainly revealed. Among its leading members we find the principal slaveholders, the chiefs of the oligarchy. It has never scrupled to sacrifice the rights of the Free States, or of the people, to the demands of the slave power.

In order to dramatize the party's decline, the *Address* portrays the submission of Northern Democrats to the slave power as itself a form of slavery, a move that dramatizes a basic assumption of the slave power strategy—that citizens and political leaders, as well as slaves, are brought low by this system and its masters.[35]

The unusual approbation given to the principles of the Democratic Party in the *Address* was part of a larger strategy that Chase would pursue throughout his political career with the Liberty Party—portraying it as the true and uncorrupted Democratic Party. The goal was to ideologically displace the Democrats as the true opponents of aristocracy, thereby (it was hoped) actually displacing the Democratic Party from its electoral base in the North. This strategy, however, was controversial to many Liberty partisans and aggravated the tension between existing and prospective Liberty constituencies, for while Chase aimed at repositioning Liberty ideology closer to traditionally Democratic ideological ground in order to convert moderate antislavery Democrats, he risked alienating many of the Liberty Party rank and file who had become accustomed to battling proslavery Democrats. It was, in fact, Chase's professed attachment to Democratic Party principles (especially a "passage styling the Liberty Party as 'The True Democracy of the United States'") that caused the most controversy in the committee responsible for revising Chase's draft of the *Address*.[36]

Scholars, too, remain puzzled by Chase's Democratic bias in the *Address*. Biographer John Niven explains this tilt in two ways: "Chase's assessment blended both the practical and the ideal. Cincinnati was solidly Democratic; but equally important was a belief . . . that Jeffersonian idealism was basically much more appropriate to the abolitionist objective than the Whig program." To Vernon Volpe, however, this "remains one of the more puzzling acts of his political career," given that "one had to look hard to discover antislavery sentiment among the northwestern Democracy. If Chase saw antislavery potential in the Democratic Party, he was . . . a rare Liberty man." Indeed, despite the opposition of some Democrats to their Party's attempts to annex Texas, Chase's efforts to sway prominent antislavery Democrats like fellow Ohioan Jacob Brinkerhoff were entirely ineffectual. Even the text of the *Address* itself admits that the Democratic Party was unlikely to turn against slavery.[37]

Northern Whigs appeared to be much more congenial partners for an antislavery coalition with the Liberty Party. During the recent Texas annexation controversy, relatively few Democrats had expressed concern about this measure's relationship to slavery or the slave power. It was largely Northern Whigs who opposed the measure on the grounds that it was designed by the slave power to expand its institution. Not only did

Northern Whigs exhibit a more spirited opposition to slavery during this recent debate, they also had much in common with the Liberty Party rank and file. Especially in the Western Reserve of Ohio, the ethno-religious similarities between Liberty partisans and traditional Whig constituencies would have made them congenial coalition partners.[38] Why, then, did Chase opt to focus on Democratic audiences? The *Address* answers this question by pointing out that while there were "zealous opponents of slavery, who are also zealous Whigs; . . . they have not the general confidence of their party; they are under the ban of slaveholders." Correspondingly, the Whig Party "proposes, in its national conventions, no action against slavery. It has no antislavery article in its national creed." As a result, "expectation of efficient antislavery action from the Whig party, as now organized, will prove delusive. Nor do we perceive any probability of a change in its organization, separating its antislavery from its pro-slavery constituents."[39]

Perhaps Chase's antipathy to the Whig Party—despite the fact that its constituency and antislavery zeal seemed to make it a more likely ally than the Democrats—is best understood as a response to one of the unique challenges faced by third parties. One way that major parties respond to third parties is by co-opting those third party agendas that appear to be compelling to large constituencies.[40] Chase's coalitional strategy only heightened this danger, for as he sought to recast Liberty Party ideology in a way that made it more appealing to antislavery Whigs and Democrats, he risked a potentially dangerous drift toward the major parties. Why leave the major parties for the Liberty Party, shrewd Democrats and Whigs might ask, when this party is already so close to Whigs and Democrats? Wouldn't the cause of antislavery be better served by joining a major party and wielding real power? In fact, such a dynamic was already in place. Antislavery Whigs like Joshua Giddings—the Ohio congressman representing the Western Reserve—sought to co-opt Liberty partisans with claims that the cause would be better served by sending antislavery Whigs to Washington than by contributing to the victory of proslavery Democrats by taking away Whig votes. In the Western Reserve, such defection had been discouraged by an insistence that the Liberty Party maintain "complete independence from the Whig party."[41]

Chase's decision to fashion Liberty Party ideology on Democratic rather than Whig grounds might also be understood as an ideological response to the potential danger Whigs posed to Liberty constituencies. Chase's plans for the Liberty Party recognized that the wholesale conversion of either major party to antislavery was as impractical as an alliance with either major party was undesirable. Rather, his strategy to gain a place within the two-party system required that the Liberty Party remain organizationally independent as its ideology was recast in a fashion enabling the party to convert increasing numbers of antislavery Democrats and Whigs. But under the circumstances of 1845, a Liberty ideology that too closely resembled Whig ideology would only increase the already existing danger of a successful bid by Northern Whigs to co-opt the Liberty agenda. This eventuality would, of course, derail Chase's plans for the party. In this respect, precisely because Whigs were much closer to Liberty men—both ethno-religiously and in term of antislavery—Chase positioned the Liberty Party ideology closer to its natural proslavery enemies. Only a Liberty Party that could resist Whig co-option of its agenda could hope to remain an independent political organization that might prevail in the electoral process and realign Northern politics on antislavery terms. A Liberty Party electorate steeped in Democratic ideals and principles might be more resistant to Whig antislavery entreaties, and a Liberty Party with Democratic predispositions would be more difficult for a Whig coalition to digest. Since there was so little danger of mainstream proslavery Democrats co-opting the Liberty agenda, on the other hand, Democratic ideology was a much safer target for appropriation than was Whig ideology. This Democratic ideological tilt might initially alienate potential Whig converts, but since antislavery Whigs already shared the Liberty Party's suspicion that the slave power was controlling their old Democratic enemies, they, too, could find a familiar niche within emerging Liberty ideology. Whatever the precise strategic calculations, the text explicitly insists on the necessity of an independent and enduring political organization: "We cannot choose between these parties for the sake of any local or particular advantage, without sacrificing consistency, self-respect, and mutual confidence." Rather, this "truly liberal and thoroughly republican party," this "truly Democratic party," is portrayed as the only appropriate electoral choice. In sum, "[t]he Liberty party of 1845 is, in truth, the Liberty party of 1776 revived."[42]

Targeted Audiences in the *Address*

The fourth section of the *Address* uses the aristocratic slave power conspiracy as a means to move a variety of different kinds of sectionally constituted audiences to support and join the Liberty Party. Within this section, the first two headings ("Anti-Slavery Men!" and "All Men of the Free States") are concerned primarily with Northern audiences, and the last three with Southern audiences ("All Non-Slaveholders of the Slave States!" "The Fruits of Slavery," and "To Slaveholders"). The "Anti-Slavery Men!" section is an appeal to the antislavery factions of the Whig and Democratic parties, and here the *Address* negotiates another complication related to the social logic of third parties. Voters frequently resist voting for third parties because they fear that their vote is squandered on candidates who have no hope of victory. The *Address* seeks to defuse this perception on both a moral and pragmatic level. On a moral level, it argues that it is "far better to act with those with whom you agree on the fundamental point of slavery." To do otherwise is to enable honest disagreements "on questions of trade, currency, and extension of territory" to be used as a means by which all are "played off against each other by parties which agree in nothing except hostility to the great measure of positive action against slavery." Far more is to be gained by "laying . . . minor difference on the altar of duty, and uniting as one man, in one party, against slavery." Such a course may, in the short term, mean that one's vote will not bring one's candidate of choice into office. Nevertheless, this course of action is said to be pragmatic in the long term: "Then every vote would tell for freedom, and would encourage the friends of liberty to fresh efforts. Now every vote, whether you intend it so or not, tells for slavery, and operates as discouragement and hindrance to those who are contending for equal rights." In this manner, the *Address* gestures to the point made by today's political scientists: "The prophecy that a [third party] candidate cannot win is self-fulfilling." Along these lines, the *Address* insists that if antislavery Whigs and Democrats would break this vicious cycle, the effect would be to "hasten" rather than "retard" the day of the Liberty Party's triumph.[43] Turning more generally to "All Men of the Free States" and "All Non-Slaveholders of the Slave States!" the *Address* returns to the slave power and its deleterious influence on the nation as a strategy of mobilizing the electorate. The slave power is positioned as a new aristocracy with extremely harmful consequences for all nonslaveholders in the North and South, and electoral cooperation with the Liberty Party is identified as the only truly empowering alternative. Finally, the *Address* asks slaveholders to follow the examples of the nation's founders, reassuring them that Liberty policy will remove slavery only from "places under the exclusive jurisdiction of the national government," leaving the institution intact within the states.[44]

The *Address* focuses its conclusion on ensuring readers that a vote for the Liberty Party is not a wasted vote but an essential first step in a larger process of partisan realignment. In this vein, the *Address* is especially concerned to develop the claim that the Liberty Party's trajectory is one of growth and eventual victory:

> The little handful of voters . . . in 1840 . . . has already swelled to a GREAT PARTY, strong enough, numerically, to decide the issue in any national contest, and stronger far in the power of its pure and elevating principles. And if these principles be sound . . . it is a libel on the intelligence, the patriotism, and the virtue of the American people to say that there is no hope that a majority will not array themselves under our banner.[45]

Such an eventual victory, of course, required political independence: "Be not tempted from the path of political duty. . . . To act with any party, or to vote for the candidates of any party, which recognizes the friends and supporters of slavery as members in full standing, because in particular places or under particular circumstances, it may make professions of antislavery zeal, is to commit political suicide." In sum, "unswerving fidelity . . . unalterable determination . . . inflexible and unanimous support . . . are the conditions of our ultimate triumph. Let these conditions be fulfilled, and our triumph is certain."[46]

The *Address of the Southern and Western Convention* was a key text in the evolution of the antislavery movement, and it anticipates most of the rhetorical strategies that would bring ultimate Republican victory fifteen years later. It was a decisive move away from the eschatological narratives and jeremiadic form of religious-minded Liberty Party supporters and Garrisonians. Chase's historical narrative more closely approximated secular civic republican narratives of decay—in which a fragile state succumbs to power-hungry factions.[47] Chase's slave power conspiracy was not that personification of evil found within radical abolitionist and universal reform jeremiadic conspiracy narratives. Rather, Chase's slave power was just another cabal—inspired by relatively ordinary motives like self-interest and love of power—of the type that civic republican ideology had always identified as a major factor contributing to the fragility of republics. Consistent with this tradition, Chase's narrative of the slave power posited not spiritual backsliding but flagging vigilance against the dangers of concentrated power and conspiracies against political liberty and the state as the primary factor enabling the rise of the slave power.[48] Such a civic republican narrative was far more consistent with the assumptions and conventions of mid-nineteenth-century partisan rhetoric than the eschatologically charged narratives of Chase's more radical allies. The *Address* also parted ways with abolitionists and anticipated later Republican strategies in directly confronting the constraints of partisan politics and the party system. Chase's slave power conspiracy rhetoric functioned in ways consistent with the demands of partisan rhetoric and of his party's circumstances. The slave power conspiracy position not only provided a common enemy that could mute the division between coalitionists and universal reformers within the convention, it also operated as a device for critique that aimed to detach Whigs and Democrats from their existing party loyalties and to redirect them toward the Liberty Party. To Democrats, Chase's refashioned Liberty ideology offered an opportunity to continue the fight against the aristocrats that had infiltrated this avowedly anti-aristocratic party; to Northern Whigs, it presented a chance to redouble their ongoing efforts against the slave power and its Democratic minions. Finally, the text negotiated several kinds of constraints related to the unique social logic of a third party within a two-party system.

Notwithstanding the optimism of Chase and the Liberty Party in the *Address*, this political movement is acknowledged as a failure in the realm of practical politics. Its failure is typically explained by reference to the party's generally ineffective strategies and tactics, particularly in terms of organization and propaganda. Tactical ineffectiveness and unwillingness to compromise, combined with a constituency holding a narrow religious and eschatological worldview, helped to ensure the eventual failure of the first antislavery political party. By 1847 even Chase was willing to admit that the Liberty Party was an entirely ineffective political instrument. In September 1847 he confided in a letter to Gamaliel Bailey that "I see few symptoms of robust vitality in the Liberty Party. What with its universal reform dreamers, its hair splitting metaphysicians, its theological politicians, its bigots, its pharisees and impracticables, the building of its tower is in a fair way to be arrested by confusion of tongues and a general scatteration."[49]

Free-Soil Interlude: 1848–1854

Chase's Rise and the Fall of Free-Soil

By 1848 the Liberty Party was all but extinct in Ohio, but in its place arose the Free-Soil Party. Here was a broader antislavery coalition composed of well-organized independent Democrats (especially New York Barnburners) and Whigs (especially from Massachusetts) as well as Liberty men and abolitionists, united behind the Wilmot Proviso's proposed prohibition of

slavery in the territories newly acquired from Mexico. Chase's hopes for
this party were moderate. No longer did he aim at the long-term conversion of Democrats and Whigs, culminating in partisan realignment. In May
1847 Chase admitted that

> to build up a new party is by no means so easy as to compel old parties to do
> a particular work. . . . [A]n anti-slavery league, operating upon both parties
> from without, aided by the anti-slavery men already in the ranks of the two
> parties . . . would, in the best manner & the shortest time, accomplish the
> great work of overthrowing slavery.[50]

In August 1848 this party organized nationally at the Free-Soil convention
in Buffalo, New York. By this time, Chase's skill at achieving compromise
within small groups of politicians had come to be recognized by his peers,
and he was largely responsible for crafting the relatively moderate platform
of the Buffalo convention. Within a few years this party, too, would fail, in
part due to its ineffective organization and corresponding reliance on ideology and moral appeals but primarily due to the continued recalcitrance of
the old party loyalties of the Whig-Democratic party system. Before it effectively ceased to exist as a national political organization, however, the
Free-Soil Party would send Chase to the Senate. In the election of 1848,
the Ohio Free-Soil Party won enough seats in the state legislature to hold
the balance between the Democrats and Whigs. While Ohio Whigs were
more strongly opposed to slavery, Democrats were willing to deal, and in
exchange for giving control of the legislature to Democrats, the Free-Soil
Party was given the soon to be vacated Ohio Senate seat.[51]

Chase had few allies in the Senate, yet he continued his efforts against
slavery. Speaking to the compromise measures of 1850, on March 26 and
27 of that year Chase delivered "Union and Freedom, Without Compromise." This speech reveals Chase's narrative of the founding period and the
slave power to be remarkably consistent with his previous efforts—in particular, the *Address*. He presented a virtually identical narrative establishing
the antislavery principles of the founding era and used most of the same
documents and sources, often in the same order, to prove that the founding policy was not one of equilibrium between North and South, freedom
and slavery.[52] Though he seemed no closer to the antislavery coalition he
had worked for since 1841, the passage of time and the course of events
had perceptibly altered the reception of Chase's rhetoric: "It makes me
smile to think of the different reception these doctrines meet with now,
from that with which they were greeted, when I first proclaimed them in

the Ohio Liberty Address of 1841." Nevertheless, Chase lamented that "the masses follow [the old parties] on, many from old usage and association,— many from the fear of being denounced as Free-Soilers and abolitionists,— and many, perhaps most of all, because they see no means of action that promises any thing else than political outlawry and defeat."[53]

Waiting for Realignment

From the perspective of the present, we know that Chase's decade of disappointment would eventually come to an end. The partisan realignment that was the goal of his rhetorical efforts on behalf of the Liberty Party would come under the auspices of the Republican Party between the years 1854 and 1860. During this time, the Republicans replaced the Whigs as the anti–Democratic Party and changed the face of the party system. According to some political historians, however, Chase's earlier attempts at crafting a third-party rhetoric of realignment were doomed from the outset by the political circumstances of the time. The political conditions of the nineteenth century were hospitable to third-party formation, but stable partisan identities and formidable institutions meant that third-party efforts, by themselves, would be unable to dissolve the party system. Rather, the realignment of the 1850s was a two-stage process. In the first stage, the old party system weakened and collapsed. It was only in the second stage, when new parties arose to fill the power vacuum, that third-party persuasions had a realistic chance of electoral success.[54]

According to political historian Michael Holt, the antebellum two-party system retained popular support only so long as voters perceived that the parties truly differed in significant ways. Under such circumstances, voters assumed that the parties were appropriate vehicles for group interests that functioned as checks on one another, and they perceived a genuine choice between competing agendas at election time. But as the 1850s approached, the Whig and Democratic programs no longer seemed to offer competing agendas and clear-cut choices to the electorate, especially as the two parties continued to concur on matters of slavery. Under these circumstances, popular confidence in the representativeness of the two-party system diminished, and the electorate became disillusioned with politicians and their party machines. The resulting disillusionment with the two-party system had two primary effects. First, as the two-party system deteriorated, a space was opened for successful third-party activity. The decay of the second party system, of course, did not proceed evenly among Whigs and Democrats. The Whig Party, not the Democratic, would wholly disintegrate in the 1850s, creating a power vacuum that was quickly filled with minor parties (like the Know-Nothings and Republicans in the North) eager to replace the Whigs in the party system. Second, disillusionment with politicians and parties fostered antiparty attitudes and encouraged the public to see traditional party politics as conspiracy. Lack of faith in establishment politicians, parties, and the political system encouraged the view that, even as political actors justified their actions in the familiar terms of the public good, they were truly pursuing their own self-interest or other sinister agendas. Such suspicions fell most heavily on the only remaining functional major party, the Democrats, and each of the anti-Democratic contenders to replace the Whigs sought to mobilize opposition by positioning Democrats as part of a conspiracy. To the growing nativists and Know-Nothing movement, Democrats were a part of a Catholic conspiracy to undermine American liberties.[55] Antislavery politicians, on the other hand, argued equally strenuously that the Democrats were instead part of a slave power conspiracy.

Nativists and Know-Nothings initially seemed to have an electoral advantage over Free-Soilers and proto-Republicans, but an increasing perception of growing Southern political unity maintained the plausibility of the notion that the slave power was seeking control of the Republic. The Nebraska bill of 1854, and its repeal of the Missouri Compromise, finally convinced many Northerners that a slave power conspiracy was a likely reality rather than just a remote possibility. But it was not the Nebraska bill itself that caused such suspicions. Rather, it was the meaning political leaders assigned to this event.[56] Antislavery forces recognized that one essential ingredient of electoral success would be to use the Nebraska bill as proof that the slave power—not the Catholic Church—represented the greatest conspiratorial threat to the nation. Chase's *Appeal* was one of the first attempts to assign conspiratorial significance to the Nebraska bill, and its assessment would become a staple of Republican slave power narratives throughout the 1850s.

The Nebraska Bill and the
Appeal of the Independent Democrats

The Nebraska Bill and the Slave Power Conspiracy

Chase's *Appeal of the Independent Democrats* is remembered as "one of the most effective pieces of political propaganda ever produced." Indeed, the ripples created by this influential text have extended well beyond its own time and animated fierce historical debates. Generations of historians have vehemently disagreed both about its effect and about the veracity of its claims. For some, Chase's claims were fundamentally erroneous, and the *Appeal* was a piece of deceptive propaganda. This group, however, also insists on the pervasive influence of the text on contemporary audiences and subsequent events—positioning it as responsible for inflaming the passions that would ensure the coming of the Civil War. Others have argued the opposite—that the charges in the *Appeal* were true and that such inflammatory rhetoric is something far less than a sufficient cause of the Civil War.[57] While historians have debated the *Appeal*'s influence and the veracity of its claims, others have considered how the text worked rhetorically. Kathleen Diffley recognizes its importance in encouraging political activity against the slave power, portraying it as "the first, best hope of an organizing rhetoric" against slavery. The *Appeal* functioned effectively in this regard, Diffley writes, because it focused on a general threat that might unify, rather than a specific policy that might divide, potential political allies. But Diffley also reads the *Appeal*'s call for a return to past purity in the face of crisis and anxiety as an indication that the text ought to be described in the terms of the jeremiad, going so far as to conclude that Chase's *Appeal* succeeded where abolitionists had failed precisely because it "couched the 'Appeal' in the older, recognizable form of the Puritan jeremiad."[58] Diffley is correct to point out the unifying function of slave power conspiracy rhetoric, but two considerations problematize the jeremiad as an interpretive strategy. For one thing, abolitionists as well as Liberty partisans were political failures despite their reliance on the jeremiad in their eschatological emplotments of American history. The jeremiad, then, cannot explain the *Appeal*'s success. In addition, as noted earlier, even as early as 1845 Chase's attempt to move antislavery into the mainstream was associated with a move away from the eschatologically charged jeremiad and toward a more secular civic republican orientation.

In any event, the authorship and title of the *Appeal* illustrate both the continuity of Chase's antislavery strategy and the very different partisan circumstances of 1854. Perhaps the most important difference in the political landscape was the lack of an organized antislavery party in 1854. Accordingly, the *Appeal* was the work not of party leaders but of Chase and a small junto of Free-Soil congressmen who saw in the Nebraska bill a great opportunity to rebuild a political antislavery coalition within the remains of the two-party system.[59] While issues of authorship highlight the radically different partisan circumstances of the *Appeal of the Independent Democrats,* its title indicates the continuity of one important component of Chase's antislavery strategy. Since the author(s) and cosigners of the text were not themselves of Democratic extraction—all were Free-Soilers and at least half were of recent Whig vintage—the title seems to be of rhetorical rather than descriptive significance. Its rhetorical significance is twofold. The title indicates Chase's continued desire to position antislavery in a Democratic fashion, and it sets up an implicit contrast between "independent" Democrats and Democrats like Stephen Douglas who were "dependent" on the patronage of the party and its ruler, the slave power. In this respect, Chase plays on the anti-party attitudes of the mid-1850s as he develops his claim about a conspiratorial threat to the Republic.

Introducing the *Appeal*

The civic republican bent of the *Appeal* is immediately indicated in its opening delineation of the duty of legislators:

> FELLOW CITIZENS: As Senators and Representatives in the Congress of the United States, it is our duty to warn our constituents whenever imminent danger menaces the freedom of our institutions or the permanency of our Union. Such danger, as we firmly believe, now impends, and we earnestly solicit your prompt attention to it.[60]

Spiritual backsliding is not the problem constructed here but rather a conspiratorial danger to the Republic. The authors and cosigners of the text privilege vigilance as the most appropriate disposition for a member of Congress. Vigilance, of course, had always been the watchword of republics, and mid-nineteenth-century civic republicanism also reiterated the necessity of vigilance against conspiracies if the Republic were to be preserved from those forces contributing to its decay.[61] The threat of which these vigilant representatives would warn their constituents was Stephen Douglas's Nebraska bill, which would allegedly "open all the unorganized territory of the Union to the ingress of slavery." Through the *Appeal,* Chase and cosigners (and, in some cases, coauthors) Charles Sumner, Joshua Giddings, Edward Wade, Gerrit Smith, and Alexander De Witt "arraign this bill as a gross violation of a sacred pledge; as a criminal betrayal of precious rights; as part and parcel of an atrocious plot to exclude from a vast and unoccupied region, immigrants from the Old World and free laborers from our own States, and convert it into a dreary region of despotism, inhabited by masters and slaves."[62]

Diffley's jeremiadic interpretation gains some grounding from the term "sacred pledge," but this language exists alongside other terms ("atrocious plot") more consistent with civic republicanism. The justification for a civic republican reading of the *Appeal* becomes more evident as the remainder of this compact seven-page text proceeds to elaborate and dramatize the danger and scope of the crisis at the same time that it seeks to move its audiences to political action against the slave power.

The Geography, History, and Consequences of Conspiracy

Following the introduction, the *Appeal*'s text is appropriately divided into several sections. First, the text moves to what one critic has called a "geographic proof."[63] Here the text invites readers, "Take your maps, fellow citizens . . . and see what country it is which this bill . . . proposes to open to slavery." Following a lengthy and detailed paragraph illustrating the enormity of the scope of the territory to be opened to slavery, the text proceeds to a "relatively cold exposition" of "irrefutable historical evidence" in the form of a "history of American slavery policy from 1784 to 1853."[64] This exposition consists of two parts. The first is a narrative of conspiracy and the second a narrative refuting Douglas's historical argument in defense of the bill.

The narrative of conspiracy opens:

> We beg your attention, fellow citizens, to a few historical facts. The original settled policy of the United States, clearly indicated by the Jefferson Proviso of 1787, was non-extension of slavery. In 1803, Louisiana was acquired by purchase from France. . . . Congress, instead of providing for the abolition of slavery in this new Territory, permitted its continuance. In 1812 the State of Louisiana was organized and admitted into the Union with slavery.[65]

The founders' antislavery policy is resurgent with the third point of the narrative as Congress, in 1818, prepared to admit the state of Missouri into the Union without slavery. But this measure was bitterly opposed, and after two years of debate characterized by "increased violence," the Missouri Compromise—by which Missouri was admitted with slavery, but slavery was prohibited in all other territory lying north of 36°30"—was widely thought to have settled the issue once and for all:

> Nothing is more certain than that this prohibition has been regarded and accepted by the whole country as a solemn compact against the extension of slavery into any part of the territory acquired from France, lying north of 36

deg. 30 min., and not included in the new State of Missouri. The same act
. . . consecrated beyond question and beyond honest recall, the whole remainder of the territory to freedom and free institutions forever. For more
than thirty years—during more than half the period of our national existence under our present constitution—this compact has been universally re-
garded and acted upon as inviolable American law.

Against this "solemn compact" and over thirty years of its operation, however, stands the Nebraska bill. As Chase describes this bill, he relies upon
the imagery of sleep and wakefulness to express the need for citizens to
wake up to the scope of the danger now facing the Republic: "It is a strange
and ominous fact well calculated to awaken the worst apprehensions, and
the most fearful forebodings of future calamities, that it is now directly
proposed to repeal this prohibition . . . and thus to subvert this compact,
and allow slavery in all the yet unorganized territory."[66]

That the *Appeal*'s narrative of conspiracy is vastly different from those
within the 1845 *Address* and the 1850 "Union and Freedom" there is little
doubt. While it has in common with Chase's previous narratives a representation of the founders and their acts as decidedly antislavery, prior
Chase narratives posited the commencement of the operation of the new
government as the key cardinal function of the conspiracy narrative—the
point at which the slave power decisively took control of national policy
and commenced its expansion westward. In the *Appeal*, however, at no
point is the slave power an all-powerful force. After describing a brief period of (apparent) slave power control between 1803 and 1812 in which
the Louisiana Purchase and the entrance of Louisiana as a slave state ex-
panded slavery westward, the *Appeal*'s narrative portrays a North reaffirming the founders' policy by seeking a prohibition of slavery in Missouri.
Though eventually forced into a compromise on the issue, the North is represented as securing the founders' antislavery policy with a prohibition of
the institution above 36°30″. In sum, the *Appeal*'s narrative is one of the
continuing triumphs of the founders' antislavery vision, even if in the at-
tenuated form of the Missouri Compromise. Only with the Nebraska bill
does the slave power appear to be on the brink of reversing the antislavery
policy of the policy of the founders. What explains this change? Why does
Chase contract his narrative of the slave power conspiracy in 1854?

The conventional wisdom regarding conspiracy narratives is that more is
better. Conspiracy rhetors typically marshal as much "evidence" as possible
in order to make the conspiracy believable.[67] When the evidence for
conspiracy consists of a historical representation—a narrative of the

conspiracy's visible actions in the world—we ought to expect that more narrative functions will provide a more compelling proof of conspiracy. Rhetors capable of presenting numerous U.S. policies—the Seminole war, the acquisition of new slave states, the gag rule, Texas annexation, and the Mexican War, to name a few—within a compelling narrative of conspiracy seem to be best equipped to persuade audiences. The contraction of Chase's narrative initially seems puzzling, but there are at least two reasons that the *Appeal*'s shortened narrative of conspiracy, consisting of only one function (the Nebraska bill), was more consistent with the goal of reaching the political audiences of 1854.

First, there is an inverse relationship between the scope of the conspiracy narrative and the possibilities for utilizing the characters, events, and documents of the American political tradition as symbolic resources against the conspiracy. On this matter, Garrison represents the extreme case. For him, American history, from the Constitution to his present, was one driven by the slave power conspiracy. This orientation—consistent with the paranoid style of conspiracy discourse—provided his narrative with the greatest possible number of conspiratorial functions. But since it also tainted all of history as the work of the conspiracy, this move required that he ground his persuasive efforts in something other than the American political tradition or its founding document—something like morality, religion, or eschatology. William Goodell and the early Chase represent a less extreme case. Because their narrative of conspiracy was preceded by an antislavery Declaration, founding, and Constitution, they were able to claim the Constitution and the nation's founders as allies and discursive resources. For this reason, their antislavery effort could be couched in political and legal (rather than moral or religious) terms, and they—like later Republicans such as Lincoln—could claim the conservative goal of returning the Republic to its first principles. The *Appeal*'s contracting narrative of conspiracy, because it made more and more elements of the American political tradition—in particular, the Missouri Compromise—available for appropriation by antislavery forces, represented a further move toward the political center in comparison to Chase's earlier efforts.

In some respects, this was a reluctant move toward the center, for Chase actually thought the Missouri Compromise gave too much to slavery. But in the *Appeal* Chase was "speaking to the conservative elites of the North, the ministers and the editors of the metropolitan press who feared for the disappearance of old landmarks such as the Missouri Compromise. . . . Chase was defending the Missouri settlement, which privately he condemned, and whose import he had publicly denied for years."[68] The extent to which Chase's voice has shifted to that of a conservative defender of sectional compromises is evidenced by his invocation of the authoritative legacy of the recently deceased Whig Henry Clay: "Were he living now, no one would be more forward, more eloquent, or more indignant, in his denunciation of that bad faith, than Henry Clay, the foremost champion of both compromises." While Chase and his radical antislavery colleagues appear conservative, the South is portrayed as violating hallowed agreements and making unreasonable demands—demands that the free states cannot meet "without the deepest dishonor and crime."[69] In situations like that of 1854, then, more extensive conspiracy narratives may be more likely to alienate rather than persuade prospective audiences. Better to reduce the scope of the conspiracy narrative and portray the conspiracy itself as threatening the landmarks of American history.

There is a second reason for Chase's narrative of conspiracy to shrink as he sought to bring the antislavery message to ever wider audiences. As mentioned, narrative emplotments construct frames that condition the possibilities for action. A comic frame positions problems in the world as subject to remediation by action. Religious-minded Liberty men and early Garrisonians initially pursued moral suasion because they believed that their efforts at reform would ultimately be successful at eliminating public error and misunderstanding. A tragic frame, on the other hand, positions evil in the world as unstoppable—at least by ordinary means. Accordingly, Garrison and his followers ultimately lost hope in the redemptive possibilities of moral suasion in a world increasingly controlled by the forces of evil. A correspondingly tragic view of the world encouraged some to withdraw from the effort and others to pursue violent means of combating slavery. Given this relationship between emplotment, frame, and action, a comic frame is much more conducive to the requirements of the rhetorical narrative, which is fashioned so as to encourage some sort of audience enactment or response.[70] Precisely because a shorter conspiracy narrative suggested a less omnipotent slave power, it was more conducive to the comic possibilities of audience enactment. Rhetors needed only to educate their audiences, and the more recently the citizen body had fallen under the deceptive influence of the slave power conspiracy, the simpler it would be to inform them of the true state of affairs. Similarly, a shorter narrative of conspiracy makes readers more likely to believe that they are capable of effectively acting against the still embryonic conspiracy.

Returning to the textual development of the *Appeal,* the second section of the historical narrative aims at refuting "the various pretences under which it is attempted to cloak this monstrous wrong." But even when refuting the historical claims of the Nebraska bill's defenders, the text simultaneously makes the case for a slave power conspiracy—it uses the very arguments and policy positions of the alleged conspirators to establish their duplicity. The most prominent "pretense"—advanced by Senator Stephen Douglas—was that "the Territory of Nebraska sustains the same relations to slavery as did the territories acquired from Mexico prior to 1850"; that, in effect, the Missouri Compromise had been superseded by more recent agreements. But according to the *Appeal,* "No assertion could be more groundless." Rather, the Compromise of 1850 is said to apply only to the acquisition from Mexico, a proposition proven from the text of the Compromise Act as well as the understandings expressed by members of Congress—even the friends of slavery—since that time. Chase writes that in 1850, "This pretense had not then been set up. It is a palpable afterthought." In sum, a review of the historical record suggested that the slave power and its Northern Democratic allies were unwilling to engage in genuine debate and deliberation. Rather, their "pretences . . . are mere inventions, designed to cover up from public reprehension mediated bad faith," and the very revelation of this deceptive justification further establishes the Nebraska bill as the work of the slave power conspiracy and its minions.[71]

Following the geography and historical sections of the *Appeal* and just prior to the conclusion, in the section delineating the expected consequences of the Nebraska bill, the text makes another shift from "relatively cold exposition" to "hot, intensely emotional, language," returning to the "hyperbolic pitch" of the introduction:[72]

> We confess our total inability properly to delineate the character or describe the consequences of this measure. Language fails to express the sentiments of indignation and abhorrence which it inspires; and no vision, less penetrating than that of the All-Seeing, can reach its evil issue. To some of its more immediate and inevitable consequences, however, we must attempt to direct your attention.[73]

The first consequence involves the effect of the Nebraska bill on the proposed Pacific railroad. The railroad will be difficult to build and unprofitable as long as the Nebraska bill makes this "a country from which the energetic and intelligent masses will be virtually excluded." The second consequence relates to the frustration of the founders' vision of westward

expansion: "patriotic statesmen have anticipated that a free, industrious
and enlightened population will extract abundant treasures of individual
and public wealth." With the Nebraska bill, "all such expectation will turn
to grievous disappointment" due to the fact that "Freemen, unless pressed
by a hard and cruel necessity, will not, and should not, work beside slaves.
Labor cannot be expected where any class of laborers is held in abject
bondage."[74]

The worst consequence of the bill relates to the larger "geographical
character of this project":

> We beg you, fellow citizens, to observe that it [the Nebraska bill] will sever
> the east from the west of the United States by a wide slaveholding belt of
> country, extending from the Gulf of Mexico to British North America. It is a
> bold scheme against American liberty, worthy of an accomplished architect
> of ruin.

This bold scheme, however, was only the first step in a plot of continental
proportions:

> It is hoped . . . by the influence of a Federal Government controlled by the
> slave power, to extinguish freedom and establish slavery in the States and
> Territories of the Pacific, and thus permanently subjugate the whole country
> to the yoke of a slaveholding despotism. Shall a plot against humanity and
> democracy, so monstrous, and so dangerous to the interests of liberty
> throughout the world, be permitted to succeed?[75]

Though the *Appeal*'s narrative of conspiracy consisted of only one point—
the Nebraska bill—this point is presented as but the first step in a larger
slave power conspiracy.

Conditioning Action:
Narratives of Decay and Renewal

The *Appeal* concludes by reaffirming the warnings with which it commenced: "We appeal to the People. We warn you that the dearest interests
of freedom and the Union are in imminent peril." Readers are implored to
ignore the advice of "demagogues," "that the Union can be maintained
only by submitting to the demands of slavery." On the contrary, the *Appeal*
insists that "the Union can only be insured by the full recognition of the
just claims of freedom and man" and entreats readers to be "mindful of the
fundamental maxims of democracy, EQUAL RIGHTS AND EXACT JUSTICE FOR
ALL MEN." Not to do so is said to entail complicity in the conspiracy, to
become an agent "in extending legalized oppression and systematized

injustice over a vast territory yet exempt from these terrible evils." The *Appeal* implores, "Let all protest, earnestly and emphatically, by correspondence, through the press, by memorials, by resolutions of public meetings and legislative bodies, and in whatever other mode may seem expedient, against this enormous crime." Finally, the authors reaffirm their understanding of the duty of legislators not only to warn of but also to confront such dangers to the Republic:

> For ourselves, we shall resist it by speech and vote, and with all the abilities which God has given us. Even if overcome in the impending struggle, we shall not submit. We shall go home to our constituents; erect anew the standard of freedom, and call on the people to come to the rescue of the country from the domination of slavery.[76]

The *Appeal*'s conclusion asks readers to act against the conspiracy and to renew the Republic from slavery's plotters. Like the Republican Party of the later 1850s, the authors aim at the conservative goal of returning the country to its original antislavery policy, to "erect anew the standard of freedom." While this call for renewal may suggest the presence of the jeremiad, when read within the overall logic of the text, it is better accounted for as enactment of the civic republican return to first principles. The text's previous narrative of conspiracy may be said to correspond to a moment of decline or decay from the purity of the early republic, one consonant with civic republican conception of the Republic as mortal and fundamentally fragile. But such moments of decay simultaneously present citizens with the opportunity to renew the Republic by returning it to its first principles. The civic republican present, in short, is a moment of decay and corruption as well as potential regeneration and rebirth. At this juncture, the connection between comic emplotments, republicanism, and organic imagery is clearest. According to Kenneth Burke, the organic imagery of decay, degeneration, and rebirth is a transcendent mode of purification associated with the comic frame.[77] In this respect, civic republicanism's organic theory of the state is strongly associated with the comic frame that shaped the slave power conspiracy narratives of Chase and later Republicans.

Despite the *Appeal*'s concern with vigilance, its preoccupation with conspiratorial threats against the Republic, and its call for a return to first principles, one might yet argue that such a republican reading is no better grounded in the text or its context than a jeremiadic reading. Both readings, one might suggest, arbitrarily situate the *Appeal* within one of the many ideological currents of the time. But the civic republican reading not only shows more fidelity to the text, it also is more consistent with Chase's own ideological predispositions, as well as with the conventions of partisan rhetoric conditioning the *Appeal*. Chase reveals his own ideological predispositions in the overt civic republican language of his contemporaneous rhetorical effort against the Nebraska bill, "Maintain Plighted Faith." This January 1854 Senate speech concluded with an explicitly civic republican vision of political decay and a call for the renewal of the Republic derived from a prominent republican: "Let me borrow from the inspiration of Milton while I declare my belief that we have yet a country 'not degenerated nor drooping to a fatal decay, but destined, by casting off the old and wrinkled skin of corruption, to out-live these pangs, and wax young again, *and, entering the* GLORIOUS WAYS OF TRUTH AND PROSPEROUS VIRTUE, BECOME GREAT AND HONORABLE IN THESE LATTER AGES.'"[78]

A civic republican reading of the *Appeal* is also reinforced by the text's place within the context of the prevailing practices of partisan rhetoric. According to Marc Kruman, within antebellum political culture, partisan rhetoric sought to involve citizens within a civic republican drama: "Party conflict offered the electorate a symbolic struggle to save the republic and white liberty and equality from corruption and tyranny. The second party system thereby institutionalized the enduring republican crisis."[79] Michael Holt agrees as to the persistent civic republican preoccupations of antebellum partisans:

> Between 1820 and 1860 Americans of all parties were obsessed with a sense of history and their historical obligation to protect the republican experiment in self-government that was the product of the Revolution. Liberty, equality, self-government, Americans were consciously educated to believe, were always threatened by tyranny, privilege, corruption, and subversion; and it was their duty to be ever vigilant that the achievements of the Revolutionary fathers were not squandered by their sons.

But the kind of vigilant activity required by citizens of a mass democracy was not the all-encompassing commitment of the ancient citizen or Revolutionary founder but the vote:

> The way they could perform that duty was to participate in politics, to monitor the men who governed them, and to cast votes for the men who seemed most loyal to republican ideals. Thus voting for Americans became a cathartic act, a way for a new generation to refight the Revolution as their ancestors had to secure freedom.[80]

While no specific party existed in 1854 to oppose the Nebraska bill, Holt suggests that this bill nevertheless provided a similar opportunity: "opposition to the Nebraska Act and the Slave power conspiracy provided a cathartic opportunity to restore political activity to its basic purposes, to regain a sense that vigilant citizens could save republican government. . . . [Citizens] were extraordinarily receptive to the rhetorical exposures of tyrannical conspiracies . . . and eager to enlist in crusades against them."[81] Situating the *Appeal*'s narrative of conspiratorial decay and renewal within a civic republican context, then, shows greater fidelity to the text and to the text's place within the generic forms of mid-nineteenth-century partisan rhetoric. Civic republicanism also helps to explain how conspiracy rhetoric, in combination with the prevailing idioms of partisan conflict in nineteenth-century political culture, served as a strategy for political mobilization and engagement. Indeed, the Nebraska bill begat the anti-Nebraska movement. Within less than two years, this loose coalition of Democrats, Whigs, Free-Soilers, Liberty partisans, and abolitionists would put aside their differences and unite against the slave power conspiracy as the Republican Party.[82] But it was more than the Nebraska bill itself that sparked such outrage in the North; it was texts like the *Appeal of the Independent Democrats*—with clipped narratives of conspiracy and emplotted within the ongoing republican drama characterizing nineteenth-century partisan rhetoric—that, within the blurred partisan lines of the 1850s, encouraged citizens to reconsider their partisan attachments.

Chase's Slave Power in Text and Discourse

Given his importance to the organization of every antislavery political party—Liberty, Free-Soil, and Republican—the trajectory of Salmon P. Chase's political career in many respects reflects the trajectory of the larger political antislavery persuasion. In Chase, one finds a figure who, over a span of decades, occupied both the fringe and center of his nation's political institutions and ideologies. Beginning in 1841, as the leader of a small and fractious Liberty Party, Chase commenced a strategy to bring antislavery to politics. Though he faced a host of political and economic elites determined to stop him, 1854 found Chase with an opportunity to capture the country's imagination and catapult the Republican Party to control of the government in 1861. Given this success story, considering the *Address* and the *Appeal* from the particular perspectives of narrative theory and partisan rhetoric reveals much about the character of slave power

conspiracy rhetoric as it approached the center of mainstream political institutions and ideologies.

Chase's 1845 and 1854 conspiracy narratives, though quite different, are
nevertheless of great value for the purposes of comprehending one pole—
the center—of this study's map of the slave power conspiracy formation.
Chase's conspiracy narratives are structurally distinct from each other but in
ways that confirm this study's expectations. In Chase's *Address,* the narrative
of American political history and the slave power propelled the text from
the past into the present and future; the slave power—ascendant since the
commencement of government operations in the 1790s—provided the key
to conceptualizing the gulf between the Republic's past and present slavery
policies. Nine years later, on the eve of the Republican Party's rapid rise into
the mainstream of American political life, the *Appeal* postulated a past relatively uncorrupted by the slave power, but it identified the Nebraska bill of
1854 as the key cardinal function of conspiracy, projecting a potential future
thick with the possibility of an expanding slave-holding despotism.
Whichever key cardinal function one considers (early 1790s or 1854), both
of Chase's conspiracy narratives are shorter than Garrison's—who viewed
the establishment of the Constitution in 1788 as the point at which the
slave power conspiracy took control of the nation. In this respect, proximity
to the center is associated with more recent key cardinal functions of conspiracy and hence shorter conspiracy narratives overall. This finding is corroborated by the fact that Chase's own conspiracy narrative shrinks
substantially as he moves from the fringe in 1845 closer to the center in
1854. In contrast to Garrison's tragic emplotments, Chase's narratives exhibit a comic emplotment. Chase's stories, driven by the slave power's ability to deceive the electorate, optimistically posit simple political action on
the part of audiences as sufficient to redeem the Republic.

From the perspective of the social logic of text, proximity to the center is
associated with a partisan social logic. Each of Chase's efforts was designed
to advance the fortunes of his antislavery political movement. In his 1845
Address, Chase continued a process of ideological innovation that sought to
steer his Liberty Party's ideology in the direction of the political mainstream
and adopt components of Democratic Party ideology. Even as the *Address*
negotiated the unique challenges faced by third parties—in particular, the
risks of co-optation and the perception that a vote for a third party is a
wasted vote—it used the slave power conspiracy as a means both to mute
internal divisions between coalitionists and universal reformers and to convert Whigs and Democrats to the Liberty Party. Nine years later the *Appeal*

used a conspiratorial interpretation of the Nebraska bill as a means to create a common enemy that might unite former Whigs and Democrats within a new antislavery coalition. The partisan social logic shared by the *Address* and *Appeal* also helps to explain the nature of Chase's narratives. Chase's conspiracy narratives were comic because they were designed for the practical purpose of mobilizing citizen action, and they were relatively short in order that the antislavery coalition might better compete within a filiopietistic culture. Chase's rhetorical texts, in sum, highlight the partisan social logic associated with conspiracy rhetoric at the center of the political mainstream.

Proximity to the center of the political mainstream brought Chase's conspiracy rhetoric not only a partisan social logic but also a civic republican ideological orientation consistent with both the norms of the party system and the mainstream political culture in general. Unlike Garrison's AASS and Goodell's faction of the Liberty Party, Chase consistently presented a relatively secular narrative in which the slave power conspiracy functioned as an agent of decay that had eroded the Republic's first principles. Consistent with the terms of the "republican drama" characterizing nineteenth-century party rhetoric, Chase's texts provided citizens with an opportunity to enact the vigilance of the founders and renew their republic through party affiliation and the ballot. In this respect civic republicanism is related to partisan social logics, as well as particular narrative forms. Structurally, civic republican conspiracy narratives, because aiming to preserve the Republic's first principles, need relatively recent key cardinal functions of conspiracy that leave the founders untainted by conspiracy. From the perspective of plot, civic republican narratives are necessarily comic insofar as they hold out the possibility of renewal.

In sum, reading the rhetorical texts of Salmon P. Chase has contributed not only to the goal of better comprehending the rhetorical strategies animating one of the most successful conspiracy theories of all time but also to better describing one pole of this study's map of the slave power conspiracy discursive formation. The interrelated dimensions of narrative, social logic, and ideology mark Chase's efforts against the slave power conspiracy as distinct from those of Garrison and his AASS. As the study moves to a consideration of Charles Sumner and Abraham Lincoln, each of these dimensions will remain important. Sumner and Lincoln, too, were party politicians whose rhetorical efforts were conditioned by this social logic. But the Sumner and Lincoln cases also provide opportunities to deepen current understanding of other essential aspects of the slave power conspiracy discourse at the center of the political mainstream.

3

Charles Sumner's "Crime Against Kansas": Conspiracy Rhetoric in the Oratorical Mold

Like Catiline, he stalked into this chamber, reeking of conspiracy,—immo etuam in Senatum venit,—and then, like Catiline, he skulked away,—abiit, excessit, evasit, erupit,—to join and provoke the conspirators, who, at a distance awaited their congenial chief. Under the influence of his malign presence the Crime ripened to its fatal fruits, while the similitude with Catiline is again renewed in the sympathy, not even concealed, which he found in the very Senate itself, where, beyond even the Roman example, a Senator has not hesitated to appear as his open compurgator.

—Charles Sumner, "The Crime Against Kansas"

Sumner's Antislavery Career and the Slave Power Conspiracy: 1844–1856

Sumner and the Whig Party

Charles Sumner was a latecomer to politics. While he had established a reputation as a philanthropist and reformer in the 1830s and early 1840s, he was not politically active until the Texas annexation controversy of the mid-1840s. As is evident by his July 4, 1845, oration, "The True Grandeur of Nations," Sumner's sudden entrance into politics was inspired largely by his pacifism and his belief that the measure to annex Texas was the work of the slave power and designed to expand slavery westward. At the time,

Massachusetts Whigs in Congress were themselves engaged in a vigorous opposition to annexation measures. Sumner made common cause with the Whigs, privately seeing the state Whig Party as a potential antislavery vehicle.[1] The Massachusetts Whig Party at the time already contained an antislavery faction. Many historians have spoken of the divide in this state between establishment Whig leaders, the "Cotton Whigs," and antislavery reformers, the "Young" or "Conscience Whigs." While Conscience Whigs like Charles Francis Adams, John Palfrey, and Charles Sumner agitated against Texas annexation, establishment Whig leaders like Daniel Webster, Rufus Choate, Robert Winthrop, and Edward Everett generally remained aloof from the movement. Seeing themselves as a "junto" or "conspiracy," Sumner and his allies entered the fray, vying with the Garrisonians for control of the anti-Texas movement. For all his radicalism, however, Sumner was not an abolitionist. He disliked both the vindictive tone of the *Liberator* and the "showy" and "noisy" mode of political action adopted by Garrison and his followers. Sumner also resisted the call for immediate abolition. Rather, like Chase, he took the more moderate position that the national government ought to have no connection with slavery, that slavery was an institution exclusively in control of the states. Sumner also followed Chase, and opposed Garrison, in his devotion to the antislavery character of the Constitution. But despite the Conscience Whigs' moderation relative to the Garrisonians, in late 1845 many establishment Whigs were pressuring Sumner and the Conscience faction to cease their agitation. But the Conscience Whigs refused, and their intransigence set the stage for a bitter feud between Conscience Whigs and Congressman Robert Winthrop for his support of the Mexican War bill in 1846.[2] This continuing rift between antislavery and establishment factions would play itself out in the Whig state conventions of 1846 and 1847, where Sumner delivered his first attacks on the slave power.

Sumner's efforts against the slave power at these Whig conventions were aimed at delivering the state Whig Party into the hands of Conscience Whigs. In the convention at Worcester on September 23, 1846, however, the Conscience Whigs revealed their political naïveté. Their antislavery resolutions were defeated by a combination of dummy resolutions and deft convention management on the part of establishment Whigs.[3] Frustration with their state party led Conscience Whigs to foster relationships with national antislavery leaders, and Sumner became an intermediary between his junto and other leaders like Salmon P. Chase and John P. Hale. Even at this early point, Sumner had come to position the slave power as a symbolic justification for the realignment of the Whig Party and political parties generally:

> I hope the time will come . . . when the Friends of Freedom may stand to-gether. There must be very soon a new chrystallization of parties, in which there shall be one grand Northern party of Freedom. In such a party I shall hope to serve by yr. Side. Meanwhile, the opponents of Slavery should aim at Union together. They should look upon each other with good will, & gen-erosity, & direct their powers,—never against each other—but always against the common enemy.[4]

Such an antislavery party was soon to come, just in time for the Con-science Whigs, who were about to realize the futility of their plan to cap-ture the Massachusetts Whig Party for antislavery.

In the Whig state convention held at Worcester on September 29, 1847, Conscience Whigs' prospects initially appeared strong. In exchange for coop-eration with an anti-Webster faction, the Conscience Whigs expected to re-ceive support for their resolution declaring that Massachusetts Whigs would support only antislavery presidential and vice-presidential candidates. In support of this resolution, Sumner delivered his "Speech for Political Action Against the Slave Power and the Extension of Slavery," in which he imitated Chase's moderate policy stands even as he followed Chase in using the slave power conspiracy as a justification for timely Whig political action:

> With every new extension of Slavery, fresh strength is imparted to the polit-ical influence, monstrous offspring of Slavery, known as the Slave Power. This influence, beyond any under our government, has deranged our insti-tutions. To this the great evils which have afflicted the country—the differ-ent perils to the Constitution—may all be traced. The Missouri Compromise, the annexation of Texas, and the war with Mexico, are only a portion of the troubles caused by the Slave Power. . . . The Slave Power is the imprisoned Giant of our Constitution. It is there confined and bound to earth. But its constant and strenuous struggles have caused, and ever will cause, erup-tions of evil in our happy country.[5]

Despite Sumner's efforts, the expected support for the resolutions was not forthcoming. This betrayal was more than Conscience Whigs could toler-ate, and it resulted in the final split of the Conscience faction from the Whig Party.[6]

Sumner and Free-Soil

Conscience Whigs were not without a political home for long. In 1848 they joined in a national coalition with Democrats, Liberty Party supporters, and abolitionists to form the Free-Soil Party. Like Chase, Sumner played an important role in organizing the Buffalo national Free Soil convention, coordinating the preconvention correspondence.[7] Prior to the national convention, however, in the "Speech for Union Among Men of All Parties Against the Slave Power," Sumner used the Massachusetts Free-Soil convention as an opportunity to define the new Liberty Party by what it stood against. Sumner insisted that the old parties and their issues—the bank, the tariff—had been made obsolete by the growing ascendance of the slave power. Like other opponents of the slave power, Sumner sought to reveal the slave power conspiracy by its profound imprint on political history:

> By the Slave Power, I understand that combination of persons, or, perhaps, of politicians, whose animating principle is the perpetuation and extension of Slavery, and the advancement of Slaveholders. That such a combination exists, will be apparent from a review of our history. It shows itself, in the mildest, and perhaps the least offensive form, in the undue proportion of offices under the Federal Constitution, which have been held by Slaveholders. It is still worse apparent in the succession of acts by which the Federal Government had been prostituted to the cause of Slavery. Among the most important of these is the Missouri Compromise, the Annexation of Texas, and the War with Mexico.[8]

Like Chase, Sumner insisted that the founders who created the Constitution were antislavery and that the early republic was relatively untainted by the slave power.[9] Sumner's present, however, was said to feature a government controlled by a slave power whose dominance was maintained through a trans-sectional alliance, an "unhallowed union—conspiracy, rather let it be called—between two remote sections of the country—between the politicians of the South-West and the politicians of the North-East; between the cotton planters and flesh mongers of Louisiana and Mississippi, and the cotton spinners and traffickers of New England; between the lords of the lash and the lords of the loom."[10] No longer part of a feeble Whig faction, Sumner was now a leader of a new antislavery party, and he sought to unify this new party on the threat—at home and in Washington—posed by the slave power conspiracy.

Despite the unifying power of a common enemy, however, Massachusetts Free-Soilers disagreed as to the best course for their party at home. Most of the former Conscience Whigs favored a complete independence from Whigs or Democrats. Others, however, sought an alliance with Democrats—an alliance solidified by a common opposition to moneyed aristocrats, the lords of the loom, the old enemies of the Democrats.

Sumner saw the advantages of a coalition with Democrats—in particular, the opportunities for office—and because he was the chair of the Free-Soil state executive committee, he was in a position to work for such a coalition. He was also in a position, as a party leader, to steer Free-Soil ideology in the direction of the Massachusetts Democracy.[11] His "Address to the People of Massachusetts, Explaining and Vindicating the Free Soil Movement," delivered at the Free-Soil convention of September 12, 1849, featured an extensive critique of slave power influence alongside a condemnation of their allies, the moneyed aristocrats. In the "Address," Sumner reiterated his claim that the old party issues were obsolete in the age of the slave power and his call for a return to the antislavery policies of the founders. The "Address" also contained Sumner's most extensive account of the slave power conspiracy to date. In language emphasizing the agency of the slave power ("It instigated," "It wrestled," "It has plunged," "It next compelled," and so forth), Sumner extensively delineated "the aggressions and usurpations by which it has turned the Federal Government from its original character of Freedom, and prostituted it to slavery." Sumner's narrative of slave power aggressions extended from the allowance of slavery within the new capital to the Louisiana Purchase, the acquisition of Florida from Spain, the Missouri Compromise, the gag rule and abolition petition controversies, Texas annexation, and the Mexican War. Sumner concluded this portion: "Such are some of the usurpations and aggressions of the Slave Power! By such steps the Federal Government has been perverted from its original purposes, its character changed, and its powers subjected to Slavery." Supplementing this account of the slave power on the national scale was a complementary account of its influence and allies in Massachusetts. Speaking of local politics, Sumner adopted a Democratic position against the many chartered corporations of the state and their alleged disproportionate influence in the legislative apportionment. "In the corporations," Sumner explained, "is embodied the Money Power of the Commonwealth. The instinct of property has proved stronger than the instinct of Freedom, and the Money Power here has joined hands with the Slave Power."[12]

Luckily for Sumner and Free-Soilers, the strategy was effective. In Massachusetts, Free-Soilers drew more Whig voters than in any other state. They were sufficiently successful, in fact, to threaten the traditional Whig legislative supremacy. Following the election of 1850, Free-Soilers held the balance of power in the legislature between Whigs and Democrats. As was the case in Ohio, in Massachusetts the Free-Soil Party threw its support behind the Democrats who, in exchange, agreed to fill the vacated Senate seat with a Free-Soiler. After lengthy wrangling, Sumner was eventually accepted by Free-Soilers and Democrats as the next Massachusetts Senator.[13]

Free-Soil Senator

In the Senate, Sumner had few allies, and his tenuous position encouraged caution. As Boston abolitionists clamored for Sumner to take early and dramatic action, he worried about instigating a brawl. The once radical Sumner was learning prudence. In defense of his silence, Sumner wrote that "the cause is now committed to my discretion, & I feel that I can best promote it by caution & reserve." In February 1852 Sumner noted, "The tone in the Senate is now such that I would be willing to enter into the discussion, if I did not feel that what I have to say come with more effect at a later day." This conservatism was based precisely in Sumner's desire to use his position in the Senate as a means to reach mainstream audiences not yet converted to the antislavery cause. Achieving this goal was made difficult by his reputation as an antislavery radical, but Sumner thought that he could overcome this stigma with time and prudence: "I think I can claim the credit of having carried the Anti-Slavery truth, & the ideas of Progress, not unsuccessfully, before audiences to which they had never been presented. But in so doing I have always borrowed something from Prudence. I still borrow from her." Finally, in August 1852 Sumner would break his silence with "Freedom National, Slavery Sectional," a speech based largely on the arguments of Salmon P. Chase, emphasizing the denationalization of slavery.[14] While gesturing at the eventual extinction of slavery, Sumner insisted that the primary work of antislavery must be more limited in scope in order to be successful. The slave power was formidable, but victory was possible by political action:

> A pecuniary interest, so enormous as that of American Slavery, fortified by time & even sanctified in many minds by religion, cannot be overthrown in a day. My hope is to tame its aggressive spirit, to banish it from the national govt, & to drive it into the states, so that it can no longer vex our politics. The way will then be open for the consideration of its true remedy, in the light of economy, morals and religion.[15]

Sumner's desire to drive the slave power from government would receive encouragement from the popular response to the Nebraska bill. Sumner joined Chase in revising the *Appeal of the Independent Democrats,* a document that helped to inspire countless anti-Nebraska mass meetings in Massachusetts. Sumner recognized in the anti-Nebraska movement the possibility for the antislavery party for which he had been hoping, and he continued to use the slave power as a justification for such a party: "My soul sickens at the names Whig & Democrat. The North must be united, & take control of the Govt., or we shall sink under the despotism of the Slave Power." Under such despotism, Sumner feared that "we shall be degraded to a serfdom worse than Russia." But to defeat the slave power would require something more than a collection of individuals or factions. Sumner insisted that the outrages of the slave power "can be wrestled with successfully by no individual; but by nothing short of a united people"[16]

Approaching "The Crime Against Kansas"

"The Crime Against Kansas": Partisan Politics as Usual

As Sumner's experiences with the Whig and Free-Soil parties suggest, one might productively read his rhetorical texts against the slave power in a manner similar to those of Chase—as instances of partisan rhetoric. Sumner's efforts at the Whig and Free-Soil conventions were certainly conditioned by a similar partisan social logic, and scholars have recognized the extent to which "The Crime Against Kansas" itself was conditioned by the political situation of the Republican Party in Massachusetts and the North in general. In Massachusetts, the Nebraska bill had provoked widespread protest and distrust of the existing party system, but in the 1854 election this protest was largely expressed through the Know-Nothing Party, rather than the Republican Party. The Know-Nothing, or American Party, of Massachusetts, however, did have antislavery predispositions. In the period prior to the election, prominent Conscience Whigs such as Charles Francis Adams and Edward Everett were courted by the Know-Nothings. Adams was even offered the senatorship by the victorious nativists, an offer that he declined because of his distaste for the party's agenda. Nevertheless, attempts at a political fusion on a Republican basis were frustrated in 1854. The following year saw further efforts by Free-Soilers to influence the Know-Nothing Party from within, but on balance Free-Soilers concluded that the party was both a poor antislavery vehicle and virtually politically unassailable. By 1856, however, there was reason for optimism. Newly organized Republicans were making electoral gains on the Know-Nothings in Massachusetts, and their national party organization was much better developed.[17]

Many historians situate "The Crime Against Kansas" within the context of Republican competition with Know-Nothings. Michael Pierson considers the speech a strategic response to Know-Nothing competition for anti-Democrat votes in Massachusetts. In 1854 much of the electorate was disillusioned with the party system and politicians in general. The Whig Party was disintegrating, and new parties were jostling to replace it as the anti-Democratic party. Disillusionment with politics and the ruling Democrats encouraged many to see politics in a conspiratorial manner. To Know-Nothings, however, Democrats were not part of the slave power conspiracy but part of a Catholic conspiracy to undermine American liberties. In this respect, voters in Massachusetts—and around the country—were faced with a choice of which conspiracy threatened their liberties most. Obviously, Republicans would prevail as long as the slave power was seen as a more vivid and present menace, and events in Kansas during 1855 and 1856 provided Republicans like Sumner with an opportunity to enhance the persuasiveness of the Republican theme that a slave power conspiracy threatened the rights of Northerners.[18] To be sure, "The Crime Against Kansas" was thoroughly immersed in partisan contexts of several sorts, but its text also provides an opportunity to consider another intriguing context of mid-nineteenth-century slave power conspiracy discourse. Sumner's text was heavily conditioned by the traditions, texts, and ideologies of oratorical culture. When considered in this light, it will be possible to discern the rhetorical operations that brought this lengthy text to persuasive life.

The Crime against Sumner and the Scholarly Deferral of "The Crime Against Kansas"

Despite the amount of scholarship concerned with Charles Sumner in general and "The Crime Against Kansas" speech in particular, surprisingly little attention has been paid to elucidating the inner workings of this important text. One reason (other than the length of the speech—119 pages) for the paucity of textual criticisms is that the speech itself has been considered primarily as a prelude to, or inspiration for, the dramatic story of Congressman Preston Brooks's caning of Sumner. Brooks, angry that Sumner's speech contained numerous base and lewd insults against his relative Senator Andrew Butler, South Carolina, and the South, resolved to respond. According to Brooks's account of the event, it was his own close reading of the text that inspired this most violent reader response: "I then went to S's seat and said, 'Mr. Sumner, I have read your speech with as much care and as much impartiality as was possible and I feel it my duty to tell you that you have libeled my State and slandered a relative who is aged and absent and I am come to punish you for it.'" Brooks proceeded to beat Sumner about the head with his metal-shod cane, getting in about thirty blows as senators sought to restrain him from continued violence against the now unconscious Sumner.[19]

The dramatic nature of these events, combined with the uproar they inspired in both the North and South, has helped to deflect attention from the text itself. Even those scholars examining the text typically focus on those portions of it that contributed to the caning. In this respect, the speech's reception history occupied the attention of scholars to the exclusion of the text itself. That the speech has been overshadowed by this violent incident and resulting fallout is evidenced in the space allotted by scholars to the speech versus its reception. The typical approach is to summarize the speech in a brief paragraph—focusing especially on the insults—and then to dedicate extensive space to the caning and the national response to the event.[20]

But the text of the speech has not been entirely ignored. Previous work has emphasized aspects of its style, organization, and argumentation. Sumner's "Crime" is said to exhibit the classical organizational pattern of exordium, narration, partition, proof, refutation, and peroration (with a digression between partition and proof) and to be characterized by literary allusions of various sorts (especially Latin quotations), the use of epithet and invective, and a generally extreme stance. One scholar has considered the issue of why Sumner resorted to insult rather than reason and a rhetoric of division rather than consubstantiality.[21] Michael Pierson provides perhaps the most complete account of the speech's text. He engages the text, providing an extensive and thoughtful interpretation of the "Crime." Pierson is especially sensitive to the rich intertextuality of the text, insisting that Sumner's allusions to Verres and Sicily represented a use of

> historical parallel [that] provides a context within which to place the remainder of the speech. First, Sumner re-enforced his own reputation as an orator by likening himself to Cicero, the man who had brought Verres to justice. Second, Verres had plundered Sicily, thus undermining Rome's long established policy of allowing its territories self-rule. Finally, . . . Cicero's orations hinted at . . . Verres's vast sexual debaucheries.[22]

Pierson also notes Sumner's other allusions to Cicero, portraying former Missouri senator David Atchison as the Catiline of the conspiracy and his army of Missouri ruffians as analogous to Catiline's corrupt and debauched force. Finally, Pierson explores the sexual connotations Sumner invokes in speaking of Douglas's popular sovereignty in terms of Milton's character "sin" from Paradise Lost.[23] By unpacking the intertextual context Sumner uses to slander his opponents and to position himself as akin to Cicero, Pierson has provided the most substantial interpretation of "The Crime Against Kansas" to date. But Pierson, too, favors for consideration those portions of the text and its intertextual context—especially the insult and epithet—that bear on Sumner's caning. It is unfortunate that the dramatic aftermath of "The Crime Against Kansas" has deflected attention away from this rich text. This chapter proposes to fill the gap in the scholarship on the "Crime" by considering the persuasive logic governing its internal dynamic along several dimensions.

Sumner, Imitation, and the Oratorical Tradition of Conspiracy

The relationship between Sumner's rhetoric of conspiracy and the oratorical tradition, as well as the internal dynamic of the text of the "Crime," is productively elucidated through a consideration of the practice of imitation, or *imitatio,* that informed classical and nineteenth-century American oratorical culture. *Imitatio* was originally a pedagogical strategy for training orators by way of examples. As Michael Leff explains, this process imprinted a particular form of intertextuality on the finished product. Because *imitatio* depended upon an orator's ability to "identify rhetorical strategies and forms as . . . embodied in a text" and re-embody these strategies and forms in a new text, this practice "established an organic link between the historical text and new composition. The old text left its impression on the rhetor's product."[24] Imitation, however, was not simply a pedagogical device but an inventional strategy for orators of all skill levels. For this reason, Leff has highlighted the utility of imitation as a hermeneutic strategy, a strategy that involves tracing the imitation of argumentative strategies and rhetorical forms in the criticism of persuasive discourse. Several scholars have put this interpretive theory into practice, identifying the appropriation by orators in the ancient world and American republic of the styles, literary devices, and argumentative strategies and themes of previous orators.[25] In "The Crime Against Kansas," Charles Sumner imitated both the textual strategies and role of Cicero (based especially on the Catilinarians), and, to a lesser extent, Demosthenes. But Sumner's "Crime" also reflected a more general preoccupation of ancient orators with conspiracy.

The Rhetoric of Conspiracy, Civic Republicanism, and the Oratorical Tradition

What might be called the "oratorical tradition" of conspiracy was rooted simultaneously in the reality of politics in the ancient world and in its political theory. In explaining the predisposition of conspiracy discourse in the classical world, Gordon Wood has emphasized the prevalence of actual conspiracies in classical politics. Given that conspiracy was a common political reality in the ancient world, it is not surprising that some of the most famous classical orations deal extensively with alleged conspiracies. Cecil Wooten recognizes the discursive manifestation of the social reality of conspiracy in the oratory of Demosthenes and Cicero when he proposes "the possibility that there is a special type of oratory evoked by certain kinds of historical situations . . . called the 'rhetoric of crisis.' This oratory is produced when an exceptional orator . . . perceives, rightly or wrongly, that the very existence of the system and all it represents is threatened by a totalitarian menace that must be stopped at all costs." The rhetoric of crisis not only involves a "threat theme" in which the patriot reveals a "fundamental threat to the existence of the state" (usually in the form of a conspiracy), however. The rhetoric of crisis, to Wooten, also invokes a temporal "renewal theme"—the necessity of turning to the old traditions of the Republic in the face of the threat. The corruption of the present (associated with the conspiracy), Wooten writes, encourages "a basically reactionary tendency of the orator to become a *laudator temporis acti* and the constant contrast in the speeches between the past, which is noble and good, which represents everything that is finest . . . , and the present, which is degenerate and unstable, mainly because of a degeneration of former standards of morality and patriotism."[26]

The two basic themes of the rhetoric of crisis, threat and renewal, have their origins in the civic republican political theory associated with these orators and the ancient world in general. The ancients are said to have perceived the state as akin to an organism—mortal. J. G. A. Pocock has formulated this recognition of the state's temporal finitude as the "problem of time":

> We have seen that the problem of the republic was the problem of maintaining a particular existence, that instability was the characteristic of particularity and time the dimension of instability. . . . [T]here was the presumption that the republic, being the work of men's hands, must come to an end in time; there was the unmistakable historical fact that Athens, Sparta and Rome had all declined and ceased to be; and there were,

inherent in the Aristotelian analysis, excellent theoretical reasons why this should be so.

According to this Aristotelian analysis, republics were doomed by contingency and human nature. Self-interest, ambition, corruption, and unexpected events constantly threatened the republic's temporal durability. In light of the thoroughly civic republican predispositions of ancient orators like Cicero, it is unsurprising that Wooten's basic themes of the rhetoric of crisis correspond to the two primary ways in which civic republican theory imagined that the state might be preserved through time.[27]

The theme of a "fundamental threat to the existence of the state" is related in some way to the possibility that the orator might help the state survive through encouraging virtue. Civic republicanism held that virtuous citizens might slow, or temporarily prevent, the state's decay. For virtuous citizens to master the flux of contingent events, however, the political body needed a way to conceptualize contingency, for civic virtue relied in part "on his [the citizen rhetor's] and his fellows' power to understand and respond to what is happening to them."[28] Within the rhetoric of crisis, the orator's delineation of a fundamental threat to the state served two distinct but related rhetorical purposes within the economy of civic republican political theory. First, fear of a fundamental threat served to assist citizens in the recognition and clarification of contingency. Second, such fear established an urgency capable of compelling the citizens—if properly guided by a virtuous orator—to deliberation. In this way, orators, by articulating a threat that encouraged a particular emotional state, may be said to have encouraged their audiences to deliberate and act virtuously.

It is not difficult to find references to the importance of fear in deliberation within the rhetorical theory and oratorical practice of the ancient world. Aristotle's *Rhetoric* and *Ethics* delineate the importance of fear: "fear makes people inclined to deliberation." Not all kinds of fear are connected with contingency, however. The rhetor must not seek to overwhelm his or her audience with "things fearful beyond human strength." In order for fear to make for good deliberation, "there must be some hope of being saved from the cause of agony." The object of fear, in other words, must be conceived as being an appropriate object of deliberation, for we deliberate about "things that are within our power," and political bodies deliberate about "things that can be done by their own efforts." Though it is important not to arouse a fear so overwhelming that it dashes all hope, a citizenry that felt continually confident (the opposite of fear, according to

Aristotle) would be incapable of recognizing, and acting upon, potential evils—thinking "they are not likely to suffer."[29] The rhetor, in other words, must steer his or her audience between the extremes of unwarranted confidence and extreme fear and create a middling kind of fear in his or her audience, the kind of fear establishing the proper frame of mind for deliberation. Examination of the rhetorical practice of Demosthenes and Cicero provides corroboration of this theoretical precept. Demosthenes' *Philippics* and Cicero's *Catilinarians* explicitly advise their audiences to avoid the excessive fear and excessive confidence alike if they are to deliberate properly about the threats facing their political communities.[30] In this respect, the theme of fundamental threat to the state said to characterize the rhetoric of crisis may be understood as an orator's enactment of civic republican political theory—a strategy of using fear to prepare citizens for the deliberation that might enable them to forestall, at least for the time being, the inevitable decline of the state.

The second major theme of the rhetoric of crisis, the contrast between the virtuous past and degenerate present, is also rooted in a civic republican understanding of time and the state. States, like mortal bodies, decayed with time, and one would expect the republic's youth to reflect a vitality and rigor not found in its old age. But the emphasis on renewal of the first principles of the republic also indicated another strategy by which civic republican political theory suggested the state might extend its life. In this respect, the tendency of those operating within the rhetoric of crisis to glorify the virtuous past is not simply a "reactionary tendency" but the corollary of the problem of time. According to classical authorities, the problem of time could be overcome, the republic's life could be extended, by way of a return to the republic's first principles: "There is nothing more true than that all things of this world have a limit to their existence. . . . I speak here of mixed bodies such as republics. . . . [T]hese bodies cannot continue to exist; and the means of renewing them is to bring them back to their first principles."[31] Such a recurrence to first principles or act of renewal, of course, was necessarily a rhetorical act. Thus it may be said that the theme of return to tradition (as well as the fundamental threat to the state) Wooten identifies in Demosthenes and Cicero was also an oratorical enactment of civic republican political theory.

In sum, one can understand the prevalence of conspiracy discourse within the oratorical tradition, at least in part, as a reflection of the prevalence of actual conspiracies as well as a series of oratorical enactments of civic republican political theory. To Demosthenes and Cicero, conspiracy (in the form of Philip and Catiline, respectively) reified and personified the forces contributing to the inevitable decay of the republic at that moment. By relaying this threat to citizens, these orators sought to encourage action to preserve the republic, while their strategy of attempting to return their audiences to the republic's first principles also offered hope of deferring its inevitable demise.

Reading the Oratorical Tradition in "The Crime Against Kansas"

Given Sumner's immersion within the oratorical tradition, it is not surprising that both imitation and the dual themes of the rhetoric of crisis provide interpretive purchase regarding his philippic "The Crime Against Kansas." The importance of the oratorical tradition to Sumner's rhetorical practice is initially underscored by his classical education as well as by the influence of his mentor, John Quincy Adams, whose opinions on the importance of imitation to oratorical education and practice were made quite clear in his *Lectures on Rhetoric and Oratory*. In addition to Sumner's education and mentor, the very political culture of Sumner's Whig Party gravitated toward oratory. Whigs often sought to imitate their role models such as Demosthenes, Cicero, and Edmund Burke. The appropriateness of imitation as an interpretive apparatus is also indicated by the text of "The Crime Against Kansas" and Sumner's favored characterizations of the speech. The text overtly invokes Cicero in the form of historical allusions to his enemies, Catiline and Verres. But the best evidence comes from the interpretations of Sumner and his contemporaries. Prior to its delivery, Sumner explicitly positioned this speech in terms of Demosthenes in a letter to Theodore Parker: "I shall pronounce the most thorough philippic ever uttered in a legislative body." Sumner further indicated his own positioning of the speech within the oratorical tradition by including in the preface to the 1874 edition a reception history emphasizing oratorical themes. Sumner included an excerpt from a correspondent for the *Missouri Democrat* of St. Louis who recognized Sumner's attempt to imitate his oratorical heroes: "That he had the great speech of Cicero and the greater speech of Burke in his mind's eye, there can be no doubt." Another excerpt, from a published sermon by Rev. Gilbert Haven, compared Sumner's effort to those of Demosthenes, Cicero, Burke, and Webster:

> But three or four in all history are its equals in beauty and strength of thought and language—Demosthenes against the Philipizing Douglas of

Athens, the keen, ready, insolent tool of her tyrants—Cicero against the Atchison Catiline of the Roman Republic,—Burke against the wholesale enslaver of India, Hastings,—Webster against the South Carolina traducer of Freedom and its fruits.[32]

In sum, Sumner's education, his political culture, and his own favored characterizations of the speech each provides good reasons to read "The Crime Against Kansas" in terms of imitation of the oratorical tradition.

Given Sumner's immersion within the oratorical tradition, it is no surprise that identification of a conspiratorial threat to the Republic and renewal of first principles are the dominant themes of "The Crime Against Kansas." On the level of threat to the Republic, this chapter considers the manner in which the "Crime" portrays the slave power conspiracy and makes it, and the threat posed by it, plausible to Sumner's audiences. As the chapter traces this narrative of conspiracy, it will consider how the text reinforces this narrative with others—how it encourages readers to view the slave power narrative in terms of the conspiracy of Catiline as well as in terms of the alleged British conspiracy against the American colonies before the Revolution. This imitative practice assisted Sumner both by invoking a particular intertextual context corroborating his narrative and by enabling him to liken himself to Cicero. On the level of renewal, the chapter examines the rhetorical devices deployed in order to reinterpret and rekindle the first principles of the Republic. This entails considering how the text invites readers to resolve the narrative of conspiracy by way of citizen action. At the same time, this task will involve consideration of the theme of time and the Republic—how the text utilized organic and temporal imagery as well as stylistic devices in order to exemplify and even synecdochically represent the Republic's first principles. Comprehending the rhetorical strategies animating this speech, however, is a difficult task. The text of "The Crime Against Kansas" is 119 pages long and complexly organized. For this reason, it is important initially to clarify the structural template within which the above themes are deployed and developed.

Organization/Textual Overview

Rhetorical scholars have noted the extent to which "The Crime Against Kansas"—like most of Sumner's other speeches—follows the organizational pattern of exordium, narration, partition, proof, refutation, and peroration. This is an interesting point, but given the goal of understanding how the text operates as a unit, how its elements are orchestrated into a functional and purposive whole, it is more appropriate to begin with the more obvious organizational structure. As the title suggests, the speech is presented as a forensic discourse prosecuting a criminal for its crimes. Located between the introduction and conclusion are three main sections organizing the speech: "The Crime Against Kansas," "The Apologies for the Crime," and "The True Remedy."[33] Each of these sections, in turn, is composed of several recognizable subunits. This basic organizational structure is an essential template within which the text develops its own variant of the themes of the rhetoric of crisis.[34]

The first theme, that of a fundamental threat to the Republic, is introduced and developed most extensively within the first section delineating the crime. The crime, or conspiracy, of course, is presented in predominantly narrative form, and the "Crime" shuttles among recent U.S. history, the American Revolution, and the political history of the classical world as it deploys its narrative of conspiracy. While the threat or conspiracy theme is found primarily in the first section, however, it is also reinforced in the second and third sections, though it loses momentum as the text's energy turns to the theme of renewal. Correspondingly, while the theme of renewal is concentrated in the later half of the speech, the component seeds for this movement are planted as early as the first section in terms of the organic imagery of states and political associations permeating the text. As the text moves from "Apologies" to "True Remedy," it increasingly positions the slave power's actions against Kansas as comparable to those of Great Britain prior to the Revolution. Through this parallel, the text invites audiences to reenact the Revolution. They are asked to position themselves within a complex performance emphasizing the indissoluble relationship among the past, present, and future in the Republic—using young Kansas itself as a synecdoche by which to reinscribe the Republic's first principles on audiences. In this manner, the text situates the present as a moment for action against the slave power primarily in terms of the formative struggles of the Republic's youth. This development, commencing in rudimentary form with section one, gains momentum as the speech progresses, receiving its most extensive attention in section three and the conclusion.

Reading "The Crime Against Kansas"
The Introduction

The introduction of "The Crime Against Kansas" follows the forensic pattern implied by the title. After introducing the importance of the issue at hand and of Kansas, Sumner proceeds to describe the crime, its motive, its enormity, and the criminal. The introduction concludes with the partition and is followed by a digression attacking Butler and Douglas. The speech text opens with the statement that "you are now called to redress a great wrong." This wrong is said to be of large magnitude and to have tremendous consequences. Unlike "ordinary legislation" in which outcomes have less effect—"The machinery of Government continues to move. The State does not cease to exist"—this issue is said to have enormous consequences for "Liberty in a broad territory . . . the peace of the whole country . . . our good name in history forevermore." That the first paragraph is exclusively concerned with the scope of the threat to the state is a clear indication of the importance of this rhetoric of crisis theme. Next, planting the first seed of the renewal theme, Kansas is introduced as "the middle spot of North America" with conditions to "nurture a powerful and generous people, worthy to be the central pivot of American institutions." Since Kansas will serve as the figural pivot from which the text's renewal theme will develop, a great deal of time is dedicated to figurally locating the territory. Anticipating the renewal theme, Kansas is described in terms of the republics of antiquity—Athens, Sparta, early Rome, and fourteenth-century London—in their early youths.[35] Although these thematic seeds of civic republican renewal will not mature for nearly one hundred pages, their presence from the beginning is important.

Having introduced the present as a fundamental crisis of state and the young republic of Kansas as a sort of center or pivot of America's geography and institutions, the text next introduces the oratorical allusions against which readers will be asked to consider the upcoming narratives of events in Kansas. Initially, Cicero's Verrine orations function as a means of comparing the crimes undertaken in Kansas to those of the depraved Verres. Edmund Burke's *Impeachment of Hastings* also illustrates the magnitude of the crimes. This time, the "Crime" imitates Burke's sentence structure in a passage that compares the crime against Kansas to that of Warren Hastings against India.[36] Such allusions perform a number of functions related to republicanism. First, because republicanism's doctrine of cyclicity and decay means that the past can be instructive to the present, such allusions clarify present events in terms of well-known crises facing past republics. Second, consistent with the "historical role-playing" encouraged by the practice of imitation, such allusions potentially invest the text's author with the credibility and heroic qualities of republican orators like Cicero or Burke.[37] After featuring Verres's violence and debauchery, the text develops the disturbing organic imagery of rape and reproduction as it sets the stage for subsequent narratives of events in Kansas. Still drawing upon the conventions of prosecutorial speeches like those of Cicero and Burke, Sumner's text identifies the motive for the crime against Kansas in the imagery of sexual violence: "Not in any common lust for power did this uncommon tragedy have its origin. It is the rape of a virgin Territory, compelling it to the hateful embrace of slavery; and it may be clearly traced to a depraved desire for a new Slave State, hideous offspring of such a crime, in the hope of adding to the power of slavery in the National Government." Having described the crime and the motive, the text turns next to the perpetrator of the crime, the slave power, a power, according to the text, surpassing Verres, Machiavelli, Bacon, and Hastings in audacity, meanness, and ability, and greater than that of any president.[38]

As the text moves toward an account of the perpetrator—the slave power conspiracy—it faces the challenge of all conspiracy texts, to expose the well-hidden conspirators by delineating the consequences of their secret machinations. The narrative of the crime, in other words, is also a narrative that reveals the conspiracy by its visible actions. This relationship between crime and the conspiracy is illustrated by way of a Norse myth revolving around a tiny cat even the strongest of gods could not lift. This apparent cat, in reality, was but the tip of a gigantic serpent. So, too, "Even the creature whose paws are now fastened around Kansas . . . constitutes in reality part of the Slave Power, which, with loathsome folds, is now coiled about the whole land." While the slave power is indeed powerful and pervasive, the text avoids slipping into a tragic mode by indicating confidence in a political resolution, an "assurance of commensurate effort by the aroused masses of the country, determined not only to vindicate Right against Wrong but to redeem the Republic from the thraldom of that Oligarchy which prompts, directs, and coordinates the distant wrong."[39] Having indicated the crime, the motive, and the criminal, the text previews its three-part structure. But the introduction has planted the seeds constituting the oratorical tradition of conspiracy—the narrative of conspiracy describing the threat to the state, historical allusion and imitation, organic imagery of the state, and Kansas as the potential redeemer of the Republic. These introductory seeds will mature as the speech develops.

Digression: Attack and Insult

Instead of proceeding to the points that have been previewed, however, the text of the "Crime" moves to what has been called a "digression" featuring personal attacks against Butler and Douglas. This section of the text

has received more extensive consideration than any other by previous critics because of its association with the caning of Sumner. Here Butler and
Douglas appear as Don Quixote and Sancho Panza, respectively. Slavery is
represented as Butler's mistress, "who, though ugly to others, is always
lovely to him,—though polluted in the sight of the world, is chaste in his
sight: I mean the harlot Slavery."[40] As mentioned earlier, the "Crime" is
best understood in terms of imitation and the oratorical tradition of conspiracy, and the lurid imagery and insulting character attacks are no exception. At least to George Campbell, Cicero's use of hyperbolic insult is
related to the need to make the conspiracy vivid and plausible to audiences. Campbell observed: "It would have been impossible even for Cicero
to inflame the minds of the people to so high a pitch against oppression,
considered in the abstract, as he actually did inflame them against Verres
the *oppressor*. Nor could he have incensed them so much against *treason* and
conspiracy as he did against Catiline the *traitor* and *conspirator*." Campbell
cites not only Cicero and the Catilinarian conspiracy, but Demosthenes and
his conspiratorial enemy as well: "How much advantage Demosthenes
drew from the known character and insidious arts of Philip of Macedon,
for influencing the resolves of the Athenians, and other Grecian states,
those who are acquainted with the Philippics of the orator, and the history
of that period, will be very sensible."[41] These passages reinforce the promi-
nence of Demosthenes and Cicero as examples for imitation in eighteenth-
and nineteenth-century oratorical circles. They also help to explain Sumner's use of insult. It was not gratuitous or malicious, nor were such insults
an example of the "exaggerated and lurid imagery" characteristic of the
paranoid style. Rather, Sumner's invective and insult represent an imitation of Demosthenes' and Cicero's synecdochical strategies for making conspiracies more compelling to audiences; if Campbell's advice is of any
relevance for reading Sumner's text, then this "digression" is actually a key
component of Sumner's practice of the rhetoric of crisis. The threat to the
state, it seems, must be presented in personal as well as abstract terms in
order to arouse an audience. As will become evident, the other theme of
the rhetoric of crisis—renewal—also receives synecdochical representation
in Sumner's text, presumably for the reason Campbell suggests. But perhaps the most important contribution of Campbell's advice is the recognition that the sole portion of the text given significant attention by previous
scholars—the rhetoric of insult—is merely a secondary characteristic of the
text's place within an oratorical tradition of conspiracy. Reading the text
within its proper context, in other words, clarifies what has heretofore

been a mystery to historians and critics—the question of why Sumner made his "Crime Against Kansas" so extreme, so insulting, so lewd, and so provocative.[42]

Section One: "The Crime Against Kansas"

The threat theme dominates section one of Sumner's "Crime" as it delineates the crime "from the beginning" by way of three narratives. Together, these narratives expose the slave power and illustrate the recent degeneration of the American republic. The first narrative, from 1820 to 1855, traces the birth of the slave power and the promise of free territories in the Missouri Compromise. During this period, the slave power gained an extension of slavery in exchange for its prohibition above 36°30". Returning to organic imagery, the text suggests that this pledge to the North is to be revoked "at the very moment of maturity." The pledge was revoked, of course, by the Nebraska bill of 1854, "a swindle of a great cause, early espoused by Washington, Franklin, and Jefferson, surrounded by the best Fathers of the Republic." Having situated the first principles of the Republic in the organic imagery of the "fathers," the text returns to organic imagery in its portrayal of the territories, insisting that the Nebraska bill had opened "to Slavery all those vast regions, now the rude cradles of mighty States."[43] The founders are "fathers," the prohibition against slavery "matures," and the territories are "rude cradles" for infant states. Organic imagery informs the "Crime"'s figurations of political communities and representations of republican themes, accumulating significance as the text proceeds, slowly at first, to develop the later theme of renewal.

With the Missouri Compromise and Nebraska bill (the "first stage" of the crime against Kansas) set within a historical framework of the birth and maturation of the slave power and free territories and with the decay from first principles, the text sets the stage for recent outrages in Kansas. The slave power is said to have commenced a two-part plan for introducing the "crocodile egg" that would give rise to the "reptile monster" of slavery in Kansas. The first part of the conspiracy involved presidential appointment of proslavery officials to all departments of the territorial government of Kansas. Next, prior to any movement from the North, "secret societies were organized in Missouri" in order to keep out Free-Soil settlers. Fortunately, the text suggests, "the conspiracy was unexpectedly balked" by Free-Soil emigration from all parts of the North. Only when this competition threatened its plan did the slave power resort to coercion: "Slavery is forcibly introduced into Kansas, and placed under the formal safeguard of pretended law. How this is done belongs to the argument."[44] Moving to the "consummation" of the crime—the forcible imposition of slavery on Kansas—Sumner's text promises "the simplest outline, without one word of color" as it moves to the series of narratives detailing the series of invasions of Kansas by Missouri ruffians between November 1854 and December 1855.

Prior to detailing these invasions, however, Sumner's text performs two moves that serve to make the conspiracy more vivid and plausible to audiences. First, the text introduces a parallel between Catiline and former Missouri senator David Atchison. Second, the text assesses and frames its evidence of conspiracy. Proceeding to portray the crime as if it were a drama, the text indicates that in "the foreground all will recognize a familiar character, in himself connecting link between President and border ruffian. . . . I need not add the name of David R. Atchison." In Atchison, the "Crime" finds its Catiline:

> Like Catiline, he stalked into this chamber, reeking of conspiracy,— *immo etuam in Senatum venit,*—and then, like Catiline, he skulked away,— *abiit, excessit, evasit, erupit,*—to join and provoke the conspirators, who, at a distance awaited their congenial chief. Under the influence of his malign presence the Crime ripened to its fatal fruits, while the similitude with Catiline is again renewed in the sympathy, not even concealed, which he found in the very Senate itself, where, beyond even the Roman example, a Senator has not hesitated to appear as his open compurgator.[45]

The parallel between Catiline and Atchison not only helps Sumner to appropriate the role of Cicero—one defending the Republic against a conspiratorial threat—it also helps to enhance the plausibility of the slave power conspiracy for audiences familiar with Catiline. The parallel between Catiline and Atchison reminds audiences of the proper way to interpret events. Within civic republican oratorical practice, "the orator is prone to assume role-models and to see the crisis that he faces in terms of patterns that have appeared in the past." The past is instructive because, as John Quincy Adams put the matter, "The future is little more than a copy of the past. What hath been shall be again. And to exhibit an image of the past is often to present the clearest prospect of the future."[46] Thus the old story of Catiline functions in a corroborative capacity that dramatically frames the soon-to-be-presented evidence of the crime.

Having established the classical template within which it frames its evidence, the text turns to a preview of the character of the evidence to be presented, seeking to "remove, in advance, all question with regard to the authority on which I rely." The evidence, consisting largely of one-sided reports from antislavery Kansans, is said to comprise "such a body of evidence as the human mind is not able to resist. It is found in the concurring reports of the public press, in the letters of correspondents, in the testimony of travelers, and in the unaffected stories I have heard from leading citizens" returning from Kansas. In order to balance this one-sided testimony, however, the text also turns to the allies of slavery, pointing out that "this testimony finds echo in the very statute book of the conspirators, and also in language dropped from the President of the United States."[47]

Initially, details of the invasions are positioned as "unquestionable evidence of the resulting crime." This new Catiline's army of Missouri ruffians invaded Kansas in order to terrorize Free-Soilers and to steal territorial elections for the slave power. The first invasion of November 29, 1854, corresponded to the first election of a territorial congressional delegate. Four months later the "grand invasion" of March 30, 1855, was orchestrated in order to carry the election for territorial legislature. By intimidation of judges and the wresting of ballot boxes, this Catiline's army is said to have gained "complete control of the election, and thus, by preternatural audacity of usurpation, impose a Legislature upon the free people of Kansas." Again, on October 1, 1855, Kansas was invaded for the purpose of securing another congressional election for slavery. The crowning outrage of this narrative was the first assault on the Free-Soil bastion of Lawrence. The murder of a proslavery man was the pretext for raising a "volunteer company" recruited from the "roadsides" of Missouri and armed with Missouri rifles and U.S. cannon. According to the "Crime," the proslavery governor of Kansas accompanied this army of eighteen hundred. "In camp with him was the original Catiline of the conspiracy." For more than a week this army harassed citizens of Lawrence, pillaged and burned their crops, and drove off their livestock. In self-defense, the citizens of Lawrence enacted vigilance, building fortifications, mustering over eight hundred armed men of their own, and sleeping "under arms, with sentinels pacing constant watch against surprise." Eventually, the standoff ended, though only days later, on December 15, 1855, another invasion by Missourians took place in order to usurp the election on the proposed constitution.[48]

Having recounted the narrative of invasion in all its horrors, the text reiterates the motive for the invasions: "As every point in a wide-spread horizon radiates from a common centre, so everything said or done in this vast circle of Crime radiates from One Idea, that Kansas, at all hazards, must be a Slave State." Even proslavery forces are heard to confess as much. Conspirator Benjamin Stringfellow is overheard before the invasions saying, "I advise you, one and all, to enter every election district in Kansas . . . and vote at the point of the bowie knife and revolver." Similarly, after the invasions, Atchison is caught reveling in the success of the usurpation: "the Abolitionist of the North said, *and published it abroad, that Atchison was there with bowie knife and revolver,—and, by God, 't was true! I never did go into that territory . . . without being prepared for all such kind of cattle.*" Other sources, such as an Independence, Missouri, newspaper, celebrated the success of the invasions, declaring that "we have made a clean sweep."[49] Significantly, the narrative of invasion ends where it began— with a parallel to the conspiracy of Catiline:

> On this cumulative, irresistible evidence—in concurrence with the antecedent history, I rest. And yet Senators here argue that this cannot be,— precisely as the conspiracy of Catiline was doubted in the Roman Senate. [Sumner next quotes Cicero in Latin, translated: "Yet there are some in this body who either cannot see what threatens us or pretend that they cannot, who have fed Catiline's hopes by their feeble decisions and put heart into the growing conspiracy by refusing to believe that it existed."] . . . These words of the Roman orator picture the case here.[50]

The Cicero quote, in particular, serves to emphasize a key lesson drawn from the oratory of Demosthenes and Cicero—the importance of recognizing threats. Reiteration of the Catilinarian case, of course, not only furthers Sumner's effort to identify himself with Cicero but also positions skeptics to his speech as either ignorant or in sympathy with the conspiracy. Either way, to doubt the evidence and to contest the claim are effectively to assist the conspiracy.

In sum, Sumner's narrative of invasions is one of both consummation and force, orchestrated by the slave power in order to secure Kansas as a slave state. The fruit of these invasions, according to the text, is a tyrannical territorial government. Accordingly, the third narrative, corresponding to the "third stage" of the crime, details actions taken by this slave power–controlled territorial government against the rights of Kansans. The new legislature's attachment to its masters is indicated by its first actions, to move the capital closer to its Missouri protectors, to adopt all of the statutes of Missouri (substituting the word "Kansas" for "Missouri" as appropriate), and to enact a series of measures against Free-Soilers. Initially, a special legislative chapter entitled "An Act to punish Offences against Slave Property" made death the penalty for interfering with slave property in any one of forty-eight ways. Next, the legislature undertook "the entire prostration of all the safeguards of Human Rights. Liberty of speech, which is the very breath of the Republic,—the press, which is the terror of wrong-doers,—the bar . . . the jury. . . . all these must be struck down, while officers are provided in all places, ready to be the tools of this Tyranny." At the same time that Free-Soil citizens were excluded from civil existence, machinations on several fronts allegedly ensured that enforcement of the laws was left to a body of officers generously supplied to the slave power by the president in his territorial appointments as well as by the legislature. Finally, because the franchise was denied to all who would not take an oath to uphold the fugitive slave law and granted to anyone who paid the sheriff $1.00, a self-perpetuating proslavery energy was invested in the legislature itself.[51]

The first section detailing the crime against Kansas concludes:

> Thus was the Crime consummated. Slavery stands erect, clanking its chains on the Territory of Kansas, surrounded by a code of death, and trampling upon all cherished liberties, whether of speech, press, the bar, the trial by jury, or the electoral franchise. And sir, this is done. . . . for the sake of political power, in order to bring two new slaveholding Senators upon this floor, and thus to fortify in the National Government the desperate chances of a waning Oligarchy.

As the first section reaches its end, the crime against Kansas is represented as the end of a tragedy commenced with the overthrow of the Missouri Compromise: "Sir, all this was done in the name of Popular Sovereignty. And this is the close of the tragedy. Popular sovereignty . . . has ended in Popular Slavery."[52]

Section one, containing the narrative of the crime, represents the core of the conspiracy position and the fullest development of the first theme of the rhetoric of crisis—the articulation of the threat to the state. The criminal arraigned—the slave power—through its widespread influence in the national government and its contacts in Missouri, is said to have consummated the very crime envisioned as early as the Kansas-Nebraska Act of 1854. When this section is read as a conspiracy narrative, the historical allusions to Catiline (and, to a lesser extent, Verres and Hastings) take on a new importance. From a civic republican perspective, the American republic was subject to the very same threats faced by ancient republics. Sumner's audiences are asked to read political events in terms of this parallel conspiratorial episode of antiquity. By literally framing the narrative of invasion in this way (the narrative begins and ends with references to Catiline), the text positions the United States as the new stage for the old civic republican struggle against demagogues and tyranny. The allusions to Catiline also emphasize the extent to which events in distant Kansas are linked to a larger conspiracy that has insinuated itself at the very center of power. In this manner, Sumner dispelled the confidence of those who viewed events in Kansas as insignificant because involving only the distant periphery of the country. Not only does this historical allusion assist in making a conspiracy appear plausible, however; by likening himself to Cicero, Sumner also engaged in his own imitative historical role-playing—role-playing that both contributes to his own credibility and dramatizes the narrative of conspiracy. Sumner portrays himself as acting as the virtuous orator ought to act in those situations where the Republic is threatened by conspiracy. Because he possesses the foresight to detect threats and the ability to communicate his knowledge to his fellow citizens, it is his duty to play the role of vigilant sentinel. This legitimizes his use of conspiracy rhetoric as a proper mode of political discourse, even as it legitimizes and valorizes Sumner himself.

Section Two: The Apologies for the Crime

The second section of Sumner's "Crime" is the midpoint of its overt organizational skeleton as well as its larger thematic structure. Somewhere between the beginning and end of the text's middle age, the threat theme recedes and the theme of renewal predominates. It is almost possible to see these themes briefly running parallel to one another before the threat declines and renewal ascends. The primary force in the growth of the renewal theme is the rapid development of parallels between the present crisis and the crisis precipitating the American Revolution, and consideration of four colorfully named apologies for the crime serves as the immediate pretext for this larger thematic development. The threat theme survives as section two begins with the assertion that the apologies for the crime are further evidence of the apologist's complicity in the conspiracy: "the Apologies for the Crime are worse than the efforts at denial. In essential heartlessness, they identify their authors with the great iniquity."[53] Former territorial governor Andrew Reeder is the author of the "Apology tyrannical" insofar as he authenticated the legislature's usurpation, giving it formal legal sanction. In summarizing the reasons to reject this apology, Sumner's text introduces a key component of the renewal theme, the parallel between events in Kansas and the American colonies at the Revolution:

> I dismiss the Apology founded on his acts, as the utterance of Tyranny by the voice of Law, transcending the declaration of the pedantic judge, in the British Parliament, on the eve of the Revolution, that our fathers, notwithstanding their complaints, were in reality represented in Parliament, inasmuch as their lands, under the original charters, were held "in common socage, as the manor of East Greenwich in Kent," which, being truly represented, carried with it all the Colonies. Thus in another age has Tyranny assumed the voice of Law.[54]

Next, the "Apology imbecile" refers to the president's claims that he lacks the constitutional authority to interfere in events in Kansas. The final two apologies relate to pretexts said to justify the outrages in Kansas as appropriate in the face of subversive antislavery movements. The "Apology absurd" relates to a document allegedly exposing a secret society, an antislavery "Legion" threatening the laws of the territory. The final apology, the "Apology infamous," relates to another antislavery organization—the Emigrant Aid Society—whose existence is said to justify the excesses of proslavery forces. This society, Sumner's speech text indicates, is far from the paramilitary organization that slavery's congressional advocates suggest.[55]

Section two concludes with a defense of Sumner's home state of Massachusetts, a defense that is the strongest articulation of the parallel between the events precipitating the American Revolution and those in Kansas. This portion of the second section is the thematic peripety of the speech. From this point on, the text rapidly develops the renewal theme at the expense of the threat theme. Massachusetts, Sumner's text suggests, "knows her rights and will maintain them firmly to the end. . . . Thus it was in the olden time, when she began the great battle whose fruits you all enjoy. . . . [B]y the voices of her poets and orators, she is now exerting an influence more substantial and commanding than ever before." In this respect, the antislavery struggle is an opportunity to surpass even the work of the Revolutionary fathers:

> [In] this battle, which in moral grandeur surpasses far the whole war of the Revolution, she is able to preserve her just eminence. To the first she contributed troops in larger numbers than any other State, and larger than all the Slave States together; and now to the second, which is not of contending armies, but of contending opinions, on whose issue hangs trembling the advancing civilization of the age, she contributes, through the manifold and

endless intellectual activity of her children, more of that divine spark by which opinions are quickened into life than is contributed by an other State.

Events in Kansas, in sum, are an opportunity to emulate the founders, an essential ingredient of the renewal theme culminating in the conclusion.[56]

Section Three: The True Remedy

Section three of the "Crime" witnesses rapid development of several components of the renewal theme—in particular, the parallel between Kansas and the Revolutionary colonies and the first principles of the Republic. "The True Remedy" is organized around "consideration of the *remedies proposed,* ending with THE TRUE REMEDY." Ideally, the remedy "should be coextensive with the original Wrong," the restoration of the Missouri Compromise's prohibition of slavery above 36°30" the "Alpha and Omega of our aim." But Sumner's text is content first to consider the spectrum of available remedies: the remedies of tyranny, folly, injustice and civil war, and justice and peace.[57] As with previous sections, consideration of these remedies is the framework within which the deeper thematic and tropological life cycle of the oration progresses.

The "Remedy of Tyranny," that favored by the president and Senator Douglas, involves congressional appropriations for the "enforced obedience of the existing laws of Kansas." The bulk of the response to this remedy is an extensive comparison of the president's message on Kansas to that of King George III's speech to Parliament in response to the complaints of the colony of Massachusetts. In order to emphasize this similarity, Sumner's text guides readers through his own reading of the text of George III's message: "Instead of Massachusetts Bay, in the royal speech, substitute Kansas, and the message of the President will be found fresh on the lips of the British King." When read in this manner, Sumner's text suggests, "The parallel is complete. The Message, if not copied from the Speech of the King, has been fashioned on the same original block, and must be dismissed to the same limbo."[58] Again the text suggests that history is repeating itself and that imitation is the habit of tyrants as well as anyone playing the role of the heroic citizen orator. From the perspective of the renewal theme, the strategy of linking the president's words to those of George III is yet another instance of the parallel between present events and those of the Revolution. Not only does the slavery controversy in Kansas offer an opportunity for Massachusetts and Kansas to equal the virtue of the founders, but the slave power is also seizing the opportunity to equal the tyranny of the British.

The "Remedy of Folly," proposed by Senator Butler, is "that the people of Kansas should be deprived of their arms." Sumner's text insists that this plan flies in the face of the Constitution, common sense, and Kansans' pressing need for self-defense and further establishes the scope of the threat, that the slave power will stop at nothing to achieve its goals. The third remedy, that of "Injustice and Civil War," consists of the proposal by Senator Douglas that the legislature of Kansas should provide for the election of delegates to a constitutional convention in preparation for eventual statehood. This plan is condemned on the grounds that "the bill recognizes the existing Usurpation" and effectively would "legalize and perpetuate the very *force* by which slavery is already planted there." Continuing to speak of political communities and the renewal theme in organic terms, the "Crime" indicates that by Douglas's plan, "You put the infant State, now preparing to take a place in our sisterhood, to suckle the wolf which you ought at once to kill."[59]

The final and "True Remedy" is the proposal put forward by Senator William Seward to admit Kansas immediately as a state. This subunit is the most extensive of the four and is concerned primarily with responding to the legal objections to this plan. Following a lengthy discussion of the law and precedent, the text again contributes to the renewal theme as it returns to first principles and positions the Declaration of Independence as a clear precedent for Seward's plan: "Again I say, do you require a precedent? I give it. . . . I plant it firmly on the fundamental principle of American Institutions, as embodied in the Declaration of Independence, by which government is recognized as deriving its just powers only from the consent of the governed." In conclusion, the text admonishes readers not to turn away from the Republic's first principles: "I appeal to the great principle of American Institutions. If, forgetting the origin of the Republic, you turn away from this principle, then, in the name of human nature, trampled down and repressed, but aroused to just self-defence, do I plead for the exercise of this power."[60] By the end of the third section, the seeds of the renewal theme have substantially grown and matured. The parallel between Kansas and the Revolution, the emphasis on the Republic's first principles, and the organic imagery of state, introduced gradually throughout the speech, by the end of the third section have come to predominate at the expense of the threat theme.

The Conclusion

The "Crime"'s conclusion commences: "an immense space has been traversed, and I stand now at the goal. The argument in its various parts is here closed. . . . But there are other things not belonging to the argument, which still press for utterance." The text has unfolded its argument, exposed the conspiracy, proposed the proper policy. As the text "closes with a political speech that sums up our duties at this moment," it gathers up the components of the renewal theme in order to enact the return to the first principles of the Republic.[61] In particular, the conclusion emphasizes the developing parallel between Kansas and the colonies before the Revolution. Kansans, "bone of your bone and flesh of your flesh . . . now stand at your door . . . claiming a simple birthright." The text asks, "will you turn them away?" Kansans are said to have earned such a birthright insofar as they have suffered and fought a tyranny similar to, though much worse than, that faced by the Revolutionary fathers: "At every stage the similitude between the wrongs of Kansas and those other wrongs against which our fathers rose becomes apparent. Read the Declaration of Independence, and there is hardly an accusation against the British Monarch which may not now be hurled with increased force against the American President." The parallel is said to extend even to the arguments on the Senate floor: "As the tyranny of the British King is all renewed in the President, so are renewed on this floor the old indignities which embittered and fomented the troubles of our fathers."[62]

Prior to completing this historical parallel, however, the text pauses to juxtapose old and new, exploiting the organic imagery of state in a manner favorable to Sumner's purposes. The text condemns Senator Butler on the grounds that he adopts the arguments of the British Parliament, but this is primarily an attack on his home state of South Carolina—an attack expressed in the organic terms of civic republicanism:

> South Carolina is old; Kansas is young. South Carolina counts by centuries, where Kansas counts by years. But a benificent example may be born in a day; and I venture to declare, that against two centuries of the older "State" may be set already the two years of trial, evolving corresponding virtue, in the younger community. . . . [I]t will be difficult to find anything in the history of South Carolina which presents so much of heroic spirit in an heroic cause as shines in that repulse of the Missouri invaders by the beleaguered town of Lawrence, where even the women gave their effective efforts to Freedom.[63]

In the penultimate move in the renewal theme, the text next connects this contrast between Kansas and South Carolina to the oratorical republican theme of imitation of examples: "Were the whole history of South Carolina blotted out of existence . . . civilization might lose—I do not say how little, but surely less than it has already gained by the example of Kansas, in that valiant struggle against oppression."[64] The renewal theme is now complete. Here are linked the parallel between the present troubles and the Revolution, the organic imagery of state, and the central importance of Kansas to the Republic. By combining these components, the renewal theme hinted at in the opening paragraphs' portrayal of Kansas as a "pivot of American institutions" culminates in a representation of Free-Soil Kansans as a synecdoche for the Revolutionary fathers. In the youthful struggles of the infant republic of Kansas, the text suggests, lie the civic vitality and virtue found in the youth of the American republic. By supporting and emulating Kansans, Americans might renew themselves and save their aging and degenerate republic from the slave power: "In this contest Kansas bravely stands forth, the stripling leader, clad in the panoply of American Institutions. . . . God be praised that Kansas does not bend ignobly beneath the yoke! Far away on the prairies, she is now battling for the Liberty of all, against the President, who misrepresents all." Kansas is the key to renewing the Republic in two senses. In the figurative sense, Kansas is a synecdoche for the virtue, independence, moral righteousness, and fortitude in the face of tyranny shown by the Revolutionary founders. Unlike the founders, however, whose temporal distance from the Republic's present might reduce the clarity and forcefulness of their example, Kansans represent the youthful vigor and virtue of the founders in the Republic's present. As such, the example of Free-Soil Kansans provides Sumner's text with a discursive means to renew the Republic despite the vast temporal distance from the founding moment. Kansas also is the means to renew the Republic in the literal sense, "since the Slave Power now stakes on this issue all its ill-gotten supremacy, the People, while vindicating Kansas, will at the same time overthrow this Tyranny."[65]

Historical Questions, Textual Answers

This chapter has illustrated how civic republican themes, tropes, and rhetorical devices animate the action within the lengthy text of "The Crime Against Kansas." But the argument that this text is best understood in the terms of the intertextual context of the oratorical tradition and the ideological context of civic republicanism is at odds with the position of an authority on both conspiracy discourse and civic republicanism, historian Gordon Wood. While Wood is an important scholar within the so-called republican synthesis, he is part of the school of thought known as "Harvard Republicanism." This faction assumes that while civic republicanism was once the paradigmatic American political ideology, it was displaced by more modern political theories early in the nation's history—around the time of the Constitution. From this perspective, Sumner and his era fall far outside the temporal bounds circumscribing civic republicanism within the United States. Wood also sharply distinguishes between ancient and modern traditions of conspiracy. According to Wood, conspiratorial interpretations after the Enlightenment were far different from those in the ancient world. As such, he would disagree with this chapter's claim that Sumner's practice of conspiracy rhetoric was based on his imitation of ancient models.[66]

Wood's arguments, and their basis in a wide spectrum of primary texts, are impressive; but insofar as Wood lacks the critical sensitivity to discursive form associated with the rhetorical perspective, as well as close familiarity with nineteenth-century oratory, his positions do little to detract from this chapter's attempt to understand the "Crime" in the terms of civic republicanism and the imitation of ancient conspiracy rhetoric. This reading, after all, has aimed at understanding the inner workings of one particular text, not the cultural currents of the eighteenth century. There are numerous reasons to understand this text in the terms of imitation and oratorical republicanism. Understanding the "Crime" in terms of imitation has elucidated the intertextual relationship between it and the oratorical tradition, the textual deployment of civic republican ideology, and the action within the text. This strategy enabled the discovery that Sumner deployed the Demosthenic and Ciceronian themes of the rhetoric of crisis—the threat to the state and renewal—throughout "The Crime Against Kansas." These themes were instantiated within particular figural vehicles—the slave power and its minions synecdochically represent the threat, while the infant republic of Kansas synecdochically represents the virtue that allows the possibility of renewal. Close attention to these themes has shown how they wax and wane in tandem—the threat theme receding as the renewal theme commenced its own life cycle within the life cycle of the text.

Sumner imitated not only the themes and textual strategies of the rhetoric of crisis and the role of orator statesman but also the more general

civic republican ideology that undergirded the rhetoric of crisis and the oratorical tradition. Sumner's text was rife with the organic figural imagery
of civic republicanism. The tropes of mortality and age permeated representations of political communities. The territories were the rude cradles of
new states; Kansas was compared to the young republics of Athens, Rome,
and Britain; Kansas's republican youth and vigor were contrasted with
South Carolina's decrepitude and decay. Throughout the text, seeds were
planted, the slave power and the western territories were born and matured, and this organic language accompanied the deployment of the
threat and renewal themes. The threat to the state was associated with its
aging and the decay of its first principles, and the possibility of renewal was
associated with the youth and vitality of the Kansas and the long-past Revolutionary republic.

The organic imagery pervading Sumner's text was not just a literary or-
nament but a reflection of the cyclical understanding of politics and the
state associated with civic republicanism. Precisely because civic republicanism perceived of states as akin to bodies, all social and political life was
cyclical in the sense that all that is born must die. But this meant that the
past could serve as a guide to the future. Pocock's account of this understanding reinforces that expressed by John Quincy Adams in his *Lectures* or
by Sumner in the "Crime":

> In the long run, therefore, everything had happened before and would hap-
> pen again; Fortune's wheel became the image of repetition as well as unpre-
> dictability, and there arose the extremely important and, within limits,
> heartening consequence that if one knew what had happened before, one
> could make predictive statements concerning the combinations in which
> things would happen again. To the extent to which this might be possible,
> Fortune's world would become more intelligible, less frightening, and even
> more manageable.[67]

This cyclical understanding of history makes the "Crime"'s historical allusions more than mere literary devices. Sumner's text asked its readers to
consider their own past and present in terms of the stories of tyranny and
demagoguery perpetuated by the oratorical canon. Seen from this perspective, Sumner's narrative of the conspiratorial threat to the Republic was
corroborated by—it showed a fidelity to—the stories of the demagoguery
of Cicero or the tyranny of Verres, Hastings, or George III. The oratorical
texts of the past, then, could guide not only orators producing speeches but
also those politicians and citizens seeking to preserve the Republic. As

Sumner sought to position himself within the role of a modern-day Cicero, he asked his audiences to emulate their Revolutionary fathers.

This chapter has been concerned with comprehending the rhetorical processes that make particular texts superior vehicles for the transmission of their conspiracy theories and with providing one of the first careful rhetorical analyses of a text whose dramatic reception has distracted generations of commentators from its inner workings. But in undertaking this critically oriented task, this chapter has also inadvertently offered a substantive, textually based answer to the question of why Sumner chose in the "Crime" to engage in a rhetorical "escalation" associated with excessive insult, invective, hyperbole, and conspiracy.[68] Several scholars have answered this question in terms extrinsic to the text—positioning the "Crime" as an attempt to compete with the Know-Nothings for anti-Democratic votes by convincing the electorate that the Republic was threatened not by a papal conspiracy but by the slave power.[69] In this respect Sumner may be said to have fought conspiracy with conspiracy, matching papal hyperbole with slave power hyperbole. In terms of his goal of mobilizing the electorate against the slave power, Sumner would succeed—though not exactly in the manner he might have hoped. It was largely the crime against Sumner rather than his "Crime Against Kansas" that resulted in the Republican electoral gains in the 1856 election. As Gienapp puts the matter, the "Crime Against Kansas," the "crime against Sumner," and continuing excesses in Kansas together served to enhance the persuasiveness of the Republican theme that a slave power conspiracy threatened the rights of Northerners. This convergence of events, Gienapp suggests, made Republican claims as to the existence of a slave power conspiracy seem like more than just political propaganda.[70]

This chapter, however, has provided another answer to the question of why Sumner's "Crime Against Kansas" is so filled with exaggeration, insult, invective, and lurid imagery. When Sumner imitated Cicero, Demosthenes, and the rhetoric of crisis, he seems to have recognized the same lesson that George Campbell had drawn from the study of these texts almost a century earlier—that audiences are more easily inflamed against conspirators than against conspiracies.[71] In other words, just as the renewal theme was expressed in terms of the heroism of the citizens of Kansas and the Revolutionary fathers, so, too, the threat theme found expression in the equally villainous Atchison, Butler, and Douglas. The rhetoric of insult and invective may be said to have been an epiphenomena of Sumner's imitation of Cicero. It was a means of making the conspiratorial threat more dramatically visible and inflaming the minds of citizens in order to inspire them to political action against the slave power. Had Preston Brooks's original (precaning) close reading of "The Crime Against Kansas" situated it within the appropriate intertextual and ideological context, his reception of the speech might have been less dramatic.

4

Lincoln, Conspiracy Rhetoric, and the "House Divided": Assessing the Judgment of History

We cannot absolutely know *that all these exact adaptations are the result of preconcert. But when we see a lot of framed timbers, different portions of which we know have been gotten out at different times and places and by different workmen—Stephen, Franklin, Roger, James, for instance—and when we see these timbers joined together, and see they exactly make the frame of a house or a mill, all the tenons and mortices exactly fitting, and all the lengths and propositions of the different pieces exactly adapted to their respective places, and not a piece too many or too few—not omitting even scaffolding—or, if a single piece be lacking, we can see the place in the frame exactly fitted and prepared to bring such piece in—in such a case, we find it impossible to not believe that Stephen and Franklin and Roger and James all understood one another from the beginning, and all worked on a common plan* or *draft drawn up before the first lick was struck.*

—Abraham Lincoln, "House Divided"

A ny study purporting to examine slave power conspiracy rhetoric in the political mainstream must consider the case of Abraham Lincoln. Salmon Chase and Charles Sumner were important national and local Republican leaders in their own right, but even they were deemed too radical to be serious presidential candidates in 1860. In contrast to comparative radicals like Seward, Chase, and Sumner, by 1860 Lincoln appeared to be a quite moderate candidate who was likely to appeal to the broadest spectrum of voters. Lincoln, in sum, was the "embodiment of availability."[1] As such, Lincoln's conspiracy texts are worthy of serious attention in terms of this study's goals. But Lincoln's ascension to the presidency and dramatic fate helped to ensure that he would become a profound symbol of political authority for subsequent generations as well as his own. As a result, countless citizens, scholars, and rhetors have subjected the Lincoln corpus to infinitely more interpretations and evaluations, praise and condemnation, than the works of prominent contemporaries like Chase and Sumner. This century and a half of attention to Lincoln's words has generated a massive "interpretive context" that inevitably conditions any hermeneutic liaison with his rhetorical texts.[2] Precisely because much of this interpretive context has grown out of the assumptions and political commitments shaping the paranoid style, negotiation of portions of this interpretive context is necessary in order to achieve the larger goal of interpreting Lincoln's "House Divided" text within its particular context.

Lincoln the Whig

One of the reasons that Lincoln was a wise strategic choice for the Republican presidential nomination in 1860 was his relative moderation. In the 1840s and early 1850s, when Chase and Sumner were gaining reputations as radicals as they worked to build an antislavery coalition upon the increasingly unstable ground of the Whig-Democrat party system, Lincoln was loyal to his Whig Party as well as to the two-party system. Lincoln strongly favored the Whig economic program of tariffs, internal improvements, and strong financial institutions. But Lincoln was more than a promoter of Whig policies; he dedicated his considerable rhetorical and organizational skills to building the Whig Party in Illinois. Lincoln was simultaneously Whig ideologue, party spokesman, and party technician. Unlike many Whigs, he was very comfortable with the machinery of party. He recognized that the organization—with its conventions, committees, party workers, and precinct captains—was a condition of party success.[3] He lamented that, in Illinois in the 1840s, "you were sure to find whigs [*sic*], not contending shoulder to shoulder against the common enemy, but divided into factions, and fighting furiously with one another." As a solution, Lincoln was an advocate of better party organization in the form of nominating conventions. He made the case for nominating conventions as a vehicle for party discipline and unity in a Whig campaign circular of 1843. This circular was also the first time that Lincoln invoked the words "a house divided against itself cannot stand" in an appeal for party unity:

> That "union is strength" is a truth that has been known, illustrated and declared, in various ways and forms in all ages of the world. That great fabulist and philosopher, Aesop, illustrated it by his fable of the bundle of sticks; and he whose wisdom surpasses that of all philosophers, has declared that a "house divided against itself cannot stand." It is to induce our friends to act upon this important, and universally acknowledged truth, that we urge the adoption of the Convention system.[4]

Lincoln's efforts on behalf of the Whigs were rewarded as his influence within the Illinois party grew. But as a good Whig, Lincoln was also a supporter of the two-party system, and he initially feared the coming of a sectional party that might replace the national character of the party system.[5]

The events of 1854 helped to change Lincoln's outlook. In Illinois, as elsewhere in the North, the Nebraska bill caused a storm of protest, and Lincoln took this opportunity to reveal his antislavery opinions. Lincoln found himself with new allies. The Illinois anti-Nebraska coalition of 1854 in which he participated consisted of a patchwork of members of the Free-Soil and Liberty parties in the North, Whigs in the central region, and independent free-soil Democrats in the South. This coalition was the beginning of what would become the Republican Party, though Lincoln initially resisted the organizational fusion of the coalition, remaining loyal to Whiggery until between 1855 and 1856.[6] Nevertheless, most commentators pinpoint 1854 as a transitional moment in Lincoln's political career, one even calling 1854 the beginning of Lincoln's "second political career." Lincoln's 1854 Peoria speech was his first foray into slave power rhetoric. Like many other antislavery politicians, Lincoln focused his wrath on Stephen Douglas's role in the plot to spread slavery. Even at this early date Lincoln condemned Douglas's stance of indifference on the slavery issue, claiming that "this declared indifference, but as I must think, covert real zeal for the spread of slavery, I can not but hate." Lincoln identified Douglas's role in the spread of slavery as that of propagandist, making "lullaby" arguments designed to lull the North into complacency as slavery insinuated itself into the western territories. With these charges Lincoln may be said to have launched into his career as conspiracy rhetor. One commentator finds no less than fifty charges of a conspiracy to nationalize slavery in Lincoln's speeches between 1854 and 1860.[7]

Lincoln and Conspiracy Rhetoric:
Historical Condemnation

Lincoln's conspiracy rhetoric—whatever its character in the context of the mid to late 1850s—has been the basis for much condemnation on the part of scholars and critics in the twentieth century. Without the appropriate correction, this condemnation is liable to color contemporary receptions of Lincoln's conspiracy texts. For this reason, it is necessary initially to review of the scope of the critiques of Lincoln's conspiracy rhetoric. The "revisionist" school of historians produced some of the first academics to find Lincoln's rhetoric of conspiracy to be a sign of his demagogy and a major contributing factor to the coming of the Civil War. The revisionists suggested that the Civil War had been repressible or avoidable, as it had been the result of a combination of fanaticism and propaganda deriving from a generation of inept statesmen, both North and South. The revisionists were especially critical of antislavery activists in this capacity. Avery Craven was one of the first and most unforgiving of revisionists. According to Craven, irresponsible politicians created a distorted picture of the opposing section, constituting "inflamed minds" and an atmosphere of "fear and hate" that made it "impossible to reason, to trust, to compromise." More specifically, the "fiction" of an evil "Slave Power," created by politicians and reformers (including Chase, Sumner, and Lincoln, according to Craven's account) for their own purposes, inflamed the minds of Northern audiences. Other revisionists have taken a similar, if somewhat more muted, position on the nexus between irresponsible and conspiratorial rhetoric and the coming of the Civil War. J. G. Randall, for instance, argues that "emotional unreason and over-bold leadership" allowed "small minorities" in both sections to draw a "blundering generation" into violent conflict. Randall, however, tends to exonerate Lincoln, emphasizing his desire for a peaceable solution and his general tendency to avoid "emotional harangues" and the tricks of the "agitator and demagogue."[8]

More recently, other historians have expressed a similar view. According to Allan Nevins, the war came because the "Slave Power" and "Freesoil Power" increasingly saw one another as bitter enemies that would stop at nothing to achieve victory for their respective sections. Nevins's account also sees mounting sectional fear as the product of irresponsible rhetoric: "Fear was largely the product of ignorance, and ignorance—or misinformation—largely the product of propaganda." In a manner similar to Kenneth Burke's "Rhetoric of Hitler's Battle," George Forgie views Lincoln's conspiracy rhetoric as sectional ritual in which "all the good brothers would band together to direct their angry passions on a scapegoat brother . . . throwing him from power (symbolically killing him), actively rid[ding] themselves of the only danger to their Union." This ritual, according to Forgie, would lead directly to the Civil War. More recently, M. E. Bradford has advanced the thesis that Lincoln was an ambitious and duplicitous demagogue whose rhetoric was largely responsible for "dividing the house." Bradford notes especially the "crisis-bringing elements" of Lincoln's rhetoric and the manner in which, by his conspiracy position (advanced, Bradford notes, over fifty times between 1854 and 1860), "[t]he seed of suspicion was planted in the fruitful soil of intersectional dispute."[9]

Lincoln's "House Divided" speech, in particular, has been the lightning rod for those twentieth-century scholars condemning Lincoln's use of conspiracy rhetoric. Roy Basler's 1939 analysis of Lincoln's use of rhetorical figures in the "House Divided" speech suggested that his "frame house" or "mill" analogy, while effective at carrying "implications of something more than rational analysis could maintain," nevertheless "seems a distortion of truth." Revisionist Craven sees the "House Divided" speech as typical of the demagogy resulting in the war, calling it an "extreme partisan appeal to unfounded fears clothed in dignified legal and Scriptural language and softened with homely humor," an appeal that helped to make compromise unthinkable. Even the more balanced revisionists condemn the "House Divided" speech. Randall faults the "usually logical" Lincoln for making his accusation of a conspiracy. At best, Randall concludes, Lincoln failed to represent correctly the events of his time; at worst, his accusation of conspiracy was "unjustified" and "fanciful." Nevins also sees the conspiracy accusation in the "House Divided" as a purely partisan maneuver that was "unfounded," an "absurd bogey." Bradford finds the alleged conspiracy of the "House Divided" text to be a "bugbear," an example of "scare tactics," and yet another instance of Lincoln's unbridled ambition and duplicitous rhetoric. Bradford notes Lincoln's shameless use in the "House Divided" speech of fallacious reasoning—in particular, the ad hominem, false dilemma, and post hoc fallacies. Finally, while not overtly condemning Lincoln, Robert Johannsen points out that the conspiracy argument in the "House Divided" was based on "no evidence" (rather, on an analogy), that the "conspiracy charge [was] a neat, simplistic, and emotionally charged stratagem," and that Lincoln "employed his best doomsday rhetoric to alarm his audiences."[10]

To be sure, other scholars have taken less condemnatory positions. Harry Jaffa, while accepting the revisionist claim that Lincoln (by destroying Douglas's hopes for an intersectional coalition) helped to precipitate the Civil War, insists that Lincoln did so for good reason (to end the injustice of slavery). Based on his analysis of the period, however, Jaffa breaks with the revisionists in concluding that there was indeed both a legal and political tendency toward slavery expansion. Jaffa's Straussian background causes him to look favorably on Lincoln's injection of moral issues into political discussion. Michael Leff suggests that Lincoln's conspiracy claim was part of a larger rhetorical device, a form of hyperbole designed to achieve an instrumental effect. Others also point to the centrality of conspiracy claims to partisan politics, the relativity of such claims to the particularities of time and space, and the instrumental value of the slave power conspiracy to Lincoln and the antislavery cause in 1858.[11]

Given this reception, it is evident that Lincoln's conspiracy rhetoric and his "House Divided" speech have been controversial to many twentieth-century commentators. While keeping these criticisms in mind, one primary goal of this chapter is to evade this massive interpretive context, focusing instead on the text in the context of the political realities, ideological assumptions, and narrative preunderstandings of June 1858. After the text has been considered in its original context, the chapter returns to the interpretive context and the issue of how the predispositions of many historians and critics have blocked a meaningful engagement with conspiracy rhetoric in general and the "House Divided" speech in particular.

The "House Divided" Text
Social Logic of the "House Divided" Text

By the time of the "House Divided" speech, Lincoln had been a Republican for two years. The Republican Party had emerged in Illinois as a result of the Decatur preorganizational meeting and its offspring, the Bloomington convention of 1856. Lincoln's support played an important role in efforts to fuse the anti-Nebraska coalition into a unified political organization. At the Bloomington convention, the Republican Party was officially organized, and Lincoln delivered his famous but "lost" speech to a diverse audience of delegates consisting of Democrats, Whigs, Know-Nothings, Germans, abolitionists, and conservatives.[12] The "House Divided" speech and its conspiracy argument were also outgrowths of the practical partisan considerations of this new party. Stephen Douglas's efforts against the proslavery Lecompton constitution (on the grounds that the popular sovereignty of Kansans was being thwarted) had problematized the ongoing Republican effort of portraying Douglas as the tool of the slave power. Some Republicans even talked of throwing their support behind him in order to broaden the Northern antislavery coalition. Don Fehrenbacher writes, "As a matter of practical politics, it [the "House Divided" speech] may be viewed as an attempt to minimize the significance and impact of Douglas's anti-Lecompton heroics and to demonstrate the folly of diluting Republican convictions with the watery futility of popular sovereignty—in short, an attempt to vindicate the nomination of a Republican candidate from Illinois." In order to ascertain how the speech accomplishes its purpose, Fehrenbacher divides the speech into three sections—the House Divided, Conspiracy, and Living Dog sections—which he claims compose a unified whole designed to define "Republicanism in terms that excluded Douglas," in sum, to "check an ill-considered retreat to the lower ground of popular sovereignty." The three parts of the speech, Fehrenbacher argues, work together to accomplish this goal: the House Divided section introduces the possibility of the slave power conspiracy making the Union all one thing; the Conspiracy section outlines the conspiracy to nationalize slavery (answering the questions "where are we?" and "whither are we tending?"); and the Living Dog section (answering the questions "what should we do?" and "how should we do it?") justifies Lincoln's leadership over that of Douglas. According to Fehrenbacher, then, the "House Divided" speech is structured to address the issue of the moment directly—Douglas and his rising popularity within the Republican Party.[13]

It is also possible to take Fehrenbacher's analysis one step further and read not just the tripartite organizational structure of the speech but also its tropes and discursive strategies as illustrations of a partisan rhetoric. At least for its original audience of political leaders at the Illinois Republican convention of June 16, 1858, Lincoln's keynote address did much more than redefine Republicanism to exclude Douglas or to validate Lincoln's nomination. Careful attention to the text in terms of its partisan convention audience and the generic conventions governing keynote addresses enables a number of interpretive insights. From this perspective, one can recognize that the famous "house divided" figure was deployed not only as a description of a troubled Union but also of the troubled national Republican coalition. The House Divided section opens:

If we could first know *where* we are, and *whither* we are tending, we could then better judge *what* to do, and *how* to do it. We are now in the *fifth* year, since a policy was initiated, with the *avowed* object, and *confident* promise, of putting an end to slavery agitation. Under the operation of that policy, the agitation has not only, *not ceased,* but has *constantly augmented.* In *my* opinion, it *will* not cease, until a *crisis* has been reached and passed. "A house divided against itself cannot stand." I believe this government cannot endure, permanently half *slave* and half *free.* I do not expect the Union to be *dissolved*—I do not expect the house to *fall*—but I *do* expect it will cease to be divided. It will become *all* one thing or *all* the other. Either the *opponents* of slavery, will arrest the further spread of it, and place it where the public mind shall rest in the belief that it is in its course of ultimate extinction; or its *advocates* will push it forward, till it shall become alike lawful in *all* the States, *old* as well as *new*—*North* as well as *South.*[14]

This passage can be read to be divided into two parts, separated by the statement "A house divided against itself cannot stand." The first half is a condensed narrative that refers to national events but, more significantly, references the natality of the Republican Party in the Nebraska bill controversy. The second half takes a predominantly national perspective, addressing the relationship of the slavery issue to the Union and introducing the slave power conspiracy as a force working to make the Union all one thing. The first half, then, is an introduction referring to the convention audience and the situation of the Republican Party and answering the question of *"where* we [the Republican Party] are"; the second half previews the argument of the Conspiracy section and answers the question *"whither* we [the Union] are tending." Given this division of the section, the "house divided" is a reference both to the Republican Party and the Union. Seen as a wrapup of the first half of the section, the claim that a house divided cannot stand resembles Lincoln's use of this figure in his 1843 Whig circular—as an admonition for Republican unity in the face of the changing course of national events. As an introduction to the second half, however, the house divided is obviously a reference to the Union and a preview of the conspiracy argument. The house divided figure, in this respect, can be read as a device linking the fate of the Union to the possibility of Republican solidarity and unity.[15]

Given the close association between growing political parties and conspiracy rhetoric, it is also possible to read the conspiracy argument in partisan terms. Conspiracy rhetoric was an effective strategy to mobilize voters in the early republic, but the conspiracy rhetoric in the "House Divided" also had the additional function—an internal one—of encouraging party unity. The conspiracy position in the "House Divided" not only provided a common enemy capable of trumping factional differences within the party, but it also appealed to the ideological predispositions of several of its factions. Finally, a partisan reading of the "House Divided" speech encourages attention to the generic conventions governing party convention keynote speeches. In particular, the "keynoter's dilemma"—the result of the need for a speaker to appeal simultaneously to the highly partisan immediate audience and to the average citizen outside the convention—helps to explain how a speech so well crafted to its original audience was easily misinterpreted by Lincoln's opponents before more general audiences.[16]

Lincoln's Conspiracy Claim in the "House Divided"

For the purposes of this chapter, concepts of party and partisanship will be enlisted primarily to interpret the Conspiracy section of the "House Divided" speech—to understand its narrative of conspiracy, not simply in terms of our own political ideologies and predispositions but in terms of its immediate context of 1858. The Conspiracy section's importance is evident based upon its predominance within the "House Divided" text. The House Divided section comprises 7 percent of the speech, the Living Dog section 21 percent, while the Conspiracy section encompasses about 72 percent of the text. Following the House Divided section's prediction of a tendency to make the Union all slave-holding, the Conspiracy section commences:

> Let any one who doubts, carefully contemplate that now almost complete legal combination—a piece of *machinery* so to speak—compounded of the Nebraska doctrine, and the Dred Scott decision. Let him consider not only *what work* the machinery is adapted to do, and *how well* adapted; but also, let him study the *history* of its construction, and trace, if he can, or rather *fail*, if he can, to trace the evidence of its design, and concert of action, among its chief bosses, from the beginning.[17]

This passage illustrates the primarily narrative mode of proof employed in the section. The conspiracy is identified and "proven" to exist by its imprint on political history. The Conspiracy section purports to establish a connection among the Nebraska bill, the Dred Scott decision, and a future "Dred Scott II" decision, a task accomplished by way of a complex linking together of acts, motives, and concert that are said to constitute a piece of machinery to nationalize slavery. It was not just the effects of the Nebraska bill or the Dred Scott decision that suggested a conspiracy was afoot, in other words, but the hidden relationship between these acts. The Nebraska bill, with its popular

sovereignty component, was sufficient to carry the 1856 election for the Democrats, but this bill allegedly created a "niche" for the Dred Scott decision
(by subordinating the territory's power to exclude slavery to the Constitution) that later made popular sovereignty null and void when the U.S.
Supreme Court ruled that a territory could not exclude slavery. It was this
conscious planning to manipulate the electorate—springing the Dred Scott
decision only after receiving popular endorsement—that constituted the
essence of the conspiracy to spread slavery into the territories. But the Conspiracy section goes one step further, pointing out the "niches" in the Dred
Scott decision that create the possibility of a Dred Scott II that would enable
slaves to be taken not only to the territories but to the free states themselves.

Classifying Conspiracy Arguments

Hofstadter's paranoid style approach provides preliminary guidance regarding the argumentative qualities of conspiracy discourse:

> The typical procedure of higher paranoid scholarship is to start with such
> defensible assumptions and with a careful accumulation of facts, or at least
> of what appear to be facts, and to marshal these facts toward an over-
> whelming "proof" of the particular conspiracy that is to be established. It is
> nothing if not coherent. . . . It is, if not wholly rational, at least intensely
> rationalistic.

The paranoid style appears to conform to argumentative language of evidence, proof, and rationality:

> The plausibility the paranoid style has for those who find it plausible lies, in
> good measure, in this appearance of the most careful, conscientious, and
> seemingly coherent application to detail, the laborious accumulation of
> what can be taken as convincing evidence for the most fantastic conclu-
> sions, the careful preparation for the big leap from the undeniable to the
> unbelievable.[18]

As rhetorical scholars have noted, Hofstadter's account of conspiracy arguments closely resembles the "quasi-logical argument"—an argument that is
persuasive because it appears to be rational. What kind of reasoning sup-
plies the rationalistic camouflage for conspiracy argument? Earl Creps's attempt to describe the conspiracy argument as rhetorical genre follows
Hofstadter, pointing out that while the mass of evidence gives conspiracy
arguments an inductive flavor, their logic is in reality deductive. Creps also
notes that conspiracy arguments are typically characterized by illogical
leaps, and he observes that "conspiracy discourse is replete with references

to 'clear' facts, 'unassailable' logic, and 'inevitable' conclusions. These are not the lessons of induction." This extreme form of deductive logic accounts for the totalizing tendencies of paranoid conspiracies. Creps observes: "This is deductive reasoning reduced to its deterministic essence. An inevitable logic gives the conspiracy rhetor the ability to subsume any fact, person, or event under the rubric of the Plot."[19]

But the conspiracy argument in the "House Divided" appears to have little in common with the conspiracy arguments considered by Hofstadter and Creps. Most notably, Lincoln's argument lacked the deductive certainty of a paranoid. He admitted in the "House Divided," "We cannot absolutely *know* that all these exact adaptations are the result of preconcert . . . [but] in *such* a case, we find it impossible to not *believe*."[20] Indeed, the character of Lincoln's conspiracy claim as argument is elucidated by considering Lincoln's explanation of what he thought he was doing in the "House Divided" speech. A month after the speech, Lincoln delivered another speech in Springfield in which he explained:

> One more point on this Springfield speech which Judge Douglas says he has read so carefully. I expressed my belief in the existence of a conspiracy to perpetuate and nationalize slavery. I did not profess to know it, nor do I now. I showed the part Judge Douglas had played in the string of facts, constituting to my mind, the proof of that conspiracy.

A fragment of speech notes provides a similar summary:

> At the Republican State Convention at Springfield I made a speech. . . . In it I arrange a string of incontestable facts which, I think, prove the existence of a conspiracy to nationalize slavery. The evidence was circumstantial only; but nevertheless it seemed inconsistent with every other hypothesis, save that of the existence of such a conspiracy. I believe the facts can be explained today on no other hypothesis. . . . I have not affirmed that a conspiracy does exist. I have only stated the evidence, and affirmed my belief in its existence.[21]

Lincoln's method appears superficially to resemble the argument strategy of the paranoid style. He strings together "incontestable facts" and concludes on the basis of these facts the existence of a conspiracy. But he expressly denies that he is certain. He does not make the final deductive leap characteristic of much conspiracy discourse. What kind of conspiracy argument, then, does Lincoln make?

Rhetorical and argument theory provide at least two analytical tools that seem best to describe the type of reasoning in which Lincoln is engaged.

The first is the figure of thought designated "accumulation" in the *Ad Her-renium*, in which "the points scattered throughout the whole case are collected in one place so as to make the speech more impressive or sharp or accusatory." Accumulation is said to be "very useful in conjectural causes, when the implications, which are petty and weak because expressed separately, are collected in one place and so seem to make the subject evident and not dubious, as follows: 'Do not, therefore, men of the jury, do not consider singly the things I have said, but join them all together and combine them into one.'"[22] The figure of accumulation seems to capture the flavor of what Lincoln was doing—the way in which the facts, taken together, converge to indicate conspiracy.

A more contemporary category explaining the type of argumentative move Lincoln made in the Conspiracy section of the "House Divided" is the conductive argument. Trudy Govier, drawing upon work in logic and ethics, places this form of argument between induction and deduction. This type of argument, not amenable to treatment by general rules, is a nondeductive, a priori, particularist way of arguing characterized as "a sort of reasoning in which (1) a conclusion about some individual case (2) is drawn non-conclusively (3) from one or more premises about the same case (4) without any appeal to other cases." The conductive argument is said to differ from deductive arguments because the premises are not put forward as being wholly sufficient for the conclusion and from inductive arguments because the hypothesis is not proved from instances. This type of argument depends, rather, on the cumulative force of several factors and deals wholly with issues of probability rather than certainty. Govier also refers to conductive arguments as "good reasons" arguments, pointing out that they thrive in contexts of uncertainty—especially those involving "practical affairs" or "disputes about the interpretation of human behavior."[23]

The conductive argument reflects not only the conditions of uncertainty regarding human actions with which conspiracy arguments deal but also closely matches what Lincoln does in the "House Divided" text. Significantly, Lincoln's "frame house" analogy—the figural key to understanding how his pieces of evidence fit together—seems to match almost precisely the kind of reasoning Govier describes:

> We cannot absolutely *know* that all these exact adaptations are the result of preconcert. But when we see a lot of framed timbers, different portions of which we know have been gotten out at different times and places and by different workmen—Stephen, Franklin, Roger, James, for instance—and when we see these timbers joined together, and see they exactly make the

frame of a house or a mill, all the tenons and mortices exactly fitting, and all the lengths and propositions of the different pieces exactly adapted to their respective places, and not a piece too many or too few—not omitting even scaffolding—or, if a single piece be lacking, we can see the place in the frame exactly fitted and prepared to bring such piece in—in *such* a case, we find it impossible to not *believe* that Stephen and Franklin and Roger and James all understood one another from the beginning, and all worked on a common *plan* or *draft* drawn up before the first lick was struck.[24]

Within the "frame house" analogy, the cumulative premises of the conductive argument may be said to correspond to the precisely fitted frames and the finished house to the conclusion. Any one piece of the frame would not be recognized for its place in the whole. It is only when the pieces are considered together and cumulatively that they begin to form the conspiratorial conclusion.

For the sake of clarity, it seems appropriate to delineate the premises corresponding to the framed timbers of the conductive argument in the "House Divided" (the tenons and mortices linking the timbers are indicated in parentheses):

1. Stephen Douglas's Framed Timbers
    a) Nebraska bill left the territories free to exclude slavery subject only to the Constitution (a niche for the Dred Scott decision)
    b) Nebraska bill refers to states and territories (a niche for Dred Scott II)
    c) Douglas refused to accept the Chase amendment (would ruin the Dred Scott decision niche)
    d) Douglas's "don't care" policy (prepares for the Dred Scott decision and Dred Scott II)
2. Franklin Pierce's and James Buchanan's Framed Timbers
    a) Incoming and outgoing presidents (and Douglas) endorse the decision before it appears (indicates collusion of presidents, Douglas, and the Supreme Court)
    b) Incoming president (and Douglas) endorse the decision after it appears (indicates collusion of president, Douglas, and the Supreme Court)
3. Chief Justice Roger Taney's Framed Timbers
    a) The Dred Scott decision was delayed until after the presidential election (would ruin Democratic election and reveal the emptiness of popular sovereignty)
    b) The Dred Scott decision prohibits territories from excluding slavery (fits into Nebraska bill niche)
    c) The Dred Scott decision does not mention the right of a state to exclude slavery (niche for Dred Scott II)

Conclusion (Strong): Douglas, Taney, Pierce, and Buchanan are involved in a concerted plan that aims at nationalizing slavery.

Conclusion (Weak): As above, but Douglas is an unwitting tool.

None of these historical facts alone would lend any credence to a conspiracy theory. It is only their cumulative force that appears to support either of the conclusions. But it was not through evidence or argument alone that the Conspiracy section made its case for complicity. Rather, Lincoln's text weaves the events comprising his evidence together in a compelling narrative—a narrative that was driven by the understandings of contemporary audiences.

Reading Conspiracy Narratives: Mimesis$_2$

The importance of narrative to conspiracy discourse generally requires no restatement here. Michael Leff's close reading of the "House Divided" speech recognizes the centrality of narrative to this text in particular. Leff utilizes narrative, among other approaches, to unlock the "rhetorical timing" of the text, how the "meaning of the speech progresses through time to reconfigure the audience's perception of both time and space relative to public events."[25] This chapter's reading will begin with the foundation laid by Leff's reading of the narrative structure in the "House Divided," but it will build upon this foundation by exploring other dimensions of narrative that are of critical importance to understanding the "House Divided" speech in its original context of 1858.

The work of Paul Ricoeur provides a valuable way of distinguishing the several dimensions of narrative. Ricoeur's theory focuses not only on the narratives as they appear in texts but also on their reception and moorings to the structure of readers' preunderstandings. Ricoeur expresses this complex relationship in terms of the concept of a threefold mimesis consisting of mimesis$_1$, mimesis$_2$, and mimesis$_3$. Together, these terms are said to comprehend the "concrete process by which the textual configuration [mimesis$_2$] mediates between the prefiguration of the practical field [mimesis$_1$] and its refiguration [mimesis$_3$] through the reception of the work." One of the advantages of Ricoeur's threefold mimesis is that it enables a nuanced account of the manner in which narratives are constructed on the basis of readers' preunderstandings of the world of action (the world of agents, goals, motives) and temporal experience, as well as the culturally specific manners in which such preunderstandings are symbolically mediated. These preunderstandings are termed mimesis$_1$, and Ricoeur writes that "to understand a story is to understand both the language of 'doing something' and the cultural tradition from which proceeds the typology of plots." Readers bring these preunderstandings to the "narrative configurations" within texts, which are synonymous with mimesis$_2$. Finally, mimesis$_3$ represents the "fusion of the text's and the reader's horizons, or of the intersection between the world of the text and that of the reader" brought about by the act of reading.[26]

The narrative theories upon which this study has depended heretofore have focused on either mimesis$_2$ or mimesis$_3$—Barthes's structural approach and explanation by emplotment each concerns a narrative's textual configuration, while Lucaites and Condit's functional approach and O'Leary's frame-centered approach each concerns how narratives condition audience actions. Leff's interpretation of the conspiracy narrative in the "House Divided" also focuses on the textual configuration. While this mimesis$_2$-centered reading is a valuable first step toward understanding the conspiracy narrative in the "House Divided," a more thorough understanding requires an exploration of mimesis$_1$ and the "narrative preunderstandings" of the speech's original 1858 audiences.[27]

In order to account for the textual configuration of the conspiracy narrative in the "House Divided," Leff divides the Conspiracy section into "three different movements [differentiated according to temporal progression] within the larger structure of the section. . . . The first subsection narrates past events, the second is grounded in the present, and the third predicts future events." The first movement, comprising over half of the Conspiracy section, begins with a narrative of events from the Kansas-Nebraska Act to Douglas's Lecompton Free-Soil heroics, followed by a nonnarrative summary or recapitulation.[28] The Kansas-Nebraska Act, opening "all national territory to slavery," is described as the "first point gained." Popular, or "squatter," sovereignty is described as a crucial component of this opening for slavery. Under this doctrine, the people are said to be left "*'perfectly free to form and regulate their own domestic institutions . . . subject only to the Constitution.'*" The "House Divided" text hints at the doctrine's proslavery bias, however, in terms of the story of the Chase amendment (which would have explicitly specified the right of territories to exclude slavery) and Douglas's hostility to this proposal. The narrative then moves from the halls of Congress to the Dred Scott case, a case said to have been commenced "in the same month" as the passage of the Nebraska bill. Next, the narrative proceeds to place the deferred Dred Scott decision in the context of the 1856 presidential election. In the campaign, Douglas is observed

to refuse to answer the question raised by the Chase amendment—
"whether the people of a territory can constitutionally exclude slavery
from their limits"—indicating "[t]hat is a question for the Supreme Court."
Democrat Buchanan is elected with the help of popular sovereignty, an
event described by Lincoln as "the *second* point gained." Meanwhile, outgoing President Pierce emphasizes the election's endorsement of the Nebraska
bill, and incoming President Buchanan exhorts the people to abide by the
upcoming Dred Scott decision (whatever it may be), which was further de-
layed by reargument. Soon after, the Dred Scott decision comes and is immediately endorsed by both Douglas and Buchanan. Only then do
Buchanan and Douglas face off on the issue of the Lecompton constitution.
While Douglas opposes the slaveholder Lecompton constitution as an
unfair imposition on the people, Lincoln emphasizes he does so with
the qualification that "he cares not whether slavery be voted down or
voted up."[29]

As Leff notes, the narrative is interrupted at this point for a digression
on popular sovereignty and a summary of the "working points" of the machinery the narrative has identified. With the Dred Scott decision that territories may not exclude slaves, "squatter sovereignty" is said to have
"squatted out of existence, tumbled down like temporary scaffolding—like
the mold at the foundry served through one blast and fell back into loose
sand—helped to carry an election, and then was kicked to the winds." The
text continues, "The several points of the Dred Scott decision, in connection with Senator Douglas's 'care not' policy, constitute the piece of machinery, in its *present* state of advancement. This was the third point
gained." Finally, the text proceeds to summarize "the working points of
that machinery." First, according to the Court in the Dred Scott case, no
"negroe" can be a citizen of any state. Second, according to the same decision, neither Congress nor territorial legislatures can exclude slavery—
enabling slaveholders to fill up the territories in order that they might "enhance the chances of permanency to the institution through all the future." Third, the Dred Scott decision deferred the question of whether
keeping a slave in a free state made the slave free for the state courts. This
third point is the jumping off point for a Dred Scott II decision that would
forbid states from excluding slavery. But the text concedes that "this point
was made, not to be pressed *immediately;* but, if acquiesced in for a while,
and apparently *indorsed* by the people at an election, *then* to sustain the
logical conclusion that what Dred Scott's master might lawfully do with
Dred Scott, in the free State of Illinois, every other master may lawfully do

with any other one . . . in Illinois, or in any free state." Douglas's "Nebraska doctrine" remains as an auxiliary to Dred Scott II, an auxiliary designed "to *educate* and *mould* public opinion . . . to not *care* whether slavery is voted *down* or voted *up.*" The first subnarrative of the Conspiracy section concludes with a summary of its accomplishment so far: "This shows exactly where we now *are;* and *partially* also, whither we are tending."[30] As the passage indicates, however, this subnarrative is not concerned solely with the past; it has already predicted the possibility of Dred Scott II, a position that will be subsequently elaborated.

Following the first narrative is a significant change in perspective. As Leff notes, "the second step in the 'conspiracy' argument reverses the temporal perspective used in the first. There Lincoln progresses forward from the past to the present. Here he stands in the present and evaluates the past." Lincoln had asked his reader/auditor to trace "evidences of design, and concert of action" in his narrative of the past. For his retrospective evaluation from the present, Lincoln again orients his reader/auditor: "It will throw additional light on the latter, to go back, and run the mind over the string of historical facts already stated. Several things will now appear less dark and mysterious than they did when they were transpiring." The first mystery elucidated is the language of the Nebraska bill that territorial legislatures' ability to exclude slavery was limited only by the Constitution: "What the *Constitution* had to do with it, outsiders could not then see. Plainly enough *now,* it was an exactly fitted *niche,* for the Dred Scott decision to afterwards come in, and declare the *perfect freedom* of the people, to be no freedom at all." So, too, with the Chase amendment: "Plainly enough *now,* the adoption of it would have spoiled the niche for the Dred Scott decision." So, too, with the delay in the decision and the endorsements of Douglas and the incoming and outgoing presidents: "These things look like the cautious patting and petting of a spirited horse, preparatory to mounting him, when it is dreaded that he may give the rider a fall." The famous "frame house" figure illustrates this retrospective evaluation of events. With this passage, as Leff notes, "Previous anticipations and suggestions are now fulfilled and elaborated. We know who the bosses are, how they work, and for what purposes they are working."[31]

The final subunit of the Conspiracy section—according to Leff, "the boldest, most controversial part of the speech"—deals with Lincoln's "speculation about the future progress of the machine."[32] Lincoln observes that "by the Nebraska bill, the people of a *State* as well as *Territory,* were to be left *'perfectly free' 'subject only to the Constitution.'* Why mention a *State?*"

Furthermore, the opinions in the Dred Scott case omit any mention of the applicability of the Court's decision to the states:

> In what *cases* the power of the *states* is so restrained by the U.S. Constitution, is left an *open* question, precisely as the same question, as to the restraint on the power of *territories* was left open in the Nebraska act. Put *that* and *that* together, and we have another nice little niche, which we may, ere long, see filled with another Supreme Court decision, declaring that the Constitution of the United States does not permit a *state* to exclude slavery from its limits. . . . Such a decision is all that slavery now lacks of being alike lawful in all the States. Welcome or unwelcome, such a decision *is* probably coming, and will soon be upon us, unless the power of the present political dynasty shall be met and overthrown. We shall *lie down* pleasantly dreaming that the people of *Missouri* are on the verge of making their state *free;* and we shall *awake* to the *reality,* instead, that the *Supreme Court* has made *Illinois* a *slave state.*[33]

Such is Lincoln's narrative of conspiracy in the "House Divided" speech, one of the many "coherent narratives that formed the premises of powerful arguments" in the subsequent Lincoln-Douglas debates.[34]

Reading Narratives against Preunderstandings: Mimesis₁

Leff's mimesis$_2$-centered reading of the narrative in the "House Divided," however, is only one part of the story. To fully understand the speech, it is essential to comprehend the preunderstandings of Lincoln's contemporary audiences and the way in which the text provides cues enabling readers/auditors to understand the logic governing the conspiracy narrative. Ricoeur's threefold mimesis enables an account of the manner in which narratives are constructed on the basis of readers' preunderstandings of the world of action as well as the culturally specific manners in which such preunderstandings are symbolically mediated. Without such understandings of the world of agents, their goals, and their motives, it is difficult to follow a story. For this reason, to Ricoeur, something like mimesis$_1$ is necessary in order to understand any narrative: "To understand a story is to understand both the language of 'doing something' and the cultural tradition from which proceeds the typology of plots."[35] These preunderstandings are said to constitute the "prefiguration of the practical field" from which any particular narrative will derive and upon which it will act. The Conspiracy section of the "House Divided" speech is concerned with just these issues. Lincoln's story of conspiracy is a tale of agents whose motives are concealed and whose actions are taken toward a secret goal—the nationalization of slavery. The application of the concept of narrative pre-understandings suggests that we ask two related questions about Lincoln's conspiracy narrative. What sorts of motives and goals (a key component of narrative preunderstandings) does the "House Divided" text assume on the part of conspirators, and how does it signal these motivations to readers? What kinds of audience preunderstandings resonate with Lincoln's interpretation of events?

The motivations of Lincoln's conspirators are revealed largely by their partisan identity. As George Forgie indicates, Lincoln's "version of conspiracy differed in important respects from the prevailing one." Most accounts of the slave power conspiracy focused on the activities of slaveholders. Lincoln, by contrast, presented a version of the slave power conspiracy in which the principals were primarily Northern Democrats. Stephen Douglas, Franklin Pierce, James Buchanan, and Roger Taney, not a slave-holding class, were engaged in a plot to nationalize slavery. Even the conspiracy rhetoric of Chase and Sumner viewed Democrats as the tools of the slaveholding class, rather than part of the conspiracy itself. But Lincoln's move resonated with the narrative preunderstandings of many audiences in 1858. Historians have emphasized that the mid-1850s was a time of antipartyism. Many citizens were suspicious that the two parties had degenerated into purely self-interested organizations that were concerned solely with the maintenance of power. With the collapse of the Whig Party, the Democrats remained a focus of antipartyism and disillusionment with politicians, party bosses, and the "powers that be." The very strategies that enabled Democratic success—for example, the strict control of party members' activities through the selective dispersal of patronage and the backroom deals—came increasingly to be seen as unacceptable and corrupt.[36]

Antipartyism, in sum, provided the major components for the narrative preunderstandings implicit in Lincoln's political narrative. The conspirators in Lincoln's slave power conspiracy were motivated not by the demonic evil of Garrison's slave power or even by the earnest desire to spread slavery attributed by Chase and Sumner. Rather, they were for the most part "doughfaces"—Northern Democrats whose desire for high office motivated them to ally themselves with the slave power. The goals of party politics, centered on the aggrandizement of power and accumulation of political resources, provided a plausible account of the motivations of the conspirators, and their association through the formal organizations and informal networks of the Democratic Party also offered a plausible explanation for the means by which the builders of the frame house coordinated their

efforts. Lincoln was well aware of the extent to which such means and motivations structured politics among the Democrats. In a letter of late 1855
he expressed to Democrat Joshua Speed the fear that the anti-Nebraska
forces would be beaten on the Kansas issue: "Standing as a unit among
yourselves, you can, directly, and indirectly, bribe enough of our men to
carry the day—as you could on an open proposition to establish monarchy
. . . [Position the issue as] . . . a democratic party [*sic*] necessity, and the
thing is done."[37] A month after the "House Divided" speech, in a speech at
Springfield, Lincoln specifically linked Douglas to the patronage machine.
Explaining the advantages held by Douglas in the Senate race, Lincoln
relates:

> All the anxious politicians of his party, or who have been of his party for
> years past, have been looking upon him as certainly, at no distant day, to be
> the President of the United States. They have seen in his round, jolly, fruit-
> ful face, postoffices, landoffices, marshalships, and cabinet appointments,
> chargeships and foreign missions, bursting and sprouting out in wonderful
> exuberance ready to be laid hold of by their greedy hands.[38]

Douglas's patronage advantage was significant, but Lincoln hoped that it
would serve to stigmatize him and his party's corrupt methods. In any
event, antipartyism helped to constitute the preunderstandings of Lincoln
and many of his contemporaries. When Lincoln's narrative is read against
such preunderstandings of the goals and motives of Democratic politicians,
its implausibility recedes.

Nonetheless, one need not rely upon historical accounts of the prevalence of antipartyism as a justification for reading Lincoln's narrative in this
way. Lincoln's conspiracy narrative itself contains rhetorical figures and
significant terms that signal the narrative preunderstandings against which
it is hoped audiences will read the narrative of conspiracy. Recognition of
the significance of these figures and terms, however, is difficult for critics
concerned solely with the narrative's textual configuration. Leff's interpretation does find significance in Lincoln's choice of figures and terms in the
opening paragraph of the Conspiracy section, and Leff makes two main
claims. He comments on several dimensions of the machine imagery and
observes that this imagery contributes to the conspiracy narrative insofar as
it "encourages the view that they are parts designed to mesh with one another." He also indicates that this imagery "suggests that the opposition is
cold, inhumane, relentless" and that the "amoral character of machine actions seems a fitting counterpart to Douglas's 'don't care' attitude." These

points seem sound, but they miss the much greater significance of the machine imagery for interpreting Lincoln's conspiracy narrative. Given the partisan character of the conspiracy narrative, the choice of machine imagery takes on new significance—for machine imagery was already being applied to the workings of political parties. In this respect, the choice of machine imagery primes the narrative preunderstandings of his audiences. Former Whigs and Democrats were equal critics of the vagaries of the Democratic Party organization. Whigs had always feared this component of the Democracy, and disaffected Democrats were acutely aware of their excommunication from their old party's organization as well as the duplicity of the remaining doughfaces.[39] Given these perceptions, the text's machine imagery provides readers with another key with which to interpret Lincoln's story, one that was more consistent with their own experiences of the workings of political parties. A similar point may be made with respect to Leff's interpretation of Lincoln's choice of the term "bosses" to describe the conspirators. According to Leff, the choice of a "simple Anglo-Saxon word [as opposed to Latinate alternatives such as "architect" or "designer"] strikes just the right note."[40] Alternately, "bosses" might be understood as another cue that the conspiracy Lincoln is about to delineate is the work of *party* bosses. The imagery of machinery and the word choice of "bosses" seem to be invocations of the narrative preunderstandings according to which readers ought to interpret the narrative of conspiracy.

Preunderstandings of the goals of party politicians, and politicians in general, were part of a larger complex of nineteenth-century civic republican ideological assumptions. As Howe notes, the nineteenth century operated largely within a "conspiracy paradigm" loosely associated with civic republicanism and English opposition ideologies. In this context, of course, conspiracy rhetoric was not deviant, though nineteenth-century political culture understood the relationship between conspiracy and politics quite differently than we do today. Conspiracy, Howe explains, once had a "broader definition" that included political parties, factions, and interest groups. Howe comments, "As long as the competition of interest groups was not accepted as legitimate, conspiracies were presumed to be a danger to the general welfare; they were very much like the 'factions' against which the Federalist Papers had warned."[41] Antiparty attitudes and civic republican ideological predispositions made for narrative preunderstandings conducive to Lincoln's conspiratorial interpretation of the events of the mid-1850s.

Reading the narrative of conspiracy (or, more specifically, its textual configuration, mimesis$_2$) in the "House Divided" against the antiparty pre-understandings of Northern audiences and recognizing the imagery with which the "House Divided" text signals the appropriateness of these preunderstandings contribute to the goal of understanding the "House Divided" in the context of June 1858. . . . In order to ground this claim, it is necessary to return to a consideration of the interpretive context of the "House Divided" and consider the preunderstandings that Lincoln's critics have brought to the text.

Pluralist Preunderstandings and the Reception of the "House Divided"

Reading Conspiracy against Political Culture

Much as Lincoln's audiences brought their own narrative preunderstandings to the "House Divided" speech, twentieth-century commentators have also interpreted the speech in terms of their own beliefs and commitments. Precisely because these commentators made assumptions remarkably similar to those underlying the paranoid style, the reception of Lincoln's conspiracy rhetoric is important to the broader goals of this study. Fully understanding the relationship between critics of Lincoln's conspiracy rhetoric and the assumptions of the paranoid style, however, requires an exercise in rhetorical hermeneutics. Such an exercise, according to Steven Mailloux, entails providing "histories of how particular theoretical and critical discourses have evolved . . . [recognizing that] . . . acts of persuasion [such as interpretations] always take place against an ever-changing background of shared and disputed assumptions, questions, assertions, and so forth. Any thick rhetorical analysis of interpretation must therefore describe this tradition of discursive practices in which acts of interpretive persuasion are embedded." Specifically, "all academic literary criticism necessarily involves participation—by omission or commission, as it were—in two interrelated sectors of rhetorical politics: that of the professional discourses within the institutionalized discipline and that of the broader domain of cultural politics reaching beyond the university."[42] As we shall see, the discourses of professional academic disciplines and the assumptions of politics beyond the university have motivated those twentieth-century commentators who have condemned both Lincoln's conspiracy rhetoric and the "House Divided" speech.

The term "political culture" seems well disposed to linking the related concepts of narrative preunderstandings and political ideologies that partially govern academic interpretations. Particular political cultural assumptions—about how political actors ought to behave, how they are motivated, and the proper role of rhetoric within political society—will tend to predispose citizens, politicians, and scholars for or against conspiracy discourse. Consideration of the political cultural context in which Lincoln made his conspiracy argument, as well as the political cultural considerations conditioning certain veins of the reception history of "House Divided," will clarify and substantiate this claim. Not surprisingly, the portion of the reception history of "House Divided" that condemns Lincoln for making irresponsible and baseless conspiracy claims was initiated by Douglas himself. For this reason, the section commences with a consideration of Douglas's view of politics and the place of conspiracy rhetoric within it. Next, the section traces the political assumptions shared by Douglas, later revisionists, and Hofstadter, the architect of the paranoid style. The background assumptions of Douglas, the revisionists, and Hofstadter, as it turns out, decisively determined their understandings of and attitudes toward conspiracy rhetoric.

Douglas the Protopluralist

Pluralism, the doctrine that politics is properly an arena for interest group competition in which competing interests are reconciled through a process of bargaining and competition, is a twentieth-century concept.[43] Nevertheless, Stephen Douglas has come to represent, for some historians and political scientists, the paradigmatic nineteenth-century pluralist. Douglas's allegedly pluralist political doctrine seems to have grown out of his experiences with party politics in an extended republic as well as his larger political aspirations. As a member of the Democratic Party, Douglas's rise to power derived, in no small part, from his ability to avoid divisive issues in favor of those amenable to compromise and bargaining. With the support of his party, Douglas hoped to establish himself as a middle point between the sectional extremes of proslavery radicals and abolitionists. Such a position, he expected, would make him an extremely strong presidential candidate in the 1860 election. Douglas understood that maintaining Democratic unity and achieving such a middle position required avoiding divisive moral issues like slavery as much as possible. Politics within a large and heterogeneous republic like the United States, he believed, required (what would later be called) a pluralist mode of politics capable of achieving practical agreement and the satisfaction of multiple competing preferences. Economic issues were the most amenable to such a political process. By contrast, issues of morality, because often difficult to resolve by the standard methods of bargain and compromise, threatened the stability of the national political consensus. Such a consensus was better maintained, Douglas insisted, by compromise and practical agreement cemented by relatively polysemous acts such as the Compromise of 1850. But this kind of democracy required extraordinary restraint on the part of politicians. It required that they were careful to respect one another's mutual preferences—however much they disagreed. It also suggested that silence was the best way to handle those controversies too explosive to be contained within a framework of horse trading and logrolling. To do otherwise was to risk inflaming competing portions of the public to the point where it would no longer be politically possible for their representatives to compromise.[44]

Within such an understanding of politics, Lincoln's slave power conspiracy strategy was an act of profound irresponsibility that threatened the very fabric of the Union. From the perspective of Douglas, Northern abolitionists and Southern radicals were equally dangerous threats to the stability of the Union. This was precisely the thrust of Douglas's primary conspiracy countercharge in the Lincoln-Douglas debates. Douglas portrayed Lincoln's attempt to realign the Whig-Democratic party system as a conspiracy to abolitionize the old parties.[45] Douglas advanced this charge at the debate in Ottawa, Illinois:

> In 1854, Mr. Abraham Lincoln and Mr. Trumbull entered into an arrangement, one with the other, and each with his respective friends, to dissolve the old Whig party on the one hand, and to dissolve the old Democratic party on the other, and to connect the members of both into an abolition party under the name and disguise of the Republican party. . . . Lincoln was to bring into the abolition camp the Old Line Whigs, and transfer them over to Giddings, Chase, Ford, Douglass, and Parson Lovejoy.[46]

While Douglas presented this position in an almost comical fashion to cheers and laughter (due to his parallelism of Lincoln's four conspirators in the "House Divided"), the implications of the charge were deadly serious. To Douglas, transsectional parties like the Democrat and former Whig parties were essential institutions making national politics possible. To consciously tear down these parties in favor of sectional parties was as irresponsible as whipping up the passions of Northerners with baseless conspiracy charges and moral appeals. Both of these courses of action would compromise the government as an arena for political interest group competition.

Pluralist Revisionism

There are striking similarities linking Douglas's pluralist assumptions with those of later revisionist historians. Not only did revisionists condemn the emotionally charged fear appeals of politicians and agitators, they did so in pluralist terms. Craven makes the pluralist point that, with the coming of the anti- and proslavery agitation of the 1850s, "[a]n emotional fervor and moral force . . . [were] thus thrown about a whole set of very practical and concrete problems." The rational bargaining and agreement that had enabled politicians in 1820 and 1850 to compromise on matters of slavery were possible only because the issue was, at that time, political rather than moral. Other revisionists have shown an appreciation for Douglas's pluralistic politics. Randall recognizes that, in 1858, Douglas faced greater constraints than Lincoln. While Lincoln's condemnations of slavery were appropriate for one concerned solely with campaign oratory, Douglas "had to think, not merely of campaign oratory, but of responsible measures to be carried out—not by one section exclusively, but by national action." From this national perspective, Randall suggests that popular sovereignty might have been the better policy: "if it was a matter of a workable national solution, Douglas was nearer to that in the peaceable sense than the Republicans." Other historians have followed this logic to the conclusion that if Douglas had been elected president in 1860, his responsible statesmanship would have avoided the Civil War.[47] But the gist of the position taken by Douglas and the revisionists—that Lincoln's conspiracy argument was baseless and politically irresponsible—is also similar to Hofstadter's attitude toward conspiracy rhetoric, and this common outlook was the outgrowth of similar political outlooks.

Pluralism and Conspiracy: Revisiting the Paranoid Style

Hofstadter shares with both Douglas and the revisionists a fundamental commitment to pluralism and the importance of consensus to politics—a commitment that heavily colors his views toward conspiracy rhetoric and the entire paranoid style category. Following Mailloux, Hofstadter's interpretive apparatus for conspiracy discourse appears to have been conditioned by the imperatives of professional disciplinary discourses and by the domain of politics beyond the university. More specifically, his work on the paranoid style was heavily conditioned by the imperatives of the "consensus school" of historians as well as by a basic commitment to pluralist politics.

The relationship between the paranoid style and the consensus school of historians illustrates the manner in which disciplinary discourses shaped Hofstadter's interpretive attitude. The consensus school, positing that American ideological conflicts and political disagreements all occurred within a fundamental liberal consensus, was an important paradigm organizing historical scholarship in the 1950s and 1960s. Louis Hartz's *The Liberal Tradition in America* may be said to exemplify the consensus view. But the consensus school historians had difficulties accounting for the ruptures and disagreements in American politics. They could not explain why those within the Lockean liberal consensus so frequently saw themselves involved in fundamental and emotionally charged conflicts with fellow citizens. The paranoid style made this kind of evidence digestible by the consensus paradigm:

> The Hartzian paradigm, to be sure, possessed strategies to contain these signs of the underappreciated emotionality. . . . The most important was the notion of the paranoid style, reconceived, not as a particular response to particular social strain, but as a constant undercurrent to the Lockean mainstream. But the recognition gathering force so rapidly in the mid-1960s that the best and brightest of eighteenth century Americans had been steeped in thought processes akin to those of McCarthyites and John Birchers was not a little troubling. . . . [T]he Hartzian paradigm was hard pressed to accommodate this challenge to the Lockean card with which it had so long trumped the Beardian signs of conflict.[48]

The paranoid style, then, sutured the growing faults within the consensus interpretation of the history of American politics, reassuring skeptics that periods of emotionally charged conflict and conspiracy charges were simply temporary departures from the liberal consensus norm.

Pluralism was both a disciplinary discourse originated by political scientists and a sensibility abstracted from the broader political culture and practice of politics. Seen from this perspective, Hofstadter's category was a pejorative label attached to a nonpluralist (or even antipluralist) way of conducting politics. Mark Fenster provides a thorough critique of the paranoid style as a category that reflected and also helped to maintain Hofstadter's pluralist allegiances. Fenster characterizes Hofstadter's consensus pluralism in a manner consistent with the sensibilities of Douglas and the revisionists—as vindicating a political order maintained by the moderate

and pragmatic sensibilities of its leaders, a commitment to rationality in political debate, and a stable two-party system. In fact, within his collection of
essays led off by "The Paranoid Style in American Politics," Hofstadter provides an extensive account of the "professional code" of the pluralist politician. According to this account, pluralist politicians first and foremost
recognize the fact that they must not only win elections but also work with
the opposing party (and opposing factions within their own party). This
means that "their partisan passions are modified by the harsh corrective of
reality" and that "under the heated surface of . . . political rhetoric . . .
there exists a certain sobriety born of experience."[49] In a passage that effectively summarizes the position of Douglas and the revisionists, Hofstadter suggests that American politics puts "a strong premium on the
practical rather than the ideological bent of mind, on the techniques of negotiation and compromise rather than the assertion of divisive ideas and
passion." Standing in contrast to this restrained rhetoric of responsible pluralist politics, conspiracy rhetoric was the strategy of extremists on both the
Left and Right, a strategy that was wholly lacking in rationality and highly
enabling to dangerous demagogues.[50]

Conspiracy's Eclipse?
Political Cultural Transition and the
Fate of Conspiracy Rhetoric

The twentieth-century aversion to conspiracy has been shown to be
rooted, in part, in liberal and pluralist assumptions about how politics
ought to be conducted and what kind of rhetoric is appropriate to such an
understanding of politics. As Howe writes, "With the coming of liberal pluralism, the conspiracy paradigm was displaced from its prominent position
in American thought. It became the property of angry minorities who did
not accept the dominant liberalism. By generalizing backward from these
groups, Hofstadter derived his notion of a 'paranoid style.'"[51] But when did
this transition occur? Scholars studying both political theory and political
rhetoric concur in identifying the 1850s as the crucial time of transition.
David Ericson suggests that liberal pluralism did not become a prominent
political ideology until the 1850s. During this decade pluralism coexisted
with the republican ideology undergirding what Howe calls the "conspiracy paradigm." With the Civil War, pluralism's victory is said to have been
complete.[52]

What is more interesting is the extent to which this account of political cultural transition is corroborated by one of the more thorough studies of nineteenth-century political rhetoric. Andrew Robertson's account of the transition from "hortatory" to "admonitory" forms of electioneering rhetoric suggests that changes in political cultural assumptions corresponded to changes in rhetorical practice. According to Robertson, electioneering rhetoric from the French Revolution to the Civil War was a "hortatory rhetoric." Hortatory rhetoric aimed at mass mobilization by way of fiery speeches and editorial appeals characterized by invective and ad hominem attacks. Robertson also notes the tendency of the hortatory style to rely on conspiracy rhetoric as a device to nurture partisan identities by portraying opposing parties and candidates as sinister and malicious. Robertson, in fact, explicitly cites Lincoln's "House Divided" speech—in particular, its conspiracy claim—as an archetype of hortatory rhetoric. Robertson's account identifies the political debates of the 1850s with hortatory rhetoric at its most shrill and extreme but notes that the Civil War itself signaled the transition to a less colorful "admonitory rhetoric." The admonitory style was much more cautious and concerned to tame the hortatory excesses that might have helped to contribute to the Civil War. Precisely because it tended to be less hyperbolic and engaging, the admonitory style is said to have been "the language of stable party competition."[53] It is not difficult to recognize the extent to which Ericson's ideological account and Robertson's account of rhetorical practice overlap. What Robertson identifies as the emotionally charged practices of hortatory rhetoric correspond to a republican/prepluralist political culture. The calmer and more cautious rhetorical practice of admonitory rhetoric, on the other hand, seems to be exactly the kind of rational pluralist rhetoric desired by the likes of Douglas, the revisionists, and Hofstadter.

Even Lincoln's rhetoric of conspiracy can be seen as indicative of this ideological transition. Douglas's pluralism ought not to be contrasted with a simplistic version of Lincoln as a prepluralist, ever suspicious of faction as conspiracy. In many respects, Lincoln was far from the premodern perspective of civic republicanism. He, too, exhibited pluralistic tendencies, and his commitment to liberalism and material progress is well established.[54] In fact, it is possible to identify this commitment to pluralism in what might be called Lincoln's "quasi-conspiracy" rhetoric. Careful attention to Lincoln's rhetorical texts between 1854 and 1860 reveals that, at many junctures, he portrays what in the "House Divided" speech appears as a conspiracy to nationalize slavery as something quite different. On many occasions, he presents the "tendency" to nationalize slavery as the work of a self-interested faction bent on pursuing material gain. The slave power conspiracy, in other words, may be just an interest group. Whatever the precise character of the agents working toward the nationalization of slavery, however, Lincoln is consistent in his insistence that this plan must be stopped.[55] In sum, Lincoln's deployment of both conspiracy and "quasi-conspiracy" positions seems a tacit recognition of the ambiguity between conspiracy, interest groups, and political parties even as early as the 1850s and reflects his place within the ambivalent pluralist and civic republican political culture of the time.

Lincoln's Conspiracy Rhetoric: Beyond the Paranoid Style

While this chapter shares with previous chapters the goal of interpreting Lincoln's conspiracy rhetoric in its original context, it has also broken with previous chapters in taking seriously the reception, and resulting interpretive context, of the influential "House Divided" speech. Consideration of the reception of the "House Divided" speech among an array of twentieth-century historians not only has cleared the way to consider the text in the context of the political realities, narrative preunderstandings, and political ideologies of 1858, but it has also enabled a more thorough understanding of the paranoid style category. Understanding the pluralist bias shared by Douglas, Hofstadter, and Lincoln critics has clarified why such a critically sensitive and productive category like the paranoid style was nevertheless subject to oversimplification and obfuscation. From a pluralistic perspective, it is possible to comprehend precisely why the paranoid style considers conspiracy rhetoric—with its irresponsibly emotional tone, basic irrationality, and tendency to make compromise difficult—pejoratively, as the strategy of the demagogue and the demented. Recognizing and interrogating this bias make it possible to simultaneously appropriate valuable aspects of the paranoid style—especially its critical sensitivity—and selectively excise that which is problematic and unproductive.

In addition to providing a jumping-off point for a discussion of the paranoid style, interpreting the text of the "House Divided" speech has contributed to the goal of elucidating the rhetorical strategies animating conspiracy texts within mainstream contexts. Thus far the study has focused largely on conspiracy narratives and the manner in which they are presented as constituting a proof for the existence of a conspiracy. Narrative has been of concern throughout the study and remains important to understanding the "House Divided" text, but this chapter emphasizes the contrasting argumentative characteristics of the paranoid style and mainstream conspiracy rhetoric. The conspiracy argument of the "House Divided" text has been shown to have little in common with the quasi-logical arguments or deductive "leap from the undeniable to the unbelievable" associated with the paranoid style. Rather, the conspiracy argument in the "House Divided" seems to correspond most closely to the conductive argument, in which premises converge to support a conspiratorial conclusion. We find in the "House Divided" speech not the deductive certainty of a paranoid but a probabilistic exercise in practical judgment.

In addition to elucidating Lincoln's conspiracy argument, this chapter has also reinforced the notion that the narrative practices of conspiracy rhetoric at the center of the political mainstream differ from those at the fringe. In previous chapters, Garrison's tragic narrative, with its extremely early key cardinal function of conspiracy, has been contrasted with the conspiracy narratives of Chase and Sumner. On the level of plot, Lincoln's text presents a comic conspiracy narrative, and the text's structure resembles those of Sumner and Chase, identifying 1854 as the key cardinal function of conspiracy—an event planting the seed for subsequent slave power outrages in the form of "bleeding Kansas" and the Dred Scott decision. In addition, the partisan figures of bosses and machines drive the three interlocking narratives in the "House Divided" by priming the antiparty narrative preunderstandings of political audiences in 1858 in order to provide a possible account of how and why the actions of Douglas, Pierce, Buchanan, and Taney could be part of a conspiracy to nationalize slavery.

So far, this account of the narrative in the "House Divided" has emphasized the fusion of narratives within texts, mimesis$_2$, with the narrative preunderstandings of mimesis$_1$. It seems appropriate to conclude with a brief consideration of the result of this fusion—mimesis$_3$—and ask how the "House Divided" text functions to reconfigure audience preunderstandings or, from the functional perspective, how the text's narrative is expected to conclude in audience action. To express the same point from the perspective of argument, this chapter has already considered the argument purporting to prove the existence of a conspiracy, but it has not yet considered the argument from conspiracy—concerning what ought to be done in light of the existence of the conspiracy. Within the text, the Conspiracy section functions to respond to "where we are" in order to better judge "what to do, and how to do it." As an instance of partisan rhetoric, the conspiracy identified in the "House Divided" speech provides a reason for Illinoisans in particular, and Northerners in general, to support the Republican Party.[56] All are invited to resolve the narrative of conspiracy by way of electoral action that would, in turn, enable the promulgation of antiextension policies. As Lincoln indicates, "I have stated in what way I thought it would be reached and passed. . . . We might, by arresting the further spread of it and placing it [slavery] where our fathers originally placed it, put it where the public mind should rest in the belief that it was in the course of ultimate extinction."[57] As an intraparty matter, the existence of a conspiracy to nationalize slavery (in which Douglas is either a conspirator or a dupe) was a reason for party unity in the face of the potential schism caused by Douglas. The conclusion of the "House Divided" emphasizes the origin of Republican unity in the struggle against the common enemy: "Of *strange, discordant,* and even, *hostile* elements, we gathered from the four winds, and *formed* and fought the battle through, under the constant hot fire of a disciplined, proud and pampered enemy." Continued unity against the conspiracy is said to be necessary if compromise is to be avoided and the crisis is to be reached and passed: "We shall not fail—if we stand firm, we shall not fail."[58] Whether warranting Republican unity or electoral support for the Republican Party at the polls, the form of action called for within the "House Divided" text remains proportional to the conspiracy. In the face of a conspiracy by party men to perpetuate their own power along with the institution of slavery, the text invites political action by citizens, in the form of voting, and party leaders, in the form of the unity that would enable the Republicans to prevail. A conspiracy by politics, in other words, is to be fought with politics.

It is appropriate that a study of the slave power conspiracy at the center of the political mainstream should conclude with Abraham Lincoln. Lincoln, after all, was not an ordinary conspiracy theorist but the very embodiment of the triumphant Republican Party in the election of 1860. One might say that Lincoln marks that coordinate on this study's map that indicates the exact middle of that vast region comprising the center of the antebellum political mainstream in the North. In addition to contributing an essential location on this study's map of the slave power conspiracy formation, Lincoln's texts also contribute uniquely to this study's critically oriented goals. Lincoln has been known for his exceptional rhetorical skills, and his conspiracy texts may be said to represent his era's state-of-the-art persuasive strategies. In respect to these cartographic and critical goals, the social logic and coalition-building function of the "House Divided" in the context of partisan institutions, its basis in conventional civic republican assumptions about politics and political motivations, and its narrative and argumentative forms confirm the appropriateness of the assumptions guiding this study. Insofar as he is perhaps the best case for comprehending the slave power conspiracy at the center, Lincoln is an appropriate last case for this study. But Lincoln is also last in a way much more significant for the purposes of mainstream conspiracy discourse. If Ericson's and Robertson's histories of political culture and rhetorical practice are correct, Lincoln may also be among the last in a long line of hortatory civic republican rhetors whose success was enabled, in part, by their practice of conspiracy rhetoric.

5

Lessons of the Slave Power Conspiracy:
Conspiracy Rhetoric at the
Center and Fringe

Critical to the tenacity and flexibility of countersubversive interpreta-
tions are their articulate champions. Politicians, religious leaders, jour-
nalists, government officials, and leading industrialists, along with other
role models, have cleared the way for ordinary men and women.

—Robert Goldberg, *Enemies Within*

It is unfortunate that at a juncture in history when conspiracy theories of various sorts increasingly populate the diverse locales of public spheres around the world, the study of conspiracy discourse continues to be hobbled, rather than enabled, by the legacy of the paranoid style. Too many scholars studying conspiracy still conceive of conspiracy discourse as uniformly deranged and dangerous. While a number of scholars have attempted to move beyond the oversimplifications and pejorative assumptions of the paranoid style in their engagements with mainstream conspiracy texts, few have brought to the issue Hofstadter's critical sensitivity and concern with discursive form.[1] In contrast, this study's goal has been to do for conspiracy discourse at the center of the mainstream what Hofstadter did for conspiracy discourse at the fringe—to develop interpretive strategies that help us to understand conspiracy discourse as a rhetorical process in

153

which texts and speeches engage and move readers and auditors. Since this study singles out one of the most successful conspiracy theories in U.S. history, it also provides insights toward understanding the rhetorical operations and processes by which mainstream conspiracy theories occasionally acquire a virulence that paranoid theories seldom possess for most people.

Following the suggestions of Zarefsky and Creps, this study has asked whether, alongside what might be called a paranoid mode of conspiracy rhetoric—one inhabiting the fringes of society's institutions and governing ideologies—there might be a distinct mode of conspiracy rhetoric that from time to time occupies the center of public discourse.[2] This question, in turn, inspired both the cartographic and critical guiding questions. First, does "place" (location within mainstream institutions and ideologies, initially conceptualized by the basic coordinates of center and fringe) condition the textual practice of conspiracy? Second (we already have approaches to thinking about conspiracy rhetoric on the fringe), what rhetorical processes best characterize these conspiracy texts that are close to the center of the political mainstream? In order to answer these questions, the study sought to "map" the discursive formation generated by abolitionists and antislavery reformers. This discursive formation, though united by a common concern that a conspiracy of slaveholders threatened the community in fundamental ways, was found to have a paranoid fringe and a more moderate center. The synthesis of often disparate academic literatures, combined with sustained attention to texts standing at the understudied (that is, from the perspective of the conspiracy literature) center of this formation, has generated a number of insights about the best means of analyzing and understanding those conspiracy texts falling outside the bounds of the paranoid style.

The map of this discursive formation identified William Lloyd Garrison and his radical AASS as representatives of the fringe of slave power conspiracy discourse. Consideration of Garrison's texts against the slave power revealed the applicability of the paranoid style category. Garrison presented the slave power as (in Hofstadter's words) a "vast and sinister conspiracy . . . set in motion to undermine or destroy a way of life," in which this "'vast' or 'gigantic' conspiracy . . . [is] . . . the motive force in historical events," and "what is felt to be needed to defeat it is not the usual methods of political give and take, but an all-out crusade."[3] In terms of its narrative of conspiracy, Garrison's slave power was the driving force in a tragic emplotment of American political history, a history in which the conspiracy gains control almost at the moment of the nation's founding. Eschewing politics, Garrison and those like him opted for withdrawal from the tragic secular world in favor of a brighter millennium or a jihad that would forever end the blight of slavery. Due to the similarity (on the level of scope, narrative, and action) between Garrison's slave power and the paranoid style of conspiracy discourse, Hofstadter's category—though profoundly ahistorical—does seem to lend strong critical purchase to some conspiracy texts. But Garrison's slave power conspiracy was found to represent only the fringe of a rich and varied discursive formation. While Garrison and other abolitionists on the political fringe practiced a form of conspiracy rhetoric consistent with the paranoid style, rhetors operating at the center of political institutions and ideologies practiced a quite different kind of conspiracy rhetoric.

The bulk of this study has analyzed the rhetorical texts of Salmon P. Chase, Charles Sumner, and Abraham Lincoln, and the fruits of these critical engagements are a number of implications and conclusions not only about the complexity of antebellum slave power conspiracy discourse but about the broader conspiracy phenomenon as well. In this spirit, this chapter will move from the particular to the general.

The Cartography of Center and Fringe: Mapping the Slave Power Conspiracy Formation

Mapping Narratives

Conspiracy rhetors have always relied on narratives of political history in order to make a hidden conspiracy recognizable to audiences, and a comparison of slave power conspiracy narratives provides perhaps the clearest indication that conspiracy discourse is significantly conditioned by its place at the center or fringe of the political community. Prior to making generalizations regarding conspiracy discourse at the map's two poles, however, it is important to note the great variety among the narratives of political history deployed by antislavery politicians. Chase's *Address* prefaced the narrative of conspiracy with a counterfactual history that speculated on the likely historical outcome of the founders' initial antislavery trajectory, then contrasted this counterfactual history with his actual present, offering the narrative of conspiracy as an explanation for the difference between this counterfactual history and the allegedly proslavery realities of U.S. policy in 1845. It also presented the commencement of the U.S. government's operation in the early 1790s as the key cardinal function of the conspiracy narrative, telling a story of the slave power whose unity of interest and empowerment by the three-fifths clause enabled it to uphold slavery in the District of Columbia and the territories, create six new slave states, dictate the choice of high officers, control foreign policy, stifle the rights of petition and free speech, and move to annex Texas in order to increase slave territory. Sumner's narratives of conspiracy in the Whig and Free-Soil conventions were rather simpler summaries of the effect of the slave power on American political history. These narratives presented the Missouri Compromise of 1820 as the key cardinal function of conspiracy, an event enabling the subsequent annexation of Texas and the Mexican War. Chase's 1854 *Appeal,* on the other hand, positioned 1854 as the point at which the slave power was poised to take permanent control of the government. While Chase's 1845 narrative looked backward, his 1854 narrative of conspiracy used its single narrative function—the Nebraska bill—as a means of looking forward to a larger plot to split the nation with a large swath of slave-holding territory. Sumner's "Crime" presented a telescoping narrative moving from 1854 to 1856. Early on, the narrative portrayed the events of 1854 (the key cardinal function of conspiracy within the narrative) in a very general fashion, while the later part of the conspiracy narrative—in particular, the narratives of invasion and tyranny—become much more detailed as the narrative approached Sumner's present. Sumner's text reinforced this telescoping narrative of events from 1854 to 1856 with corroborating narratives drawn from the American Revolution as well as the orations of Cicero and Demosthenes. Finally, the narrative of conspiracy in the "House Divided" exhibited a more sophisticated narrative structure that helped to lend the text its unique "rhetorical timing."[4] Lincoln's narrative also posited 1854 as the cardinal function of conspiracy, and it operated with three parts—a narrative of events from 1854 to 1858, a retrospective evaluation from the standpoint of the present, and speculation as to the trajectory of the conspiracy in the future.

The particular conspiracy narratives of Chase, Sumner, and Lincoln are quite variable, but what is most important for the purposes of this study are their common characteristics and the vast gulf separating them from the conspiracy narratives of Garrison and the radical abolitionists. From the perspective of plot, Garrison's narrative emplotted American political history tragically, as the work of an all-powerful demonic conspiracy that seemed unstoppable. By contrast, each of the Chase, Sumner, and Lincoln conspiracy narratives considered in this study was emplotted in a distinctly comic manner—the conspiracy maintained itself by the ordinary political means of patronage and deceptive demagoguery and could be defeated by the ordinary political means of coalition building and electioneering.

It is on the level of narrative structure, however, that one finds the clearest association between "place" and discursive form. In every case considered, proximity to the fringe was associated with an earlier key cardinal function of conspiracy—the point in the narrative at which the slave power was said to have gained control of the nation. At the extreme of the fringe, Garrison's narratives of conspiracy exhibited the earliest key cardinal functions of conspiracy—finding the root of the slave power in the Revolution and its absolute ascendancy in the Constitution. Next, we find William Goodell's narrative of the slave power, in which the slave power was not ascendant until after the commencement of the operation of the national government. The early Chase, circa 1845, told a story that was very similar to Goodell's on the structural level, although Chase may be said to have secularized Goodell's eschatological saga. For Chase and Goodell, the conspiracy arose only after the operation of the new government, leaving the Revolution and Constitution as discursive resources for the antislavery cause. Shortly after the agitations of Chase, Goodell, and other Liberty Party partisans, the early Sumner was crafting narratives in which the key cardinal function of conspiracy did not occur until the Missouri Compromise of 1820. At the same time that relatively radical antislavery politicians like Chase and Sumner told stories of conspiracy commencing in the 1790s or 1820s, their more mainstream counterparts within the party system—Thomas Morris, John Quincy Adams, Joshua Giddings, Jacob Brinkerhoff, and Thomas Hart Benton—were telling stories of a slave power conspiracy that had only recently arisen in the form of the gag rule of the 1830s or the measure to annex Texas in the 1840s.

Whether considered synchronically or diachronically, proximity to the center of the political mainstream is associated with much later key cardinal functions of conspiracy. On the synchronic plane, Lincoln, the later Chase, and Sumner, show the latest cardinal functions of conspiracy. In the *Appeal,* the "Crime," and the "House Divided," American political history is unsullied by a significant slave power conspiracy until the Nebraska bill of 1854. Consideration of how Chase's and Sumner's slave power narratives evolved over time suggests that this rule holds on the diachronic plane as well. Both Chase and Sumner gradually moved closer to the center of American political institutions and ideologies as they entered the Senate and as the Wilmot Proviso and Free-Soil movement made the conversion of moderates a real possibility; as Chase and Sumner did so, the key cardinal function within their narratives of conspiracy moved closer to their present (from the 1790s to 1854 in Chase's case and from 1820 to 1854 in Sumner's case). On the structural level, then, the rule seems to be that as conspiracy narratives move into the mainstream, they become shorter, their key cardinal functions of conspiracy appear later in political history. Shorter conspiracy narratives enable rhetors to utilize larger portions of the American political tradition (its events, documents, and persons). Equally important and contrary to the expectations of the paranoid style, shorter conspiracy narratives may be more believable to mainstream audiences. It is likely a simpler matter to persuade audiences that their republic has recently become corrupted by conspiracy than to convince them that all of their history is a lie and their republic was corrupt from the beginning. On the level of narrative configurations, then, a comic emplotment and later cardinal function of conspiracy provide quite tangible formal characteristics distinguishing conspiracy texts at the center of political institutions and ideologies.

In addition to these narrative characteristics corresponding to the dimension of mimesis$_2$, the region of interaction between readers and narratives implied in mimesis$_3$ provides additional factors distinguishing the conspiracy texts of center and fringe. Unlike the logic of the tragic narrative, which suggests an apolitical response (withdrawal or violence), the comic narratives of the slave power considered in this study invite audience enactment in the form of political engagement—usually in the form of partisan identification and electoral support. This tragic-comic distinction also overlaps with narrative length. Longer conspiracy narratives with earlier cardinal functions of conspiracy tend toward a tragic logic, while later cardinal functions of conspiracy and shorter conspiracy narratives provide audiences with greater hope of overcoming the conspiracy. Within these shortened comic narratives, then, political action resolves the American narrative by delivering the government from the slave power.

Mapping Sacred and Secular Ideologies

Conspiracy discourse at the fringe and center of this study's map also represents very different ideological valences, a distinction that may best be characterized by the opposition between sacred and secular. The fringe of the slave power conspiracy formation relied heavily upon the assumptions of sacred ideologies, especially millennialism and the jeremiad. That William Lloyd Garrison and the AASS saw their efforts as part of a grander eschatological plan relating to the coming of the millennium has been well established. Early on, the movement adopted an optimistic postmillennial ideology that saw reform efforts as essential in order to prepare for the coming of the millennium and the return of Christ. Later, disillusioned by repression and lack of success, much of the movement abandoned comic postmillennial assumptions in favor of a grimmer premillennial ideology associated with tragic assumptions. Whether in postmillennial or premillennial modes, Garrison and the AASS also relied upon the ideological assumptions of the jeremiad as they sought to redirect the increasingly slave-holding trajectory of the nation and redeem a backsliding people from the evils of slavery.[5] While the fringe of the slave power conspiracy formation (including Garrison and the AASS as well as Goodell and much of the Liberty Party) tended to draw upon and express sacred ideologies like millennialism and the jeremiad, antislavery politicians at the center of the political mainstream distanced themselves from such perspectives in favor of the assumptions of civic republican ideology and the partisan ideologies of their time.

The place of Chase's, Sumner's, and Lincoln's conspiracy texts within the center of political institutions—in particular, partisan institutions— helps to explain the importance of political ideologies, understood as the set of symbolic systems utilized by rhetors to gain the assent of political audiences to their efforts. Because each of these politicians needed to reach as wide an audience as possible, partisan political ideologies have loomed large. In 1845 Chase couched his slave power conspiracy rhetoric in the terms of Democratic ideology. His slave power was both similar to and allied with the moneyed power that had been the conspiratorial enemy of Jeffersonian Republicans and remained the ideological opponent of Jacksonian Democrats. Chase's conspiracy rhetoric was heavily conditioned by Democratic ideology. Sumner's early efforts on behalf of the Free-Soil Party also represent a "Democratized" slave power, portraying the lords of the lash as equivalent to and allied with the lords of the loom in Massachusetts. More Whiggish figures such as John Quincy Adams, Abraham Lincoln, and the later Sumner (in the "Crime"), on the other hand, presented the slave power conspiracy in terms of the conspiracy of demagogues and party bosses that had animated Whig (and Federalist) Party ideology. Careful attention to the appropriation of these political ideologies has assisted in the interpretation of the conspiracy texts and helps to explain the success of the mainstreamed slave power conspiracy theory among former Whig or Democratic partisans.

The civic republican ideology that served as the deep structure of eighteenth- and early-to-mid-nineteenth-century politics comprises another important secular ideology characterizing slave power conspiracy discourse at the center of the mainstream. This ideological substratum, in fact, arguably served as the foundation of the partisan ideologies discussed earlier.[6] Civic republican ideology, in other words, was of a different order than partisan ideologies. While rhetors consciously manipulated partisan ideologies in their texts for political purposes, civic republican ideology constituted the antebellum period's deeper political consciousness. Scholars have long recognized the nexus between civic republicanism and conspiracy. The fragility of the republic within this worldview was a measure, in part, of the ever-present danger of conspiracies against liberty and the public good. From the ancient world to the early republic, rhetors warned of the need for eternal vigilance against conspiracies if the republic was to be preserved. In fact, the pervasiveness of civic republican assumptions may be said to account for the prevalence of concern about conspiracy within the mainstream of nineteenth-century political discourse.[7] Enabled by these assumptions, each of the rhetors considered in this study spoke as the vigilant citizen or farsighted leader warning the political community of a hidden threat to its survival. This was the role of Demosthenes, Cicero, Edmund Burke, John Trenchard and Thomas Gordon, John Dickinson, James Madison, and Andrew Jackson, not that of the crackpots and fanatics of the paranoid style.

Recognition of the nexus between conspiracy texts and civic republican contexts not only explains the place of conspiracy during the antebellum period, but it also elucidates the inner workings of the Chase, Sumner, and Lincoln texts and helps to explain the success of this conspiracy theory in the political mainstream. The civic republican theme of a return to first principles structured the texts considered by this study in important ways. Chase, Sumner, and Lincoln each recognized the necessity of constituting the founding moment in antislavery terms. In good civic republican form, they told a story of antislavery first principles—principles that were threatened with the passage of time and the work of the slave power. If the slave power conspiracy was an agent of degeneration, however, political action against the conspiracy promised the possibility of regeneration—a comic resolution to the political narrative in which citizens rediscovered the virtues of their founding principles and emulated the vigilance of the founding generation. Emulation of the founders, in turn, reinforced the pervasiveness of conspiracy discourse, for consideration of the founders' texts revealed the extent to which the Revolution was itself undertaken in the name of opposition to a conspiracy against liberties.[8]

The nexus between the Chase, Sumner, and Lincoln texts and the first principles of the Republic is clear. Chase's *Address* was especially concerned to chart the antislavery principles of the founders and to position the Liberty Party as the true heir of these principles. Furthermore, he positioned the slave power of 1845 as another aristocratic conspiracy—the type against which Americans had revolted in 1776. Sumner focused on the temporal dimension of republicanism expressed in Pocock's formulation of "the problem of time."[9] Guided by ancient orators, Sumner wove civic republicanism's temporal tropes and themes of threat and renewal into an explicit parallel between the conspiracy inspiring the Revolution and the crimes against Kansas. Citizen action, guided by the examples of the Revolutionary founders and the citizens of Kansas, was conceptualized as the means for the renewal of the Republic in the face of the threat posed by the slave power.

In addition to elucidating particular slave power conspiracy texts, the nexus between conspiracy and the civic republican ideology occupying the center of mid-nineteenth-century American political discourse also has important implications for the intertexts of mainstream conspiracy discourse. Hofstadter derived the paranoid style from studying Barry Goldwater's rhetoric and generalizing backward to other paranoid fringe groups (anti-Masons, Know-Nothings, and others) within the American political tradition. Essentially, Hofstadter reads Goldwater's practice of conspiracy against an intertextual network of previous paranoid rhetoric. This study has followed (and extended) a different trajectory, one emphasizing that in order to understand the conspiracy discourse of nineteenth-century American political discourse, it is necessary to consider it in terms of a civic republican intertextual network that extends from the ancient orators through English opposition writers, American revolutionaries, and the tracts and luminaries of the first and second party systems.[10] As the reception of Lincoln's "House Divided" speech among historians illustrated, however, the republican assumptions nurturing conspiracy discourse in the nineteenth century receded in favor of a liberal pluralist ideology that not only legitimized activity once seen as conspiratorial but also considered conspiracy rhetoric as irresponsible. Nevertheless, this observation only highlights the extent to which civic republican ideological contexts are essential in order to understand antebellum conspiracy discourse.

Mapping Social Logics

Consideration of the vastly different narratives, arguments, and ideological valences of the fringe and center of the slave power conspiracy formation has important implications regarding the social logic of conspiracy discourse. Put simply, texts possessing vastly different rhetorical characteristics will operate differently upon societies, institutions, and individuals. It is evident how the rhetorical strategies of the radical abolitionist fringe texts served to intensify social movement group identities and inspired some individuals to action, but these same characteristics seemed to sabotage the prospects for these conspiracy theories among broader mainstream audiences. On the level of narrative, we have seen how Garrison's premillennial narratives of an all-powerful and demonic slave power conspiracy were relatively politically ineffectual. To be sure, Garrison's perfection of the slave power scapegoat helped to build and affirm abolitionist identity, but its tragic narratives foreclosed the possibility of genuine political engagement. For most abolitionists, the increasingly tragic logic of Garrison's conspiracy narratives encouraged inaction and political disengagement. Insofar as these tragic narratives with millennial overtones inspired action at all, it tended to be an extreme response consistent with the vast scope of the conspiratorial enemy. John Brown's fervent embrace of the call to a holy war against slavery may be said to illustrate this principle of proportionality between the scope of the conspiratorial enemy and the kind of action it inspires. To put the matter simply, although fringe slave power conspiracy texts may have helped to maintain abolitionism's status as a social movement, these rhetorical efforts were ill equipped to break out into the political mainstream. The fringe texts appealed to the eschatological predispositions of a relatively narrow Christian sect and contained narratives of conspiracy that encouraged pessimism and discouraged political engagement.

On the other hand, the comic narratives and ideologies associated with conspiracy texts at the center of the political mainstream encouraged audiences to build a political coalition against slavery. Comic narratives of recent slave power control fostered an optimism that saw victory against the conspiracy as virtually inevitable and enabled antislavery politicians to use the prevailing filiopiety to their advantage. In addition, the texts of antislavery politicians drew upon compelling party ideologies and the familiar assumptions of civic republicanism, rather than fantastic millennial ideologies. Utilizing the organic and temporal language of decay and renewal associated with civic republicanism as well as the comic frame, antislavery politicians followed their peers within the second party system by seeking to involve their audiences in a conspiracy-driven "republican drama" or "republican crisis" that sought to encourage audience enactment.[11] Within the conspiratorial republican dramas built by the rhetorical texts of Democrats, Whigs, or Republicans, voting became a "cathartic act" in which voters emulated the vigilance of their Revolutionary fathers by "re-fighting the Revolution" at election time.[12] Simple partisan loyalty at the ballot box was represented as sufficient to defeat the conspiracy in question. The conspiracy, whether of designing aristocrats, power-hungry demagogues and party bosses, or the slave power, is invariably represented within the republican drama as vulnerable, subject to the normal coalition-building and electioneering methods of politics. In sum, slave power conspiracy rhetoric at the center of the political mainstream was designed to construct party identities and build party coalitions. While the conspiracy rhetoric at the fringe was the rhetoric of a narrow social movement, conspiracy rhetoric at the center cannot be considered independently of the social logic of party institutions.

From the beginning, American political parties have relied on conspiracy rhetoric in order to establish and reinforce partisan identities and mobilize the electorate. This mobilization function was readily apparent in all of the cases considered. In 1845 Chase used the claim that a slave power conspiracy had captured the major parties and the national government as a means to convert moderate antislavery Whigs and Democrats to the Liberty ticket. Later, in 1854, Chase again used the Nebraska bill as a justification for the mobilization of a new opposition to the slave power. In 1856 Sumner used the outrages against Kansas to convince citizens that the slave power, not the Catholic Church, ought to be the primary target at the ballot box. Lincoln, in 1858, aimed at convincing audiences that, appearances to the contrary, Douglas and the slave power posed a dangerous threat that ought to remain the focus of citizens' energies. Confirmation of the mobilization function in the texts of Chase, Sumner, and Lincoln contradicts the widely held impression that conspiracy rhetoric is the strategy of the fringe, an ineffective strategy for political engagement and coalition building.[13] Conspiracy rhetoric at the center of the political mainstream served practical functions—legitimation, identity formation, and mobilization—that were vital to the creation and maintenance of party constituencies.

Not only was conspiracy rhetoric a means by which leaders sought electoral support and built party constituencies, but it also was an important instrument by which party leaders sought the unity within their own ranks that was necessary for the maintenance of partisan institutions. Both Chase's *Address* and Lincoln's "House Divided" speech were heavily conditioned by their association with the partisan convention, one means by which parties coordinated their efforts. The partisan convention, like its predecessor, the legislative caucus, was designed to coordinate the efforts of a national political party. The convention was, in some respects, a miniature republic. Delegates came from far-flung state and local parties to—in theory—deliberate about the party's goals and candidates. But precisely because it was more democratic than the legislative caucus, party conventions could easily slip into disunion and disarray—eliminating the possibility of the united effort that was necessary in order to succeed in national elections.[14] This possibility was especially apparent to Chase in 1845, when he utilized the slave power conspiracy as a means of trumping the potentially fatal division between coalitionist and universal reform factions within the Liberty Party. The common conspiratorial foe reminded factions of the need to submerge differences if they were to succeed. At the Massachusetts Whig conventions of the mid-1840s, Sumner, too, used the slave power conspiracy as a means to convince state party leaders to adopt a determined antislavery posture. In 1858 Lincoln utilized the conspiracy argument, in part, as a means to reunite former Whigs, Democrats, and abolitionists against Douglas. Party conventions posed other unique restraints on speakers and texts. While conventions are generally composed of party leaders and activists (who tend to be more extreme than the electorate), the platforms, nominees, and addresses generated by conventions need to be acceptable to the general public. Convention speakers experience this tension between party insiders and outsiders in the form of the "keynoter's dilemma," in which the convention speaker must craft a speech equally effective for the immediate audience of partisan leaders and for members of the electorate who will receive the speech text detached from its immediate convention context. Chase appears to have successfully negotiated this constraint in the *Address*, in which the Liberty Party is presented in quite moderate terms. On the other hand, Lincoln's "House Divided" speech, while expertly crafted to its immediate convention audience, was caught on the horns of this dilemma when its polysemous character was exploited by opponents such as Douglas.[15]

While conspiracy discourse has been found to be symbiotically related to partisan institutions generally, the cases considered also highlight the manner in which the conspiracy strategy negotiates the particular constraints posed by various configurations of the party system. In 1845 Chase's

Address illustrated the constraints and opportunities faced by a third party within a relatively smoothly functioning two-party system. His text sought to realign the party system along antislavery lines by converting Whigs and Democrats in order to replace one of the major parties with a broadened Liberty Party. Later, with the Free-Soil Party, Chase and Sumner would opt for the more realistic goal of using the existing parties for antislavery purposes. In Ohio and Massachusetts, this strategy succeeded, as Free-Soilers held the balance in the state legislatures, enabling them to win antislavery policy goals at the state level and place both Chase and Sumner in the Senate. Chase's 1854 *Appeal* might best be classed as a "prepartisan" effort designed to bring persons of all partisan persuasions together against a specific measure. Sumner's "Crime" confronted a party system in disarray, with Republicans and Know-Nothings competing as the anti-Democratic heirs to the Whig Party. Lincoln's "House Divided" speech, on the other hand, was deployed within a new two-party system (at least in the North) in the face of the Dred Scott decision and Douglas's efforts to gain the support of Republicans. Whatever the particulars, the slave power conspiracy texts at the center of the political mainstream were part of a decidedly partisan and political social logic, one conducive to the creation of the coalitions and party institutions necessary to prevail in the electoral process.

Two Vectors

One must admit that any map possessing only two poles will not be entirely adequate for navigating the vast array of conspiracy theories populating diverse societies and polities. But given the rhetorical perspective taken throughout this study, the map provides important insights into an issue at the heart of the conspiracy phenomena—how conspiracy theories spread. Conspiracy discourse at the fringe and center seems to be so distinct that, far from being part of the same "explanatory framework," the texts and theories at the poles of the map appear to represent entirely different modes of expression and action. If we follow those commentators who think of conspiracism as a sort of disease, this study's map suggests one clear conclusion: there are at least two distinct species of slave power conspiracy theories, each with its own unique vector of attack.

On the political fringe, William Lloyd Garrison exemplified the paranoid style. He presented a conspiracy of overwhelming power and demonic character, a conspiracy that discouraged political engagement. Garrison exhibited the paranoid certainty, the apocalyptic determination of the all-out crusade, the tragic and lengthy narratives of conspiracy, the slippery self-sealing arguments, and the lurid and exaggerated imagery we have come to expect from the paranoid style. Like the many paranoid conspiracy theories espoused by marginalized social movements, Garrison's conspiracy theory lacked a real virulence—it was unable to spread far beyond the confines of his own marginalized social movement. The slave power conspiracy theory espoused in the texts of Chase, Sumner, Lincoln, and others has been shown to have been highly adaptable and hence extremely virulent. On the one hand, this conspiracy theory was able to spread by way of exploiting not only pervasive partisan ideologies but also more foundational ideologies like civic republicanism. On the other hand, the mainstreamed slave power conspiracy theory spread by its symbiotic relationship with the partisan institutions that were so essential to nineteenth-century mass politics. At the same time, these conspiracy texts possessed shorter comic narratives with later cardinal functions that made the wider public more susceptible to their conspiratorial interpretations. In sum, the virulent form of slave power conspiracy theory that captured the Northern antebellum political mainstream actually had very little in common with the less virulent strain that remained on the margins of society.

Two Traditions of Conspiracy Discourse

This chapter's claim that the theories espoused by the slave power conspiracy discourse of the fringe and center are in fact entirely different species with very divergent vectors would be more firmly buttressed if one could document their distinct origins. According to Thomas More Brown, the genealogy of conspiracy discourse extends only as far back as the English tradition of antipapal rhetoric. During the Reformation and Enlightenment periods, Brown suggests, antipapal rhetoric provided an eschatological framework of international and cosmic scope for conspiracy theories that was profoundly influential within the emerging American colonies and may have set a mold for subsequent fears of conspiracy.[16] This study has highlighted the findings of a number of scholars who suggest that Brown is mistaken to trace the roots of conspiracy discourse only as far back as Reformation England, but since Brown's genealogy of conspiracy focuses primarily upon the kind of conspiracy discourse falling within the purview of Hofstadter's paranoid style or Davis's literature of countersubversion, his historical observation might be accurate as applied solely to these types of fringe paranoid rhetoric. The conspiracy-centered rhetorical efforts of the English Reformation, focused as they were on vast global or even universal conspiracies of superhuman evil, may have provided a template for the kind of conspiracies feared by the fringe social movements of the eighteenth, nineteenth, twentieth, and twenty-first centuries. The fantastic theories and superhuman conspirators of such eschatologically charged conspiracy narratives, once detached from the context of Reformation England, would tend by their very nature to inhabit the fringes of narrow social movements, providing a truly "perfected" scapegoat against which the identity of such groups could be managed and constructed. The eschatologically charged and relatively apolitical conspiracy narratives of Garrison and his followers seem to fit comfortably within this mold. In such an instance, the application of Hofstadter's category is entirely appropriate—it seems possible simply to replace a popish Antichrist with a new abolitionist incarnation of evil in the form of the slave power without altering the underlying "explanatory framework." Brown's account of the roots of conspiracy discourse suggests that, while the paranoid style was the first and most enduring category of conspiracy discourse within the academy, its historical origins may be relatively recent.

As a number of scholars—and the findings of this study—have made clear, however, a very different and much older form of conspiracy discourse characterizes the texts at the center of this study. Gordon Wood, Cecil Wooten, and others have highlighted the role of conspiratorial interpretations in the political life of the ancient Greek and Roman republics, and Sumner's "Crime" has illustrated that this particular mode of conspiracy discourse remained alive and well in the antebellum period. Following Wood, we know that conspiracy was a prevailing mode of regime change in the ancient world, an extremely common political practice. Wooten's study of the texts of Demosthenes and Cicero has attested to the presence of conspiracy discourse in ancient rhetorical practice.[17] The prevalence of conspiracy in ancient political and rhetorical practice provides an initial foundation for a tradition of conspiracy discourse at the political center. The foundation enlarges substantially when one considers the importance of appeals to fear within Aristotle's political and rhetorical theory. Aristotle initially indicated the relationship between regime preservation and fear in book five of the *Politics:*

> Regimes are preserved not only through the things that destroy them being far away, but sometimes also through their being nearby; for when men are afraid, they get a better grip on the regime. Thus those who take thought for the regime should promote fears—so that they will defend and not overturn

the regime, keeping watch on it like a nocturnal guard—and make the far away near.[18]

As mentioned in chapter 3, Aristotle's rhetorical and ethical theory provided reinforcing explanations for the prevalence of appeals to fear of conspiracy in ancient rhetorical practice. Precisely because it helps citizens recognize events as contingent rather than necessary, Aristotle's *Rhetoric* suggests that "fear makes people inclined to deliberation." At the same time that Aristotle's rhetorical theory cites the importance of fear to deliberation, however, it makes a clear distinction among different types of fear appeals—a distinction that parallels this study's findings regarding the distinction between conspiracy rhetoric at the fringe and center. Since citizens deliberate only about "things that can be done by their own efforts," fear makes for good deliberation only when there is "some hope of being saved from the cause of agony."[19] Rhetors warning of all-powerful conspiracies can take fear appeals too far, to the point that they discourage deliberation and action. The most famous ancient conspiracy rhetors, however, limited the scale and power of the conspiracy to the point that it was contingent and not necessary, meaning that citizen action remained an appropriate and viable remedy. In this respect, Aristotelian prudence helped to ensure that ancient conspiratorial interpretations resembled neither the fantastically powerful conspiracies of the English Reformation nor the paranoid style more generally.

The tradition of conspiracy discourse at the center of politics continued well beyond the horizon of the ancient polis or republic. Bailyn, among others, identifies an English opposition mode of conspiracy discourse that was concerned to maintain the political community against threats of concentrated power. While the English and later colonial and U.S. governments were very different from ancient republics, the conspiracy theories of Bolingbroke, Trenchard and Gordon, and other English opposition writers undoubtedly resembled ancient conspiracy discourse much more than the historically contiguous tradition of English millennialism. They, like their ideological descendants in North America, aimed at a particularly political effect and identified banal conspiratorial enemies that were the proper objects of conventional political action. Within the social logic of antebellum American politics, the general contours of the ancient and English tradition of conspiracy discourse were given specific shape by the partisan institutions at the center of the political community's political and deliberative life. In this respect, while differences between the ancient republics and later democratic republics conditioned conspiracy discourse accordingly, it is nevertheless possible to identify a mode of conspiracy discourse that remained at the center of politics and public discourse.

This study's synthesis of existing literatures, along with its contextually sensitive critical work, provides reinforcing reasons to generalize beyond the particularities of the antebellum period and the slave power conspiracy toward a bifurcated view of conspiracy discourse more broadly. The poles of the study's map seem to represent two distinct yet, at least after the English Reformation, parallel species of conspiracy discourse with distinct traditions—one eschatologically charged and often paranoid, the other secular and political. The paranoid style, despite its pejorative connotations and extensive scholarly baggage, remains perhaps the most appropriate way of talking about conspiracy discourse at the fringes. But the longer tradition of conspiracy at the center of political life and discourse has yet to be labeled. Previous scholars have suggested the term "mainstream"; this study has preferred the spatial terminology of the "center," and along with others, has highlighted the importance of this mode of conspiracy discourse to politics and deliberation. Perhaps the term "political style" might best characterize the distinct mode of conspiracy discourse that has been at the heart of political discourse from ancient times to the nineteenth-century United States. But the question remains: has the political style of conspiracy discourse been wholly eclipsed by the rapid political, social, and ideological changes of the twentieth and twenty-first centuries?

Contemporary Conspiracy Discourse
Ideology and Conspiracy in the Twentieth and Twenty-first Centuries

The prospects for the applicability of this study's map to contemporary conspiracy discourse are clouded by the rapid ideological changes following the Civil War. As noted in chapter 4, most scholars concur that the civic republican ideological assumptions nurturing conspiracy discourse through the antebellum period have receded in favor of liberal and pluralist understandings that legitimate activity once viewed as conspiratorial. Alongside such studies of ideological change we find corroborating studies of changes in rhetorical practice—a move from a conspiracy-centered and hyperbolic "hortatory" style to a more moderate "admonitory" style suited to the assumptions of liberal pluralism. Under such an ideological and discursive climate, the account goes, conspiracy discourse became increasingly confined to the margins of society. Such ideological explanations for the marginalization of conspiracy discourse in the twentieth century, however, may oversimplify the diversity of conspiracy discourse and its continued presence at the center of political discussions. Conspiracy theories, in fact, still find their way into the mainstream, and such allegations continue to characterize discourse at the center of American politics.[20] Consider, for example, Hilary Clinton's allegations of a "vast right-wing conspiracy" against her husband, Ralph Nader's contention that a conspiracy of corporate plutocrats aided by the communication-industrial complex dominates American politics and policy, Michael Moore's belief that the Bush family and other prominent Republicans rigged the presidential election in Florida in 2000, or Trent Lott's insistence that members of the liberal establishment conspired to demonize him and remove him from the Republican leadership. Conspiracy discourse continues to flourish at the mainstream as well as the fringes, and this continued presence suggests questions about the manner in which contemporary liberal and pluralist ideologies condition conspiracy discourse, the continuing role (if any) of civic republicanism in contemporary conspiracy discourse, and the applicability of this study's two traditions of conspiracy discourse within contemporary settings.

As mentioned earlier, civic republican suspicions of conspiracy during the antebellum period were based, in part, on this ideology's assumption that political parties and interest groups were little more than organized conspiracies against the public good. In contrast to these civic republican assumptions, liberalism's valorization of the pursuit of self-interest and pluralism's sanction of interest group and party competition seem to leave very little room for conspiratorial views of politics. Under such ideological assumptions, one might argue, conspiratorial interpretations like those generated by slave power conspiracy rhetors are fundamentally misguided. Why label the slave power a conspiracy, one might ask, when it is equally possible to view it as an interest group that, while sectional, is nonetheless legitimate? From the perspective of liberalism and pluralism, it initially seems inappropriate to label the slave power as conspiratorial—despite its reliance on secrecy, propaganda, and less than transparent discursive practice. Further consideration of liberalism and pluralism, however, reveals a more complicated view of the place of contemporary conspiracy discourse.

For one thing, liberalism is more nurturing of conspiracy discourse than has been imagined, and it, too, provides fertile ideological ground for contemporary conspiratorial interpretations. Previous scholars have noted the association between conspiracy discourse and agency. Wood, Howe, and others have emphasized that the logic of conspiracy tends to identify all so-cial and political conditions as the result of human agency. Lincoln's con-spiracy position effectively illustrates this tendency. Rather than considering the Nebraska bill and the Dred Scott decision as the outcomes of complex social, economic, and political processes, Lincoln characterized these events as the work of a small cabal. Within a conspiracy theory, someone is responsible for the existing state of affairs, and this nexus be-tween conspiracy and agency finds hospitable ideological ground within the liberal assumptions of the twentieth century. Timothy Melley echoes Gordon Wood's pronouncement that the modern world is governed largely by impersonal social and economic systems that are much too complex to explain in terms of agency, but he posits this increasing complexity as the leading cause for many of the paranoid conspiracy theories of the twenti-eth century. Such conditions are said to collide with the "liberal individual-ism" continuing to characterize contemporary ideologies, precipitating an "agency panic" that is the "result of liberal individualism's continuing pop-ularity despite its inability to account for social regulation." Insofar as con-spiracy narratives restore the agent and the individual to the center of the modern world, they provide a discursive solution to "agency panic" that sustains a sense of individualism that is in reality outdated. Conspiracy dis-course, in this respect, continues to find ideological support in more mod-ern ideologies like liberalism, despite the fact that such agent-centered views most often are serious oversimplifications of complex systems and processes.[21]

Conspiracy discourse may also find an ideological niche within contem-porary pluralism. This claim initially seems to contradict that scholarship finding pluralism's valorization of competition among interest groups and political parties to flatly contradict older civic republican suspicions of these activities and organizations. But pluralism's very assumptions may also nurture a sort of residual civic republicanism conducive to conspiracy dis-course. Despite pluralism's endorsement of kinds of interest group and po-litical party competition that antebellum civic republicanism condemned as conspiratorial, pluralism retains a faith that the political outcomes gener-ated by such competition, on a level playing field, reflect the public good, or at least a basic procedural justice.[22] But what of situations in which in-terest group competition is inherently unfair or skewed? Under such con-ditions, another of civic republicanism's assumptions may be more relevant than ever. While it is undoubtedly the case that civic republicanism's suspi-cion of interest groups and parties is outdated in a contemporary setting, civic republicanism also nurtured another kind of suspicion that remains salient even within a pluralist paradigm—its suspicion of concentrations of power. In the contemporary setting, such suspicions are far from outmoded and may even contribute to the health of the pluralist polity. Again, the case of Abraham Lincoln is instructive. Alongside Lincoln's explicit conspiratorial interpretations were other interpretations of the political scene more conducive to modern pluralist understandings. By the time of the Cooper Union speech in 1860 in particular, Lincoln more closely resembled William Seward, portraying the South as an extraordinarily powerful interest group whose interests and goals (the expansion of slavery) were contrary to the interests of the North and the public good and whose immense power had enabled Southerners to unfairly control political outcomes. Such a perspective, in its legitimation of interest group competition, is no longer civic republican, but it retains a residual civic republican suspicion of concentrations of power that might warrant the label "vigilant pluralism."

Conspiracy Discourse at the Contemporary Center and Fringe

If conspiracy discourse remains an important phenomenon within the contemporary mainstream and continues to find succor within contemporary liberal and pluralist ideologies, then the story of conspiracy discourse's confinement to the fringe within liberal-pluralist societies is either incomplete or wholly inaccurate. Under such circumstances, it seems hasty to conclude that the political style of conspiracy discourse identified and distinguished by this study was merely an artifact of civic republicanism that declined along with this ideology, leaving only the paranoid style in its wake. Rather, it seems prudent to begin asking questions about how this study's map might provide a means to think about the complexity of contemporary conspiracy discourse. At this point a qualification is in order, for Robert Goldberg has amply documented the extent to which conspiracy theories have infiltrated the contemporary mainstream. But Goldberg and scholars such as Goodnight and Poulakos characterize this process of "mainstreaming" in a manner distinct from this study. They assume that it is the paranoid style itself that migrates into the mainstream, rather than entertaining the possibility that there is something like a political style of conspiracy discourse, an entirely separate species with its own distinct textual characteristics and social logic, that is indigenous to the mainstream of political discourse.[23] The likelihood that something approaching the political style persists alongside the paranoid style within contemporary conspiracy discourse can be established in two ways. First, Mark Fenster's analysis of conspiracy discourse functions as a powerful corroboration of the continued political relevance of this practice. Second, this study's findings about the characteristics of conspiracy rhetoric at the center of the slave power conspiracy formation provide basic criteria with which to recognize the contemporary political style and classify contemporary conspiracy discourse.

Fenster has suggested that the paranoid style and even the very term "conspiracy theory" itself are each part of a larger strategy of "delegitimization" that seeks to place conspiracy theorists outside the bounds of "proper" democratic politics. Although Fenster considers conspiracy theories generally, he seriously entertains the possibility of a somewhat more political role for contemporary conspiracy theories. To Fenster, conspiracy theories are best understood as populist expressions of democratic culture, expressions that might provide the basis for political resistance. The tendency of conspiracy theory to divide the world into the categories of "the powerful" and "the people," he writes, is increasingly appealing in an era in which distrust of ruling elites "saturates the everyday lives of a considerable portion of the public" and opportunities for citizens to engage in meaningful political activity have receded. Under these conditions, "conspiracy theory constitutes a profoundly satisfying politics." More important for the purposes of this study, Fenster insists that conspiracy theory constitutes a theory of power that provides one means to understand social and political inequalities and the instrumental uses of power by elites. Such theories are said to have appeal both to the political left and right, and are especially salient to subaltern identities.[24]

But Fenster qualifies this populist potential, suggesting that conspiracy theories, because emphasizing the actions of plotters and de-emphasizing the systemic sources of injustice and iniquity, are relatively simplistic, constituting "an ideological misrecognition of power relations." Conspiracy theory's elision of systemic factors in society and politics is said to make it an "unstable element in populism" that is more likely to be associated with authoritarian or fascist regimes and become a justification for racism and scapegoating, rather than an effective basis for genuine political engagement and reform. Fenster finds conspiracy theory to be a "disabling theory of power." Too many conspiracy theorists, he suggests, are more concerned to amass evidence than to build political coalitions with other groups; echoing the findings of this study, Fenster concludes that when a given

theory posits the conspiracy's control to be complete, "then effective resistance is unlikely, or it at least requires the most desperate of measures."[25]

It is not surprising, given Fenster's attempt to consider contemporary
conspiracy theories broadly, that his analysis is of two minds on the issue of
conspiracy's populist potential. Indeed, this study has suggested that such
confusion is precisely to be expected when one is considering such a broad
spectrum of conspiracy theories. Recognizing the essential distinctions between conspiracy discourse at the contemporary fringe and center may enable a more nuanced account of conspiracy in politics and enable one to see
Fenster's conclusions about the apolitical and/or extreme tendencies of conspiracy theory as applicable narrowly to conspiracy theories in the paranoid
style. Consideration of conspiracy discourse solely at the center, in the form
of the political style, on the other hand, may generate different and less
problematic conclusions about conspiracy theory's political potential.

To be sure, the paranoid style continues to thrive at the contemporary
fringe, dominating the attention of many critics and scholars, and the logic of
these kinds of eschatological conspiratorial interpretations still encourage adherents toward the apolitical alternatives of withdrawal or a violent crusade.
Individuals and groups expressing fear of all-powerful global conspiracies
(like the New World Order, for instance) withdraw not only from political
engagement but often withdraw even further into the confines of hidden
bunkers and enclaves in order to escape the continued terrors of their demonic nemeses. When not withdrawing, opponents of global conspiracies of
the kind associated with the paranoid style frequently turn to violent crusades. In this respect, holy warrior, crusader, and terrorist John Brown may
find a contemporary counterpart in the likes of Timothy McVeigh.

While the paranoid style is undoubtedly alive and well in the twenty-
first century United States, further study will likely document the continuing presence of the political style of conspiracy discourse as well.
Fortunately, this study's map of antebellum slave power conspiracy discourse suggests a number of dimensions to consider as criteria for discover-
ing the apparently more elusive political style of conspiracy rhetoric within
the setting of current political discussions. First, since a partisan social logic
seems to be associated in important respects with the political style, one
ought to look toward explicitly political movements utilizing some sort of
conspiracy rhetoric as a means of electoral mobilization and coalition
building. Second, one ought to look at those political movements positing
relatively banal conspiratorial opponents. One extremely promising candidate for the contemporary political style of conspiracy discourse is the

anticorporate conspiracy theory expressed by Ralph Nader. Nader's efforts with the Green Party beginning in 1996 seem to provide a textbook example of the political style. In his acceptance speech at the Greens' national convention of that year, Nader posited that a corporate or plutocratic conspiracy, motivated by greed and love of power, had become a threat to democracy and the public good. According to the conspiracy narrative, the plutocracy, by means of control of the media and the two political parties, had in recent decades taken control of the U.S. government. Nader uses this banal conspiratorial enemy as a means to build a Green partisan identity, justify the creation of broad coalitions, and energize and mobilize voters. Alongside this comic narrative with recent key cardinal functions of conspiracy, Nader uses filiopiety to enact a vigilant pluralism that ultimately aims at dethroning the corporate menace. Michael Moore provides another variant of corporate conspiracy theory. In *Stupid White Men*, he aims at entertaining and mobilizing citizens with a comic conspiracy narrative that relates how George W. Bush and his corporate supporters conspired to steal the 2000 presidential election.[26]

Nader and Moore clearly represent only a small sample of contemporary anticorporate conspiracy rhetoric, and such anticorporate conspiracy theories are but one variant of what is likely a much larger body of conspiracy discourse in the political style. Nevertheless, these examples indicate that there remains in the twenty-first century a species of conspiracy discourse indigenous to the center of the political mainstream, a style of conspiracy that is not fruitfully understood in terms of the paranoid style. Contrary to those scholars whose approach to the mainstreaming of conspiracy is to trace the intrusion of the paranoid style into the mainstream, this is a political rather than paranoid style, with its own unique social logic and narrative form, a parallel tradition of conspiracy that is indigenous to the mainstream of political discourse.

Reevaluating Conspiracy Discourse:
Arguments, Ethics, and Paranoia

Kenneth Burke's landmark work on the conspiratorial dimensions of Hitler's rhetoric, alongside Hofstadter's paranoid style, has set the stage for the marginalization of conspiracy discourse by establishing the presumption that conspiracy rhetoric is fundamentally irrational, unethical, and unhealthy for the political system. Many other scholars, even those critical of the paranoid style category itself, continue to echo the belief that conspiracy rhetoric is both logically flawed and an ethically problematic and

even dangerous phenomenon—a political pathology—that encourages social strife, fascism, totalitarianism, ethnic conflict, hate crimes, and, in its
most extreme version, even genocide. Consider, for example, the manner
in which Hofstadter critic and revisionist Robert Goldberg concludes his
study: "The cancer of conspiracism has begun to metastasize. Without a
new awareness of its character and quick intervention, countersubversion
may overwhelm the body politic."[27] This extensive body of condemnation
seems warranted as applied to much paranoid conspiracy discourse—
especially that of the Far Right. Questions remain, however, as to the rationality and ethical status of the political style of conspiracy discourse.
Two questions in particular are of great moment for the purposes of this
study. First, if we do not assume at the outset that all conspiracy claims are
fundamentally incorrect, how are citizens and critics to determine which
conspiracy claims are worth being taken seriously? Second, what is the
ethical status of the political style that this study has identified as indigenous to the mainstream of U.S. political discourse?

Evaluating the rationality of conspiracy discourse is an important task
for critics on all sides of the issue. For those who view conspiracy discourse
as fundamentally irrational and even dangerous, it is essential that they
provide some means by which to debunk and discredit such manifestations
of political pathology. For those holding a more generous view of conspiracy discourse, one recognizing that conspiratorial interpretations are sometimes correct and may provide a means for critiquing inequalities of power,
the issue of evaluation is also important, for citizens and critics alike must
be able to recognize those instances (however rare they may be) when
conspiratorial interpretations are the most appropriate explanations for
events. Despite recognition that conspiracy arguments are difficult to evaluate, the literature provides a number of possible solutions to the problem
of evaluation, alternatives that approach conspiracy rhetoric from a variety
of perspectives.

One approach follows Hofstadter in understanding conspiracy arguments as irrational, or instances of "quasi-logical" argument. Hofstadter assumed from the outset that rhetors in the paranoid style made claims
about vast and sinister conspiracies that were fundamentally false, and
much of his analysis of the logic of conspiracy proceeds to unravel the puzzle of how paranoid authors attempted to "prove" these fundamentally irrational and absurd claims. For Hofstadter, and those who follow in his
footsteps, then, conspiracy argument can aspire, at best, to the status of the
"quasi-logical" argument, an argument whose logical form is merely a kind

of camouflage for a fundamentally irrational claim.[28] Under this set of assumptions, evaluating a conspiracy argument is irrelevant; the question becomes one of removing the logical camouflage rather than determining the truth or falsity of the claims. This debunking approach is undoubtedly appropriate in many cases, but the case of the slave power conspiracy has suggested that these assumptions may not be appropriate to a political style of conspiracy discourse. Rather than entirely dismissing the issue of evaluating conspiracy arguments, some scholars have suggested that although "conspiracist rhetoric purports to be an evidentiary process . . . what makes the rhetoric work is its narrativity." From this perspective, it may be most appropriate to apply concepts such as narrative coherence and fidelity to evaluating conspiracy rhetoric. But while Hofstadter's approach may be said to be entirely too harsh (in automatically dismissing almost all conspiracy claims), a narrative approach to evaluation may allow conspiracy rhetoric to pass muster too easily. Such is the perspective of Marilyn J. Young, Michael K. Launer, and Curtis C. Austin, who suggest that conspiracy arguments must be held to more rigorous standards of "formalistic criteria," or the "traditional forms of argument analysis."[29]

This study's findings have gestured in directions that may contribute to unraveling the complex puzzle of evaluating conspiracy rhetoric. Initially, the association of conspiracy arguments in the political style with the probabilistic "conductive" argument form may assist in the task of evaluation. According to Trudy Govier, there are "no precise rules" for evaluating conductive arguments, but she provides some basic guidelines. Following conventional wisdom, Govier initially suggests the need to assess the strength of the premises as well as their positive relevance to the conclusion, but against these premises Govier insists on the need to weigh what she calls "counter considerations." Since a given conspiratorial interpretation is only one of many possible explanations for a particular state of affairs, Govier's emphasis on "counter considerations," alongside Michael Billig's insistence on the importance of the "argumentative context" of competing arguments and claims, is especially relevant to the evaluation of conspiracy arguments.[30]

Evaluation of conspiracy arguments in terms of the "counter considerations" that are part of their argumentative context seems a promising avenue, but how might such a contextual approach to argument evaluation work when applied to a case like the slave power conspiracy? Slaveholders undoubtedly wielded disproportionate power in the antebellum republic, but was there really a conspiracy, and were the arguments purporting to prove the existence of this conspiracy rational? Such questions are impossible to answer on this level of generality, but case studies focusing on particular arguments and their broader contexts may yield some answers. One such study focused on the claims of some dissenting Whig and Democratic politicians that the 1844 measure to annex Texas was the work of a slave power conspiracy. These politicians, in good civic republican form, insisted that the measure was part of a scheme by slave-holding aristocrats and their allies to expand slavery and thus aggrandize their power over the Democratic Party and the nation. Rather than considering this claim in a vacuum, the case study in question posited that such claims were best evaluated comparatively. If the conspiratorial interpretation was only one of many competing claims, narratives, or frames explaining Texas annexation, the question then became one of determining which of the alternate interpretations of the measure was the most reasonable explanation for events. While the study failed to make any certain determinations, it found that the slave power conspiracy interpretation held up better than many alternate explanations and justifications for the measure.[31]

Despite this study's failure to make decisive determinations about the rationality of the slave power conspiracy interpretation circa 1844–45, an evaluative approach that compares conspiracy claims to alternate interpretations within thoroughly contextualized accounts of political controversies seems more sensible than outright dismissal of all conspiracy claims. This approach also imposes stricter standards than narrative fidelity and coherence and is more contextually sensitive than standards derived from formal argument. The virtues of this comparative-contextual approach to evaluating conspiracy arguments are especially important in a discursive climate in which critics will encounter instances of both the paranoid and political styles. It may help critics to recognize that some conspiracy claims—especially those concerned with the increasing concentrations of economic and political power—deserve our serious attention if not outright support.

Recognition of a political style of conspiracy discourse alongside a paranoid style also has important implications for the ethical status of conspiracy rhetoric. At least since Burke's analysis of Hitler's conspiracy rhetoric, scholars have recognized that this form of discourse—in part due to its identification and perfection of a scapegoat—is often associated with or responsible for instances of extremism, violence, totalitarianism, war, and genocide.[32] This study has validated these findings to some degree. At least at the political fringes of the slave power conspiracy formation, the slave power was a "perfected" scapegoat whose vast scope and demonic nature required an extreme response, such as Garrison's "all-out crusade" or radical abolitionist John Brown's acts of terrorism. This study has accounted for the excesses of conspiracists in terms of a relationship of proportionality between the scope of the conspiracy and the response suggested by the rhetor. Simply put, tragic narratives of conspiracy driven by gigantic demonic conspiracies require extreme responses (if there is to be a response at all). Under such circumstances, however, all too often alleged conspirators themselves become victims of the most horrendous kinds of abuses. The horrific consequences of such turns of events for these innocent scapegoats need no restatement here.

But this principle of proportionality also suggests that conspiracy rhetoric at the center of the political mainstream may be less ethically problematic. Paranoid abolitionist variants of the slave power conspiracy may have helped to move John Brown to slaughter innocent farmers in Kansas and prepare for guerilla warfare and servile insurrections, but the relatively banal conspiracies posited by Chase, Sumner, and Lincoln suggested the appropriateness of a very limited domain of action. In terms of chapter 4's distinction between arguments alleging to prove the existence of a conspiracy and arguments from conspiracy (which use the conspiracy as a warrant for audience action), Chase's, Sumner's, and Lincoln's versions of the slave power conspiracy were used as a means to justify a narrow political response on the part of audiences. They employed the alleged existence of the conspiracy as a means to encourage citizens to organize politically within party institutions. To put the matter in Burkean terms, for the rhetors at the center of this study's map, the scapegoat is most certainly not perfected. So too, the political style, which, because concerned to involve citizens in a comic resolution to the conspiracy narrative, tends to concern itself with banal conspiracies composed of political and economic elites who are themselves merely pursuing their self-interest. Conspiracies consisting of relatively "perfected" scapegoats, this study has suggested, simply do not lend themselves to the imperatives of the political and ideological contexts nurturing the political style of conspiracy discourse. In this respect, the political style of conspiracy discourse is not ethically problematic in the same sense as the paranoid style, and it seems erroneous to equate ethically, for example, the paranoid, eschatologically charged, and anti-Semitic New World Order conspiracy theories inspiring contemporary terrorist Timothy McVeigh with the corporate conspiracy theories of Ralph Nader.

Postscript: Criticism and Conspiracy

Timothy Melley has characterized the paranoia-inspiring conspiracy theory as an "interpretive disorder."[33] If this is the case, then it is surely appropriate that the phenomenon of conspiracy discourse be approached from a rhetorical perspective that is both critically and hermeneutically oriented. Richard Hofstadter's paranoid style, despite its shortcomings or oversimplifications, was extremely critically and hermeneutically sensitive and remains an authoritative guide to understanding conspiracy rhetoric at the fringes of society. Since Hofstadter has provided the means to interpret and critically engage paranoid conspiracy texts, his work has also elucidated the persuasive strategies that tend to consign the paranoid style to the fringes of society. While much of this study may appear to have been written against Hofstadter, it has aspired nevertheless to do for conspiracy discourse at the center what Hofstadter has done for conspiracy rhetoric at the fringe. It has aimed to develop interpretive strategies that elucidate the rhetorical operations that characterize conspiracy rhetoric in the political style and in so doing has helped to explain the persuasive strategies that contribute to the success of conspiratorial interpretations within public discourse. This study, then, shares with Hofstadter a commitment to the belief that, whatever one's orientation to conspiracy discourse—whether one is suspicious of its claims, paranoid about its possible consequences, or hopeful about its potential as a strategy of resistance—a critical and hermeneutic approach is essential to understanding and responsibly responding to the broader conspiracy phenomenon. Only a textually sensitive approach is capable of providing critics and citizens with the means to make sense of and evaluate the barrage of conspiratorial interpretations increasingly characterizing early-twenty-first century discourse. Such an approach may also provide the keys to comprehending and explaining the increasing appeal, documented by Robert Goldberg, of conspiracy theories and conspiratorial interpretations to mainstream audiences worldwide. But whether conspiracy theories are a pathology to be feared, a corrective to inequalities of power, or both, only a rhetorically sensitive approach is capable of comprehending the primary means by which conspiracy theories reproduce themselves. Conspiracy theories propagate themselves by way of the persuasive strategies embedded in rhetorical texts, a fact suggesting that rhetorical scholars have an increasingly important role to play in understanding the complexities of conspiracy in contemporary discourse.

Notes

1. Problems of Interpretation: Approaching Conspiracy in Text and Discourse

1. Richard Hofstadter, "The Paranoid Style in American Politics," in *The Paranoid Style in American Politics and Other Essays* (Cambridge, Mass.: Harvard University Press, 1964), 3–6.
2. According to Hofstadter, the "content" of the paranoid style remains the same even when it is used by different groups against different conspiratorial enemies at different times and places. See Hofstadter, "Paranoid Style," 4, 6.
3. Hofstadter, "Paranoid Style," 29.
4. Hofstadter, "Paranoid Style," 17, 32.
5. Kenneth Burke, "The Rhetoric of Hitler's Battle," in *The Philosophy of Literary Form: Studies in Symbolic Action* (Berkeley: University of California Press, 1973), 191–220, esp. 192–93, 202–3, 218. The scapegoat is also discussed in Kenneth Burke, *A Grammar of Motives* (Berkeley: University of California Press, 1969), 406–8; Kenneth Burke, *On Symbols and Society,* ed. Joseph R. Gusfield (Chicago: University of Chicago Press, 1989), 121, 280, 294–95. On perfecting the scapegoat, see Kenneth Burke, *Permanence and Change* (Indianapolis: Bobbs-Merrill, 1965), 284–94. Rhetorical scholars have long noted the nexus between conspiracy discourse and scapegoating. See Nicholas Burnett, "The Impetus for Rebellion: A Rhetorical Analysis of the Conditions, Structures, and Functions of Conspiracy Argumentation during the American Revolution" (Ph.D. diss., University of Pittsburgh, 1989), 184–85, 195. Burnett underlines the importance of the "perfection of the scapegoat" to conspiracy rhetoric.
6. Hofstadter, "Paranoid Style," 5–6, 36–38. Some rhetorical scholars have referred to the leap from reasonable evidence to fantastic conclusions as the "evidence-inference dichotomy." See note 12.
7. Hofstadter, "Paranoid Style," 3, 6, 39. One explanation for the occurrence of the paranoid style that is conspicuously absent, especially

given the author's concern with style and text, is that some conspiratorial interpretations are presented more compellingly than others, that rhetorical strategy rather than social ills might explain occasional surges in paranoia.

8. Hofstadter, "Paranoid Style," 7, 30. Hofstadter admits that from time to time—as in the case of the anti-Masons and Know-Nothings—adherents of the paranoid style revert to party politics. He also recognizes the increasing marginalization of the paranoid style within the twentieth century (22–23).

9. David Brion Davis, "Some Themes of Counter-Subversion: An Analysis of Anti-Masonic, Anti-Catholic, and Anti-Mormonic Literature," *Mississippi Valley Historical Review* 47 (1960): 205–24, esp. 207, 212–15, 223–24. On the fusion of Hofstadter and Burke, see David Brion Davis, *The Slave Power Conspiracy and the Paranoid Style* (Baton Rouge: Louisiana State University Press, 1969), 4, 26, 30–31. On recurring metaphors see Davis, *Slave Power Conspiracy*, 48; David Brion Davis, *The Fear of Conspiracy: Images of Un-American Subversion from the Revolution to the Present* (Ithaca, N.Y.: Cornell University Press, 1971), xiv–xv.

10. On Davis's less pejorative assumptions regarding conspiracy discourse, see Davis, *Slave Power Conspiracy*, 6; Davis, *Fear*, xvi. On the credibility of some conspiracists and conspiracy theories, see Davis, *Slave Power Conspiracy*, 6, 7, 11–12, 29, 63–64; Davis, *Fear*, 103–6.

11. Earl Creps, "Conspiracy Argument as Rhetorical Genre" (Ph.D. diss., Northwestern University, 1981), 4–5, 36, 71, 96–97. On the fusion of poetic and dialectic, see 214. On the poetics of conspiracy arguments, see 59, 60, 73. On the logic of conspiracy arguments, see 4, 42–43, 45. On the possibility of mainstream conspiracy arguments, see 58, 212–13.

12. Keith R. Sanders and Robert P. Newman, "John A. Stormer and the Hofstadter Hypothesis," *Central States Speech Journal* 22 (1971): 218–27; Craig Allen Smith, "The Hofstadter Hypothesis Revisited: The Nature of Evidence in Politically 'Paranoid' Discourse," *Southern Speech Communication Journal* 42 (1977): 274–89. Smith coins the term "evidence-inference dichotomy," his name for what Hofstadter describes as the paranoid style's "characteristic leap" from reasonable evidence to fantastic conclusions.

13. G. Thomas Goodnight and John Poulakos, "Conspiracy Rhetoric: From Pragmatism to Fantasy in Public Discourse," *Western Journal of Speech Communication* 45 (1981): 299–316, esp. 310–11; David Zarefsky, "Conspiracy Arguments in the Lincoln-Douglas Debates," *Journal of the*

American Forensic Association 21 (1984): 63–75, esp. 73–75; Marilyn J. Young, Michael K. Launer, and Curtis C. Austin, "The Need for Evaluative Criteria: Conspiracy Argument Revisited," *Argumentation and Advocacy* 26 (1990): 89–107, esp. 89, 102.

14. Charles Griffin, "Jedediah Morse and the Bavarian Illumaniti: An Essay in the Rhetoric of Conspiracy," *Central States Speech Journal* 39 (1988): 293–303; Marouf Hasian, "Understanding the Power of Conspiratorial Rhetoric: A Case Study of *The Protocols of the Elders of Zion*," *Communication Studies* 48 (1997): 195–214.

15. Bernard Bailyn, *Ideological Origins of the American Revolution* (Cambridge, Mass.: Belknap Press of Harvard University Press, 1967), 34–93, 144, 150–51, 156–58.

16. Gordon Wood, "Conspiracy and the Paranoid Style: Causality and Deceit in the Eighteenth Century," *William and Mary Quarterly* 39 (1982): 401–41, esp. 409–11, 432, 441.

17. See, for instance, James H. Hutson, "The Origins of the 'Paranoid Style in American Politics': Public Jealousy from the Age of Walpole to the Age of Jackson," in *Saints and Revolutionaries: Essays on Early American History,* ed. David D. Hall, J. Murrin, and T. Tate, 332–72 (New York: W. W. Norton, 1984).

18. Creps, "Conspiracy Argument," 58, 212–13; Goodnight and Poulakos, "Conspiracy Rhetoric," 300, 311; Zarefsky, "Conspiracy Arguments," 63, 71–75; Burnett, "Impetus for Rebellion."

19. Robert Goldberg, *Enemies Within: The Culture of Conspiracy in Modern America* (New Haven, Conn.: Yale University Press, 2001), x-xi, 240, 242–59, 260.

20. This approach might also provide an additional answer to the question, why is conspiracy rhetoric so prominent at particular times? Hofstadter and Davis suggest that conspiracy rhetoric increases during times of rapid socioeconomic change and social strain. Hofstadter ("Paranoid Style," 39) suggests that the paranoid style travels in waves—waxing and waning according to circumstances. According to Davis ("Some Themes of Counter-Subversion," 223–24), rapid social and economic change determines the persuasiveness of the conspiracy argument. For both Davis and Hofstadter, then, the conspiracy text is irrelevant— extrinsic factors make conspiracy seem plausible to audiences. This study, on the other hand, looks to the persuasive strategies that animate conspiracy texts in order to account for why conspiracy theories become plausible to audiences.

21. Davis, *Fear,* xvii–xviii. Davis's edited collection of conspiracy texts includes prominent leaders of the Revolution, Jeffersonian Republicans, Federalists, Free-Soilers, and Republicans. Davis also indicates the extent to which conspiracy rhetoric was the strategy of political opportunists. See Davis, *Slave Power Conspiracy,* 63–64. On the relative realism of some conspiracy theories, see Davis, *Fear,* xiv. On the Republican versus abolitionist theories, see xviii.

22. Davis, *Slave Power Conspiracy,* 7–10. Following Davis, Leonard Richards has also recognized that opponents of the slave power ranged from centrist politicians to the lunatic fringe, but he, too, fails to develop this observation and its implications for reading conspiracy texts. See Leonard L. Richards, *The Slave Power: The Free North and Southern Domination, 1780–1860* (Baton Rouge: Louisiana State University Press, 2000), 2.

23. Richards, *Slave Power.* On prominent Republicans with whom this study is concerned, see 1–27, esp. 2. On the original controversy over the three-fifths clause, see 28–45. On the string of slave power victories, see 75–87. What is remarkable about Richards's account, however, is not only his extensive history of the slave power but his status as a true believer. Richards endorses the thesis that Southerners—enabled by the three-fifths clause and support of Northern "doughfaces"—indeed gained a disproportionate advantage both in terms of policy and offices until well into the 1850s. See Richards, *Slave Power,* 57, 69, 111, 127, 138, 148, 153, 179, 188.

24. Daniel Pipes defines the "mainstream" in terms of socially sanctioned ideas and institutions that enjoy the patronage of the government and leading private institutions, and the "fringe" in the opposite manner. See Daniel Pipes, *Conspiracy: How the Paranoid Style Flourishes and Where It Comes From* (New York: Free Press, 1997), 29.

25. Larry Gara, "Slavery and the Slave Power: A Crucial Distinction," *Civil War History* 15 (1969): 5–18.

26. On the contrast between the ACS and AASS, see William Freehling, *The Road to Disunion: Secessionists at Bay, 1776–1854* (New York: Oxford University Press, 1990), 126–27, 157–61. On Garrison, the *Liberator,* and hostility to the AASS's activities, see 289–352, esp. 273, 289–290.

27. William Lloyd Garrison, *Selections from the Writings and Speeches of William Lloyd Garrison* (1852; reprint, New York: Negro University Press, 1969), 138, 260. On the slave power's propaganda machine and control of political and religious institutions, see 142, 181, 249, 254, 256.

28. Garrison, *Writings and Speeches,* 314. See also 241, 245, 248 for instances of slave power interference with the right of free speech and inquiry.

29. Joseph Barker, *Proceedings of the American Anti-Slavery Society at its Second Decade* (1854; reprint, Westport, Conn.: Negro University Press, 1970), 12 (hereafter cited as *AASS Proceedings*); Charles Burleigh, *AASS Proceedings,* 63, 72; Wendell Phillips, *AASS Proceedings,* 85, 112; Joseph Barker, *AASS Proceedings,* 41; Henry C. White, *AASS Proceedings,* 23; Wendell Phillips, *AASS Proceedings,* 113; J. Miller McKim, *AASS Proceedings,* 149.

30. Hofstadter, "Paranoid Style," 29.

31. On the importance of narrative to conspiracy theory generally, see Hofstadter, "Paranoid Style," 6; Davis, *Slave Power Conspiracy,* 4–5, 69, 72; David Zarefsky, *Lincoln, Douglas and Slavery: In the Crucible of Public Debate* (Chicago: University of Chicago Press, 1990), 103. Several other rhetorical scholars have also emphasized the importance of narrative in conspiracy texts of the eighteenth and nineteenth centuries. See Michael Leff, "Rhetorical Timing in Lincoln's 'House Divided' Speech" (Van Zelst Lecture in Communication, Northwestern University, May 19, 1983), 10–11; Stephen Browne, *Edmund Burke and the Discourse of Virtue* (Tuscaloosa: University of Alabama Press, 1993), 19. Zarefsky gestures toward the importance of narratives of political history when he notes how Lincoln inferred "Douglas' participation in the plot— from some external manifestation that is taken to be a sign of it." Zarefsky, *Lincoln, Douglas and Slavery,* 76. This study will be concerned more specifically with the narrative configuration of several such "signs" into a political history of the slave power. On the importance of historical narratives to conspiracy rhetoric during the Revolution, see Burnett, "Impetus for Rebellion," 46–47.

32. Barthes's structural approach reads narrative in terms of three hierarchically related structures—function, action, and narrative (function is the most basic level, narrative the highest). For the purposes of this study, it is primarily at the level of function that Barthes's analysis is especially useful. Functions are the basic "narrative units" that serve to "inseminate the narrative with an element that will later come to maturity." Functional units, according to Barthes, are divisible into at least two subsets. Catalyses are functional units whose purpose is solely to "fill narrative space"—that is, to create a sense of realism and continuity. Narrative descriptions are frequently full of such details, though these details have no relationship to subsequent narrative events. Cardinal functions (according to Barthes, the "true functions"), on the other hand, are the actual hinges, or moments of choice, within a

narrative. Cardinal functions establish temporal continuity and relate to the larger unfolding of the narrative. Identification of such functions will help to elucidate the political histories with which this study is concerned. See Roland Barthes, "An Introduction to the Structural Analysis of Narrative," *New Literary History* 6 (1975): 244, 246–49.

33. On the Revolution, see Garrison, *Writings and Speeches* , 239, 311, 313. On the Constitution, see Garrison, *Writings and Speeches*, 140, 250, 302–3.

34. Garrison, *Writings and Speeches*, 256, 307.

35. Garrison, *Writings and Speeches*, 137.

36. Hofstadter, "Paranoid Style," 29.

37. Hayden White, *Metahistory: The Historical Imagination in Nineteenth-Century Europe* (Baltimore: Johns Hopkins University Press, 1973), 2. Though White's *Metahistory* is concerned primarily with the accounts of historians, both his approach in this work and his later writings suggest that White's methods adequately subsume the historical representations of professional historians as well as more politically minded uses of history.

38. John Lucaites and Celeste Condit, "Reconstructing Narrative Theory: A Functional Perspective," *Journal of Communication* 35 (1985): 93–94, 100.

39. As O'Leary explains: "Tragedy and comedy are differentiated not only by the substantive elements that each proposes for the dramatic emplotment of history, but as strategies for living and coming to terms with the world. . . . The comic assumption that human beings are free actors and the tragic assumption of divinely ordained fate do not only shape the form of the historical narratives; they also serve as elements of self-definition that constrain and enable arguments for different audiences. Likewise, conceiving of evil as a demonic and malevolent cosmic force, or as the natural functions of human limitation and fallibility, will have significant consequences for discursive practice in that such conceptions provide the rhetor with models for understanding both one's audience and the rhetorical exigence. . . . the tragic and comic frames offer a working logic . . . a configuration of motives, which both govern the individual's participation in the apocalyptic movement and enable scholars to make sense of the movement's formal developments as it conceives of and strives to achieve its own modes of perfection." See Stephen O'Leary, "Reading the Signs of the Times: A Topical and Dramatistic Analysis of the Logic of Apocalyptic Advocacy" (Ph.D. diss., Northwestern University, 1991), 181–82.

40. On the tendency of paranoid style spokespersons to imitate the enemy's tactics, Hofstadter cites the Klu Klux Klan's imitation of Catholic priests' robes and the John Birch Society's organization around the notion of Communist cells. See Hofstadter, "Paranoid Style," 32.
41. Garrison, *Writings and Speeches,* 139, 142.
42. Garrison, *Writings and Speeches,* 256; Charles Burleigh, *AASS Proceedings,* 68.
43. Hofstadter, "Paranoid Style," 29.
44. On Garrison's nonviolence, see John Demos, "The Antislavery Movement and the Problem of Violent Means," in *Articles on American Slavery: Antislavery,* ed. Paul Finkelman, 115–40, esp. 116–17, 136–37 (New York: Garland, 1989). See also Bertram Wyatt Brown, "William Lloyd Garrison and Antislavery Unity: A Reappraisal," in Finkelman, *Articles on American Slavery,* 511–30, esp. 519–22, 525–26.
45. O'Leary, "Reading the Signs of the Times," 40, 127, 133. O'Leary relies on Burke for the notion of tragic and comic frames. See Kenneth Burke, *Attitudes toward History,* 3rd ed. (Berkeley and Los Angeles: University of California Press, 1984).
46. On the initial comic assumptions of the abolition movement, see O'Leary, "Reading the Signs of the Times," 127–77, 185–86, 191–94. On the postmillennial perception among early abolitionists that their reform efforts were part of God's plan to perfect the world in preparation for God's return, see Demos, "Violent Means," 115, 127; Merton L. Dillon, "The Failure of the Abolitionists," in Finkelman, *Articles on American Slavery,* 165–83, esp. 169–70; Anne C. Loveland, "Evangelism and 'Immediate Emancipation' in American Antislavery Thought," in Finkelman, *Articles on American Slavery,* 318–34, esp. 326; Lewis Perry, "Versions of Anarchism in the Antislavery Movement," in Finkelman, *Articles on American Slavery,* 384–98, esp. 394–95, 389. On the abolitionist transition to a tragic frame, see O'Leary, "Reading the Signs of the Times," 196, 254, 263. On the split between the AASS and the AFASS, see Vernon L. Volpe, *Forlorn Hope of Freedom: The Liberty Party in the Old Northwest, 1838–1848* (Kent, Ohio: Kent State University Press, 1990), xvii. The Liberty Party retained a comic postmillennial perspective. In the face of the slave power, the Liberty Party still hoped to resolve the corrupted American narrative by way of a comprehensive reform of all religious and political institutions. Its goal, in short, was a democracy repurified by Christianity in preparation for the eventual erection of the government of God on earth. Douglas M. Strong, *Perfectionist*

Politics: Abolitionism and the Religious Tensions of American Democracy
(Syracuse, N.Y.: Syracuse University Press, 1999), 7, 42, 118–19.

47. On the large number of defections from Garrison's pacifistic position in
the 1850s, see Demos, "Violent Means," 136–37; Joseph Barker, *AASS
Proceedings*, 16; Wendell Phillips, "Harpers Ferry," November 1, 1859, in
Speeches, Lectures and Letters by Wendell Phillips (Boston: Lothrop, Lee and
Shepard, 1891), 263, 270, 275–76.

48. Garrison, *Writings and Speeches*, 307; O'Leary, "Reading the Signs of the
Times," 196, 254, 263; James Darsey, *The Prophetic Tradition and Radical
Rhetoric in America* (New York: New York University Press, 1997),
72–73, see, more generally, 61–84. Scholars have long recognized that
the doctrine of "immediatism" held by radical abolitionists was as
much a sign of an individual's "calling"—the mark of an "internal
transformation"—as a call to pursue a realistic policy option. See David
Brion Davis, "The Emergence of Immediatism in British and American
Antislavery Thought," in Finkelman, *Articles on American Slavery*,
83–104, esp. 228; Loveland, "Evangelism," 326. O'Leary writes that
"the function of argument in the tragic mode is not to convince, but to
retrace the pattern of divine revelation. Argument becomes . . . primarily ritual, a fulfillment of prophecy, a symbolic enactment that constitutes its own proof even (and perhaps especially) when it fails to
convince." O'Leary, "Reading the Signs of the Times," 173–74.

49. Mark Fenster, *Conspiracy Theories: Secrecy and Power in American Culture*
(Minneapolis: University of Minnesota Press, 1999), xv. Davis has
noted the difficulty of cooperation among anticonspiracy groups. Each
tends to resist compromise, insisting that its version of the conspiracy
reveals the true enemy. See Davis, *Slave Power Conspiracy*, 14. Garrison
himself is recognized to have been politically inept. His belligerent attitude and quarrelsome nature are said to have alienated him from
many of his allies and hurt the abolitionist cause overall. See Betty L.
Fladeland, "Revisionists vs. Abolitionists: The Historiographical Cold
War of the 1930s and 1940s," in Finkelman, *Articles on American Slavery*,
227–47, esp. 229; Richard Hofstadter, "Wendell Phillips: The Patrician
as Agitator," in Finkelman, *Articles on American Slavery*, 267–93, esp.
277; Brown, "Garrison," 512.

50. This expectation has been borne out by previous studies of conspiracy
rhetoric in the mainstream. Burnett, in particular, emphasizes that the
conspiracy rhetoric of the Revolution was expected to mobilize, unify,
and move audiences to action. As a result, it was necessary to maintain

some optimism about the possibility of defeating the conspiracy. See Burnett, "Impetus for Rebellion," iv, 159, 171.

51. On the importance of the slave power conspiracy to Republican ideology and efforts at political mobilization, see Eric Foner, *Free Soil, Free Labor, Free Men: The Ideology of the Republican Party before the Civil War* (New York: Oxford University Press, 1970, 1995), 73–102, esp. 102; Zarefsky, *Lincoln, Douglas and Slavery*, 103–6. Creps postulates that mainstream conspiracy arguments are probably more moderate in terms of the exaggeration, urgency, and lurid imagery that he found to characterize the conspiracy argument as a rhetorical genre. See Creps, "Conspiracy Argument," 58, 211. Goodnight and Poulakos also explore the "manner in which conspiracy rhetoric unfolds in mainstream political drama" in the case of the Watergate scandal. See Goodnight and Poulakos, "Conspiracy Rhetoric," esp. 302.

52. The distinction between abolitionists and political antislavery is well known. One of the clearest expressions of the distinction comes from Larry Gara, who distinguished between opposition to slavery and opposition to the slave power. Opposition to the slave power was the alternative of practical politicians because it did not disturb the racial prejudices of most Northern whites. See Gara, "Slavery and the Slave Power," 5–18. William Lee Miller defends antislavery politicians from the charge that they were less pure than abolitionists. Miller insists that "politicians may get some moral credit for attending to what actually happens in the real world, and operating within its constraints in the attempt to change it. . . . It is a false morality indeed that places William Lloyd Garrison on a higher moral plane than Abraham Lincoln." See William Lee Miller, *Arguing about Slavery: The Great Battle in the United States Congress* (New York: Alfred A. Knopf, 1996), 498–99. It has been established that one of the more paradoxical results of the political mode of antislavery was its racist tendencies. Many political actors sought to prevent slavery's expansion in the name of avoiding the population of the western territories by African Americans. On the racial prejudices driving the antislavery attitudes in the territories, see Eugene H. Berwanger, *The Frontier against Slavery: Western Anti-Negro Prejudice and the Slavery Extension Controversy* (Urbana: University of Illinois Press, 1967), esp. 30–59.

53. By linking the slave power to the "monster bank," Morris fashioned one of the first Democratic variants of the slave power conspiracy. See Foner, *Free Soil*, 91; Thomas Morris, Speech to the Senate, February 9,

1839, *Congressional Globe Appendix*, 25th Cong., 3rd sess., 167–68, 170–71, 173, 174.

54. John Quincy Adams, "Speech of John Quincy Adams of Massachusetts, upon the Right of the People, Men and Women, to Petition on the Freedom of Speech and of Debate in the House of Representatives of the United States; on the Resolution of Seven State Legislatures, and the Petitions of more than one hundred thousand Petitioners, relating to the Annexation of Texas to the Union. Delivered in the House of Representatives of the United States, in fragments of the morning hour, from the 16th of June to the 7th of July, 1838, inclusive" (Washington D.C.: Gales and Seaton, 1838), 54–55, 62, 99.

55. Thomas Hart Benton, Speech to the Senate, May 16, 1844, *Congressional Globe Appendix*, 28th Cong., 1st sess., 474–86; Thomas Hart Benton, Speech to the Senate, June 15, 1844, *Congressional Globe Appendix*, 28th Cong., 1st sess., 607–11; Jacob Brinkerhoff, Speech to the House, January 13, 1845, *Congressional Globe Appendix*, 28th Cong., 2nd sess., 120–22. Other anti–slave power Democrats include George Rathbun, Speech to the House, January 22, 1845, *Congressional Globe Appendix*, 28th Cong., 2nd sess., 131–34; David Seymour, Speech to the House, January 23, 1845, *Congressional Globe Appendix*, 28th Cong., 2nd sess., 212–16. Rathbun, too, spoke of Southerners' control of the party by patronage (which he called "loaves and fishes") as the "crack of the Virginia lash."

56. Joshua Giddings, Speech to the House, May 21, 1844, *Congressional Globe Appendix*, 28th Cong., 1st sess., 704–8; Joshua Giddings, Speech to the House, January 22, 1845, *Congressional Globe Appendix*, 28th Cong., 2nd sess., 342–47; Jacob Miller, Speech to the Senate, February 25, 1845, *Congressional Globe Appendix*, 28th Cong., 2nd sess., 351–55. According to Luther Severance of Maine, the annexation measure served to confirm the kind of charges made by Adams that the United States had sanctioned the rebellion of its citizens in Texas in order to acquire the territory for slavery. Against this policy, Severance claimed to stand with the "founding fathers" in considering slavery as a blight on the national character. Luther Severance, Speech to the House, January 15, 1845, *Congressional Globe Appendix*, 28th Cong., 2nd sess., 367–73.

57. Walter Dean Burnham, "Party Systems and the Political Process," in *The American Party Systems: Stages of Political Development*, ed. William Nisbet Chambers and Walter Dean Burnham, 277–307, esp. 296 (New York: Oxford University Press, 1967).

58. Robert F. Berkhofer, *Beyond the Great Story: History as Text and Discourse* (Cambridge, Mass.: Belknap Press of Harvard University Press, 1995), 22.

59. Hofstadter, "Paranoid Style," 39; Davis, *Slave Power Conspiracy,* 12–13.

60. Fear of moneyed aristocrats was a special concern of the English opposition tradition. Both J. G. A. Pocock and Lance Banning have noted the extent to which Republicans and Democrats self-consciously modeled themselves after the English opposition. See J. G. A. Pocock, The *Machiavellian Moment: Florentine Political Thought and the Atlantic Republican Tradition* (Princeton, N.J.: Princeton University Press, 1975), esp. 506–52. Banning even goes as far as to label Republican John Taylor of Caroline an "American Bolingbroke." See Lance Banning, *The Jeffersonian Persuasion* (Ithaca, N.Y.: Cornell University Press, 1978), 200. The tendency of Federalists in general, and Fisher Ames in particular, to fear demagogues is noted in Wendell Knox, *Conspiracy in American Politics: 1787–1815* (New York: Arno Press, 1972), 4–5. The influence of Cicero in particular on another prominent Federalist—John Adams—is discussed in James M. Farrell, "John Adams and the Ciceronian Paradigm" (Ph.D. diss., University of Wisconsin–Madison, 1988). Chapter 3 is dedicated to the influence of Cicero's Catalinarians on Adams's *Novanglus.* See also James M. Farrell, *"Pro Militibus Oratio:* John Adams' Imitation of Cicero in the Boston Massacre Trial," *Rhetorica* 9 (1991): 233–49. On Whig suspicion of demagogues, see Daniel Walker Howe, *The Political Culture of the American Whigs* (Chicago: University of Chicago Press, 1979), 8, 79–81. Howe also emphasizes the importance of English opposition thought to the Whig tendency to identify political conspiracies.

61. On the concept of filiopiety and its importance to mid-nineteenth-century rhetoric and politics, see George Forgie, *Patricide in the House Divided: A Psychological Interpretation of Lincoln and His Age* (New York: W. W. Norton, 1979). Several rhetorical studies have emphasized the importance rhetors attached to appropriating the authoritative symbols of the American political tradition and the interpretive possibilities of reading texts in these terms. Zarefsky and Leff, in particular, have studied Lincoln's texts from the perspective of tradition. Zarefsky's study of how Lincoln and Douglas sought to appropriate influential political symbols such as the Declaration of Independence, Henry Clay, and so forth effectively illustrates filiopiety in action. See Zarefsky, *Lincoln, Douglas and Slavery,* 141–65. Leff has also examined Lincoln's appropriation of key aspects of the American political tradition from the

perspective of hermeneutic rhetoric. See Michael Leff, "Hermeneutical Rhetoric," in *Rhetoric and Hermeneutics in Our Time: A Reader,* ed. Walter Jost and Michael J. Hyde, 196–214 (New Haven, Conn.: Yale University Press, 1997).

62. Ideology has long been defined as a set of ideas and assumptions that impose a "false consciousness" conducive to the rule of a dominant class. See Terry Eagleton, *Ideology: An Introduction* (New York: Verso, 1991), 28–30. Eagleton reviews the definition of ideology as false consciousness as he seeks to complicate and enrich the concept. See 1–32. Michael McGee's definition of ideology as "political language, preserved in rhetorical documents, with the capacity to dictate decision and control public belief and behavior" is somewhat consistent with this pejorative understanding. See Michael C. McGee, "The 'Ideograph': A Link Between Rhetoric and Ideology," *Quarterly Journal of Speech* 66 (1980): 1–16, esp. 5. This study uses Clifford Geertz's understanding of ideology. According to Geertz, "it is through the construction of ideologies, schematic images of social order, that man makes himself for better or worse a political animal." He continues, "The function of ideology is to make an autonomous politics possible by providing the authoritative concepts that render it meaningful, the suasive images by means of which it can be sensibly grasped." See Clifford Geertz, "Ideology as a Cultural System," in *The Interpretation of Cultures* (New York: Basic Books, 1973), 218. Three fine historical studies utilizing Geertz's conception of ideology include Foner, *Free Soil;* Banning, *Jeffersonian Persuasion;* and Josiah Ober, *Mass and Elite in Democratic Athens* (Princeton, N.J.: Princeton University Press, 1989). To Foner, ideology is almost synonymous with "belief-system," and he defines ideology as "the system of beliefs, values, fears, prejudices, reflexes and commitments." Foner, *Free Soil,* 4. Banning defines ideology as a "more or less coherent body of assumptions, values and ideas." Banning, *Jeffersonian Persuasion,* 15. For Josiah Ober, ideology is a "set of ideas [or a "more or less integrated set of beliefs, values, feelings, and attitudes"] sufficiently well organized to facilitate decision and action." Ober, *Mass and Elite,* 39. For Foner, Banning, and Ober, ideology is first and foremost an interpretive tool for reconstructing the context of political belief and action.

63. For a review of the "republican revision" of the study of the history of political thought, see Daniel T. Rodgers, "Republicanism: The Career of a Concept," *Journal of American History* 78 (1992): 11–38. The most prominent resuscitators of republicanism in American history include

Bernard Bailyn, *Ideological Origins;* Pocock, *Machiavellian Moment;* and Gordon S. Wood, *The Creation of the American Republic, 1776–1787* (New York: W. W. Norton, 1969). The precise character of the influence of republicanism in the American experience remains in dispute. A number of scholars have resisted republican interpretations of American political texts in favor of a view of the liberal character of American ideology. The Lockean liberal view of American political discourse was most prominently articulated by Louis Hartz, *The Liberal Tradition in America* (New York: Harcourt Brace Jovanovich, 1955). A subsequent elaboration of the Lockean liberal thesis is provided by Thomas Pangle, *The Spirit of Modern Republicanism* (Chicago: University of Chicago Press, 1988). More recent proponents of the liberal thesis focus upon the influence not of Locke, but of the Scottish Enlightenment. Joyce Appleby continues to apply the liberal thesis to the Jeffersonian Republicans and the early national period. See Joyce Appleby, *Capitalism and a New Social Order* (New York: New York University Press, 1984); Joyce Appleby, "Republicanism in Old and New Contexts," *William and Mary Quarterly* 43 (1986): 20–34. The other major proponents of this thesis are John Patrick Diggins, *The Lost Soul of American Politics* (New York: Basic Books, 1984), and Paul Rahe, *Republics Ancient and Modern* (Chapel Hill: University of North Carolina Press, 1992).

64. On the prevalence of conspiracies in the ancient world, see Wood, "Conspiracy and the Paranoid Style," 409–10. On the nexus between the fragility of a republic and the necessity for vigilance against conspiracies in the context of nineteenth-century American republicanism, see Michael F. Holt, *The Political Crisis of the 1850s* (New York: John Wiley and Sons, 1978), 134; Howe, *American Whigs,* 8, 79–80; Jean H. Baker, *Affairs of Party: The Political Culture of Northern Democrats in the Mid-Nineteenth Century* (Ithaca, N.Y.: Cornell University Press, 1983), 147; David Ericson, *The Shaping of American Liberalism: The Debates Over Ratification, Nullification and Slavery* (Chicago: University of Chicago Press, 1993), 12, 17–18; Michael A. Morrison, *Slavery and the American West: The Eclipse of Manifest Destiny and the Coming of the Civil War* (Chapel Hill: University of North Carolina Press, 1997), 170–71. Even when not serving the practical function of maintaining vigilance against conspiracies, conspiracy discourse also served the psychological function of providing scapegoats for the perceived failures of the American political system. Americans often preferred to blame such potential failures in the republican experiment on conspiracies rather than to admit either that their political institutions were flawed or that their citizens might

lack sufficient virtue to maintain the republic. See Knox, *Conspiracy,* 316–18; Howe, *American Whigs,* 80; Morrison, *Slavery,* 169–70.

65. Spiegel advocates thinking about the text's "location within a broader network of social and intertextual relations, that we best become attuned to the specific historical conditions whose presence and/or absence in the work alerts us to its own social character and function, its own combination of material and discursive realities that endow it with its sense of historical purposefulness." See Gabrielle M. Spiegel, "History, Historicism, and the Social Logic of the Text in the Middle Ages," *Speculum* 65 (1990): 59–86, esp. 85.

66. According to Daniel Sisson, within such a "classical conception of politics," the emergence of "organized political groups" was seen as a "threat to the administration in power," leading many of the founding generation to believe "in the one or non-party state." See Daniel Sisson, *The American Revolution of 1800* (New York: Alfred Knopf, 1974), xvi. Richard Hofstadter's *The Idea of a Party System: The Rise of Legitimate Opposition in the United States, 1740–1840* (Berkeley and Los Angeles: University of California Press, 1969), one of the most extensive considerations of political parties in the new republic, concurs as to Sisson's explanation for the prevalent suspicion of parties (see esp. 13–22). On civic republican inspired attitudes toward political parties in the mid nineteenth century in particular, see Major Wilson, "Republicanism and the Idea of Party in the Jackson Period," *Journal of the Early Republic* 8 (1988): 419–42. On the prevalence of antiparty attitudes in Jacksonian Illinois, see Gerald Leonard, "The Ironies of Partyism and Antipartyism: Origins of Partisan Political Culture in Jacksonian Illinois," *Illinois Historical Journal* 87 (1994): 24, 28. On the nexus between conspiracy, unanimity, and faction, see Knox, *Conspiracy,* 27; Howe, *American Whigs,* 53.

67. For an example of how this strategy was deployed in a particular rhetorical text, see Michael William Pfau, "The House That Abe Built: The 'House Divided' Speech and Republican Party Politics," *Rhetoric and Public Affairs* 2 (1999): 625–51. The tendency of conspiracy charge to beget conspiracy charge is noted both by Knox, *Conspiracy,* 275, and Zarefsky, *Lincoln, Douglas and Slavery,* 109. A countercharge is a more effective tactical response than a refutation.

68. Joel Silbey, *The Partisan Imperative* (New York: Oxford University Press, 1985), 59. On the reinforcement, mobilization and conversion functions of party rhetoric, see Silbey, *Partisan Imperative,* 60; Thomas Brown, *Politics and Statesmanship: Essays on the American Whig Party* (New York: Columbia University Press, 1985), 13–14. On the special impor-

tance of rhetoric to new parties like the Republicans, see Steven J. Rosenstone, Roy L. Behr, and Edward H. Lazarus, *Third Parties in America* (Princeton, N.J.: Princeton University Press, 1984), 15–16. On the function of party ideologies, see William Chambers, *Political Parties in a New Nation* (New York: Oxford University Press, 1963), 47–48; Silbey, *Partisan Imperative*, 61, 100, 175. On conspiracies as common enemies, see Marc Kruman, "The Second American Party System and the Transformation of Revolutionary Republicanism," *Journal of the Early Republic* 12 (1992): 524. See Foner, *Free Soil*, 102, on the importance of the slave power conspiracy to the rise of the Republican Party.

69. The 1844–45 texts of Whig and Democratic antislavery politicians provide an initial basis for this interpretation of the relationship between party ideologies and slave power conspiracy rhetoric. For more general accounts of the "Democratic" variant of the slave power conspiracy, drawing on the symbolism of Jackson's bank war and featuring the role of the moneyed power in the conspiracy, see Foner, *Free Soil*, 90–91. For a general account of the Whig variant of the slave power conspiracy, emphasizing the Democratic Party and its demagogic leaders as the instruments of the slave power, see Howe, *American Whigs*, 53, 67–68.

70. This basic structuralist approach is delineated in J. G. A. Pocock, "Introduction: State of the Art," in *Virtue, Commerce and History: Essays on Political Thought and History, Chiefly in the Eighteenth Century* (New York: Cambridge University Press, 1985), 1–34. For an example of the interpretive possibilities of reading texts against partisan ideologies, see Pfau, "House That Abe Built."

71. On increased Southern unity and perceptions of conspiracy, see Davis, *Slave Power Conspiracy*, 18. On the acceptance of the slave power among Northerners, see Foner, *Free Soil*, 95.

72. Seward was excluded on the basis that his "irrepressible conflict" centered not so much on conspiracy as it did on the radical divergence of the Northern and Southern economic and political systems. Seward, to be sure, worried about the slave power and the threat it posed to the North's way of life, but within his accounts the slave power was not a conspiracy, it was merely an interest group pursuing its self-interest in the national arena. Conflict was inevitable because the South and North lived under radically different economies, political systems, and ways of life, and the slave power was to be opposed. But Seward may be said to have submerged the issue of agency (central to conspiracy) within an account of conflict between differing economic and political systems. See Richards, *Slave Power*, 4–11.

2. The Slave Power According to Salmon P. Chase: Entering the Mainstream of Partisan Rhetoric, 1845–1854

1. Foner, *Free Soil*, 73, 80–81.
2. On the distrust of Chase by many of his contemporaries, see John Niven, "Salmon P. Chase and the Republican Conventions of 1856 and 1860: Bolingbroke or Sincere Reformer," in *A Crisis of Republicanism: American Politics in the Civil War Era*, ed. Lloyd Ambrosius, (Lincoln: University of Nebraska Press, 1990), 55–72.
3. On the context of the *Address*, see Foner, *Free Soil*, 80–81. On the importance ascribed to the *Appeal* by generations of historians, see Dick Johnson, "Along the Twisted Road to Civil War: Historians and the 'Appeal of the Independent Democrats,'" *Old Northwest* 4 (1978) 119–41.
4. On Chase's years in Washington under Wirt and his reaction to Jackson's victory, see Frederick J. Blue, *Salmon P. Chase: A Life in Politics* (Kent, Ohio: Kent State University Press, 1987), 1–13, esp. 10–13. Regarding Chase's early association with Ohio's anti-Jacksonians, see Blue, *Chase*, 16–21. On Chase's marginalization from Ohio Whigs, see John Niven, *Salmon P. Chase: A Biography* (New York: Oxford University Press, 1995), 57.
5. Chase to Charles D. Cleveland, August 29, 1840, in *The Salmon P. Chase Papers*, ed. John Niven (Kent, Ohio: Kent State University Press, 1994), 2:71. According to Foner, Chase prefigures virtually all of the discursive strategies that would eventually bring the Republicans to power. See, generally, Foner, *Free Soil*, 73–102. On the antislavery versus abolition distinction, see Chase to Charles D. Cleveland, October 22, 1841, in *Chase Papers*, 2:80. Regarding Chase's strategy, see Chase to James G. Birney, January 21, 1842, in *Chase Papers*, 2:84; Chase to Joshua R. Giddings, February 15, 1842, in *Chase Papers*, 2:88; Chase to William Emery Channing, May 3, 1842, in *Chase Papers*, 2:95.
6. Chase to Henry B. Stanton and Elizur Wright, September 23, 1845, in *Chase Papers*, 2:119.
7. Chase to Gerrit Smith, May 14, 1842, in *Chase Papers*, 2:96. On the importance of this distinction between the slave power and slavery, see Gara, "Slavery and the Slave Power," 5–18.
8. For a portrait of Chase as pragmatic politician, see Foner, *Free Soil*, 78. An excellent example of the conventional wisdom regarding the pragmatism of Liberty Party supporters is found in John Mayfield, *Rehearsal*

for Republicanism: Free Soil and the Politics of Slavery (Port Washington, N.Y.: Kennikat Press, 1980), 66.

9. Volpe, *Forlorn Hope*, xvii. On the religious goals of Liberty partisans, see Volpe, *Forlorn Hope*, 12. Historians still disagree as to the actual mix of sacred and secular in the Liberty Party and whether the party ought to be seen in religious terms, political terms, or both. See Alan M. Kraut, "Partisanship and Principles: The Liberty Party in Antebellum Political Culture," in *Crusaders and Compromisers: Essays on the Relationship of the Antislavery Struggle to the Antebellum Party System*, ed. Alan M. Kraut, 71–99, esp. 72 (Westport, Conn.: Greenwood Press, 1983). But insofar as this section of the chapter is concerned primarily with Chase and his party in Ohio, Volpe's judgments—because based on a careful study of the Liberty Party in Ohio—seem most credible.

10. Garrison, *Writings and Speeches*, 302–3. On the Liberty Party narrative, see William Goodell, *Slavery and Anti-Slavery: A History of the Great Struggle in both Hemispheres; with a view of the Slavery Question in the U.S.* (1852; reprint, New York: Negro University Press, 1968). Goodell is an excellent representative of the party. Not only is he cited as a "representative" Liberty leader, he represented the anticoalitionist wing of the Liberty Party that opposed Chase's efforts at broadening the base of the party. See Mayfield, *Rehearsal*, 70; Strong, *Perfectionist Politics*, 65. While the Goodell narrative reconstructed here was articulated in 1852— seven years after the Southern and Western Convention—it nevertheless helps us to understand the religious postmillennial orientation of the Liberty Party. On Goodell's jeremiad, see Goodell, *Slavery and Anti-slavery*, 119–38. On the jeremiad, see Sacvan Bercovitch, *The American Jeremiad* (Madison: University of Wisconsin Press, 1978). On the many victories of the slave power, see Goodell, *Slavery and Antislavery*, 119–38, 241, 268–71, 274–75, 295–303.

11. Strong, *Perfectionist Politics*, 7, 42, 118–19. On politicized moral suasion, see Mayfield, *Rehearsal*, 65. On the church as basic organizational unit, see Volpe, *Forlorn Hope*, xii–xiv. On the party's general rejection of conventional political tactics, see Volpe, *Forlorn Hope*, 76, 109; Kraut, "Partisanship and Principles," 85; Mayfield, *Rehearsal*, 65.

12. The schism between perfectionists, or universal reformers, and nonperfectionists, or coalitionists, is discussed in Strong, *Perfectionist Politics*, 147; Volpe, *Forlorn Hope*, 109. This schism would persist until 1847, when Goodell led the universal reformers out of the party to form the Liberty League. See Kraut, "Partisanship and Principles," 87. Chase's desire for a coalition with Whigs and Democrats is discussed in Volpe,

Forlorn Hope, 108; Foner, *Free Soil,* 81; Mayfield, *Rehearsal,* 66. On the regional and organizational dichotomy, see Volpe, *Forlorn Hope,* 111–12. Not only Chase's political goals and strategy but his religious life also reflected his alienation from the Ohio Liberty Party rank and file. Even while most Liberty Party members viewed slavery as a terrible sin, Chase continued to attend a church that took no condemnatory position regarding slavery. See Volpe, *Forlorn Hope,* 111–13.

13. Martin Van Buren, the ideological father of the party, followed Bolingbroke's justification of party—claiming that party was essential in order to counter the plots of designing aristocrats. But Van Buren took Bolingbroke's argument one step further. Since aristocratic conspiracies were an ongoing and perpetual threat, Van Buren reasoned, the Democratic Party must acquire a similar permanence. See Wilson, "Idea of Party," 419–42, esp. 433–34. To Democrats, all of history was a struggle by the masses to control the powerful. See John Ashworth, *"Agrarians" and "Aristocrats": Party Political Ideology in the United States, 1837–1846* (Atlantic Highlands, N.J.: Humanities Press, 1983), 17, and, more generally, 7–51. On the similarity between Federalists, National Republicans, Whigs, and monied aristocrats, see Mayfield, *Rehearsal,* 13. On the necessity of the effective organization of majority sentiment, see Martin Van Buren, *Inquiry into the Origin and Course of Political Parties in the United States* (1867; reprint, New York: A. M. Kelley, 1967), 226. On the tools of the Albany Regency, see Robert Remini, *Martin Van Buren and the Making of the Democratic Party* (New York: Columbia University Press, 1959), 9–10. On party organization and structure, see Michael Holt, *Political Parties and American Political Development* (Baton Rouge: Louisiana State University Press, 1992), 41. On the party's use of printed materials to relay its messages to the electorate, see Baker, *Affairs of Party,* 109.

14. On Democratic policy positions, see Holt, *Political Parties,* 36–37; Mayfield, *Rehearsal,* 15; Ashworth, *"Agrarians" and "Aristocrats,"* 34, 42–45. Democrats also opposed high tariffs. See Ashworth, *"Agrarians" and "Aristocrats,"* 40–41. Democratic support for strict construction is discussed in Ashworth, *"Agrarians" and "Aristocrats,"* 19–21. On the nexus between strict construction and the curbing of aristocratic policies, see Van Buren, *Inquiry,* 212. On the importance of states' rights and federal limitation to Democratic ideology, see Baker, *Affairs of Party,* 146–47. On Democratic support of westward expansion, see Ashworth, *"Agrarians" and "Aristocrats,"* 37–39; Michael A. Morrison, "Westward the Curse of Empire: Texas Annexation and the American Whig Party,"

Journal of the Early Republic 10 (1990): 221–49, esp. 226–29. On the importance of territorial expansion to Democrats, see also Baker, *Affairs of Party*, 146. On the small landholder as ideal Democratic citizen, see Ashworth, *"Agrarians" and "Aristocrats,"* 22.

15. On the Whig coalition generally, see Brown, *Politics and Statesmanship*, 215. The Whigs styled themselves after the English Whigs, whose opposition to executive tyranny undergirded Revolutionary ideology. See Michael Holt, *The Rise and Fall of the American Whig Party: Jacksonian Politics and the Onset of the Civil War* (New York: Oxford University Press, 1999), esp. 19–32; William R. Brock, *Parties and Political Conscience: American Dilemmas, 1840–1850* (Millwood, N.Y.: KTO Press, 1979), 9. On Whig opposition to demagogues and party machines, see Howe, *American Whigs*, 30. On the danger of party machines to republican government, see Brown, *Politics and Statesmanship*, 7, 216.

16. On Whig antipartyism, see Howe, *American Whigs*, 30; Wilson, "Idea of Party," 427. The Whig imperative on independence is discussed in Leonard, "Ironies of Partyism," 37; Howe, *American Whigs*, 52. The Whig ideal of the independent statesman is delineated in Brown, *Politics and Statesmanship*, 8–9, 32; Ashworth, *"Agrarians" and "Aristocrats,"* 57; Wilson, "Idea of Party," 422. At election time, Whigs compensated for their relative lack of organization by a reliance on exceptional campaign oratory: "Moral appeals were the Whigs' substitute for party loyalty. Less well knit than the Democrats by patronage and organization, the Whigs emerged as a party only intermittently, at election time. This gave their campaigns something of the flavor of religious revivals." Howe, *American Whigs*, 32. On the Whig policy program, see Ashworth, *"Agrarians" and "Aristocrats,"* 55, 69, 78–82; Morrison, "Westward," 224; Howe, *American Whigs*, 34–37. Whig antipathy to rapid expansion is discussed in Ashworth, *"Agrarians" and "Aristocrats,"* 76; Morrison, "Westward," 234.

17. For this definition of a two-party system, see William N. Chambers, "Party Development and the American Mainstream," in Chambers and Burnham, *American Party Systems*, 3–32, esp. 6. On the parties' need to keep the slavery issue out of politics, see Burnham, "Party Systems," 277–307. On the "federal consensus" narrative, see Robert Alexander Kraig, "The Narration of Essence: Salmon P. Chase's Senate Oration against the Kansas-Nebraska Act," *Communication Studies* 48 (1997): 234–53, esp. 236.

18. On the centrality of rhetoric to parties, see Silbey, *Partisan Imperative*, 59. The reinforcement and mobilization functions are discussed in

Silbey, *Partisan Imperative*, 60; Brown, *Politics and Statesmanship*, 13–14. On the nexus of conspiracy rhetoric and party rhetoric, see Silbey, *Partisan Imperative*, 61, 100, 175; Kruman, "Second American Party System," 524. For the distinction between externally and internally mobilized parties, see Martin Shefter, *Political Parties and the State: The American Historical Experience* (Princeton, N.J.: Princeton University Press, 1994), 5. The Liberty Party was an externally mobilized party. Federalists, Jeffersonian Republicans, Jacksonian Democrats, and Whigs, on the other hand, were internally mobilized parties. They were mobilized by persons already holding political power. On third parties' lack of resources, see Rosenstone, Behr, and Lazarus, *Third Parties in America*, 15–16.

19. On ideological versus coalitional partisan styles generally, see Gary Orren, "The Changing Styles of American Party Politics," in *The Future of American Political Parties: The Challenge of Governance*, ed. Joel L. Fleishman (Englewood Cliffs, N.J.: Prentice-Hall, 1982), 6. Political parties have always faced the tension between rewarding party activists (who often tend to be extremists) and nominating moderate centrists (who are more electable). See Ronald P. Formisano, *The Transformation of Political Culture: Massachusetts Parties, 1790s–1840s* (New York: Oxford University Press, 1983), 307. In the case of party convention keynote addresses, this tension between inside and outside gives rise to what is known as the "keynoter's dilemma," in which party convention speakers are required to appeal simultaneously to the highly motivated partisan crowds at the convention and to the broader audience of citizens. See Wayne N. Thompson, "Barbara Jordan's Keynote Address: Fulfilling Dual and Conflicting Purposes," *Central States Speech Journal* 30 (1979): 272. Thompson cites Robert L. Smith, "A Keynoter's Dilemma: A New Dimension," *Forensic* 47 (1962): 9–11.

20. On the connection between partisan rhetoric and party ideology, see Silbey, *Partisan Imperative*, 173. On the duty of party leaders to stimulate the faithful and convert the wayward, see Richard P. McCormick, *The Second American Party System: Party Formation in the Jacksonian Era* (Chapel Hill: University of North Carolina Press, 1966), 350. On the special importance of party leaders in the earliest stages of party formation and the need for further study of partisan leadership, see McCormick, *Second Party System*, 351–52.

21. John Gerring, *Party Ideologies in America: 1828–1996* (New York: Cambridge University Press, 1998), 271–72.

22. On the Liberty Party convention, see Niven, *Chase,* 90. On partisan conventions in the nineteenth century generally, see McCormick, *Second American Party System,* 95, 348–49; Richard P. McCormick, "Political Development and the Second Party System," in Chambers and Burnham, *American Party Systems,* 90–116, esp. 105. On the issue of intraparty democracy and deliberation generally, see Jan Teorell, "A Deliberative Defence of Intra-Party Democracy," *Party Politics* 5 (1999): 363–82.

23. Chase to Quintus F. Atkins, July 2, 1845, *Chase Papers,* 2:110. According to the text, "the Chairman of the Committee which reported this very able address, and by whom the same was written, was S. P. Chase, Esq., of Cincinnati." See Salmon P. Chase, *The Address of the Southern and Western Liberty Convention held at Cincinnati, June 11 & 12, 1845, to the People of the United States, with Notes by a Citizen of Pennsylvania* (Philadelphia: Office of the American Citizen, 1845), 1, Ohio State Historical Society, PA Box 735, item 23. On Chase's extensive experience with party statements and platforms, see Blue, *Chase,* 50–51. For Chase's discussion of his revisions, see Chase to Quintus F. Atkins, July 2, 1845, *Chase Papers,* 2:109–111. See also Niven, *Chase,* 90; Volpe, *Forlorn Hope,* 116; Blue, *Chase,* 51. On the "representative principle" within party meetings and conventions, see Silbey, *Partisan Imperative,* 65. On party leaders and innovation, see Gerring, *Party Ideologies,* 271–72. According to Shefter, successful party leaders usually manage to harmonize their own goals and interests with the need to be "representative" of the party as a whole. See Shefter, *Political Parties,* 4.

24. Chase, *Address,* 1.

25. On the concept of filiopiety and its importance to mid-nineteenth-century rhetoric and politics, see Forgie, *Patricide;* Chase, *Address,* 1.

26. Chase, *Address,* 2–3. Characterizing slavery as an exclusively state institution, Chase writes. "They [the founders] sought to impress upon the national character and the national policy the stamp of Liberty, but they did not . . . attempt to interfere with the internal arrangements of any State."

27. Chase, *Address,* 3–4. Other arguments against a proslavery Constitution include the claim that the due process clause is an implicit prohibition against national government support of slavery and the observation that the words "slave" and "slavery" do not appear in the document.

28. Chase, *Address,* 4–5.

29. Chase, *Address,* 6.

30. Chase, *Address,* 6.

31. Chase, *Address,* 7.

32. Chase, *Address,* 7–8.
33. Chase, *Address,* 8.
34. On the durability of partisan identities, see Rosenstone, Behr, and Lazarus, *Third Parties,* 39–41. Chase, as a converted Whig, recognized the intractability of established partisan identities. See Blue, *Chase,* 11–12; Niven, *Chase,* 57. Chase's decision to leave the Whig Party is said to have been a painful one. See Niven, *Chase,* 60; Blue, *Chase,* 44. During the course of a letter-writing campaign on behalf of the Liberty Party in 1842, Chase expressed the obstacle posed by partisan loyalties in this way: "But many are timid and many cannot yet summon resolution enough to break their old party ties. I do not wonder at this feeling when I recur to the difficulty which I experienced myself in coming to the conclusion that I ought to separate myself from the party with which I have acted ever since I had a vote." See Chase to James G. Birney, January 21, 1842, *Chase Papers,* 2:84.
35. Chase writes: "Like Sir Pertinax McSycophant, its northern leaders believe that the great secret of advancement lies in 'bowing well.' No servility seems too gross, no self-degradation too great, to be submitted to. They think themselves well rewarded, if the unity of the party be secured, and the spoils of victory be secured." See Chase, *Address,* 9.
36. Volpe, *Forlorn Hope,* 116–17. See also Niven, *Chase,* 90.
37. Niven, *Chase,* 88; Volpe, *Forlorn Hope,* 117. On Chase's lack of success in converting Democratic leaders, see Niven, *Chase,* 92–93. Niven notes that Chase's pro-Democratic strategy was effective a year later when Hale and other "independent Democrats" of New Hampshire temporarily fused with the Liberty Party there. But of the two major parties, the Democrats were most consistently opposed to antislavery. See Joel H. Silbey, "'There Are Other Questions Beside That of Slavery Merely': The Democratic Party and Anti-slavery Politics," in Kraut, *Crusaders and Compromisers,* 143–75. On the prospects for turning the Democratic Party away from slavery, Chase wrote: "Political concert with that party, under its present leadership, is . . . plainly impossible. Nor do we entertain the hope . . . that the professed principles of the party will . . . bring it right upon the question of slavery. Its professed principles have been the same for nearly half a century, and yet the subjection of the party to the slave power is, at this moment, as complete as ever." Chase, *Address,* 9.
38. Northern Whigs are said to have provided some of the first political meeting places for abolitionists and antislavery activists. See James Brewer Stewart, "Abolitionists, Insurgents, and Third Parties: Section-

alism and Partisan Politics in Northern Whiggery, 1836–1844," in Kraut, *Crusaders and Compromisers*, 25–43, esp. 30. On similarities between Ohio Liberty Party men and the Whigs, see Volpe, *Forlorn Hope*, 82; John R. McKivigan, "Vote as You Pray and Pray as You Vote: Church-Oriented Abolitionism and Anti-slavery Politics," in Kraut, *Crusaders and Compromisers*, 179–203, esp. 182.

39. Chase, *Address*, 9.
40. Rosenstone, Behr, and Lazarus, *Third Parties*, 8, 44.
41. Volpe, *Forlorn Hope*, 42, 117.
42. Chase, *Address*, 9–10.
43. On the "wasted vote" issue and its nature as self-fulfilling prophecy, see Rosenstone, Behr, and Lazarus, *Third Parties*, 39–41; Chase, *Address*, 10–11.
44. Chase, *Address*, 12–14.
45. Chase, *Address*, 15.
46. Chase, *Address*, 15.
47. Power hungry factions were considered an important element contributing to the fragility of republics. For a review of the "republican revision" of the study of the history of political thought, see Rodgers, "Republicanism," 11–38. The most prominent resuscitators of republicanism in American history include Bailyn, *Ideological Origins of the American Revolution;* Pocock, *Machiavellian Moment;* and Wood, *Creation of the American Republic.*
48. On the nexus between the fragility of the Republic and the necessity for vigilance against conspiracies in the context of nineteenth-century American republicanism, see Holt, *Political Crisis*, 134; Baker, *Affairs of Party*, 147; Ericson, *Shaping of American Liberalism*, 12, 17–18; Morrison, *Slavery*, 170–71.
49. Strong, *Perfectionist Politics*, 7, 42, 118–19; Blue, *Chase*, 44; Mayfield, *Rehearsal*, 65; Volpe, *Forlorn Hope*, 136, 144. Volpe relates an illustrative anecdote that, while taking place after the dissolution of the Liberty Party, nevertheless exhibits the ineffectiveness of propaganda efforts in Ohio's Western Reserve. As Volpe relates, "In . . . 1848 a Dayton lieutenant of Salmon Chase complained that the local Free Soil organization was 'scandalously destitute' of campaign materials to circulate. All that was available, the former Liberty man explained, were some 'old Abolition documents, which were not very appropriate to the occasion.'" See Volpe, *Forlorn Hope*, 140. On Chase's surrender, see Niven, *Chase*, 102; Chase to Gamaliel Bailey, September 14, 1847, in *Chase Papers*, 2:157.

50. Chase to John P. Hale, May 12, 1847, in *Chase Papers,* 2:153.
51. Strong, *Perfectionist Politics,* 63. While most delegates were happy with the moderate goals of the Wilmot proviso, Chase again found himself responding to dissent from radicals—this time by selling nonextension to abolitionists as merely a first step. See Mayfield, *Rehearsal,* 82–85; Niven, *Chase,* 108–9. On the eventual failure of the Free-Soil Party, see Mayfield, *Rehearsal,* 187–89. On Chase's ascension to the Senate, see Niven, *Chase,* 115–23.
52. Salmon P. Chase, "Union and Freedom, Without Compromise, Speech of Hon. S. P. Chase of Ohio, on Mr. Clay's Compromise Resolutions delivered to the United States Senate March 26 & 27, 1850" (Boston: Redding, 1850), esp. 1–6.
53. Chase to unknown, May 8, 1850, in *Chase Papers,* 2:294; Chase to John Brough, October 27, 1851, in *Chase Papers,* 2:342.
54. Walter Dean Burnham defines a partisan realignment as a massive change in voting behavior that results in fundamental consequences for the political system, such as major changes in "the way the political system as a whole is articulated," "the identity and circulation of dominant national elites," and the policy outputs of government. See Walter Dean Burnham, "Critical Realignment: Dead or Alive," in *The End of Realignment: Interpreting American Electoral Eras,* ed. Byron E. Shafer, 101–39, esp. 115–16 (Madison: University of Wisconsin Press, 1991). There is a consensus that a partisan realignment occurred sometime between the mid-1850s and 1860. See Joel H. Silbey, "Beyond Realignment and Realignment Theory: American Political Eras, 1789–1989," in Shafer, *End of Realignment,* 3–23, esp. 5, 8–10; Holt, *Political Crisis,* 3. For collections of essays by the major realignment scholars, see Chambers and Burnham, *American Party Systems;* Shafer, *End of Realignment;* Jerome Clubb, William H. Flanigan, and Nancy H. Zingale, *Partisan Realignment: Voters, Parties, and Government in American History* (Boulder, Colo.: Westview Press, 1990), 11. On the inability of third parties to dissolve healthy party systems, see Holt, *Political Parties,* 4, 18–19. Third parties may, in fact, strengthen a two-party system by draining away dissenters. See Holt, *Political Parties,* 88. On this multistage process, see William E. Gienapp, *The Origins of the Republican Party 1852–1856* (New York: Oxford University Press, 1987), 443; Holt, *American Whig Party,* 838.
55. Holt, *Political Crisis,* 4, 238; Holt, *Political Parties,* 272. On the emerging space for third-party success, see Rosenstone, Behr, and Lazarus, *Third Parties,* 126–27. For a detailed account of the decay of the Whig Party

between 1850 and 1856, see Holt, *American Whig Party*, 635–985. On the antiparty attitudes associated with the decay of the second party system, see Holt, *Political Parties*, 146, 150, 279. The tendency of each of the emerging third parties in the 1850s to characterize the Democrats as part of a conspiracy is discussed in Holt, *Political Parties*, 118, 146, 150, 279.

56. On the increasing plausibility of a slave power conspiracy, see Davis, *Slave Power Conspiracy*, 18. The role of the Nebraska bill is discussed in Foner, *Free Soil*, 95. According to Gienapp, "the role of party leaders was ultimately crucial" to the realignment. One of the important functions of these leaders, he writes, was to give meaning to events and place them in a larger ideological context. Events, in other words, were not sufficient to make the slave power threat seem real. Rather, events required interpretation by party leaders such as Chase. See Gienapp, *Origins of the Republican Party*, 447.

57. On the importance of the *Appeal*, see Niven, *Chase*, 152; Blue, *Chase*, 94. On the historical debate over Chase and the *Appeal*, see Dick Johnson, "Along the Twisted Road to Civil War: Historians and the 'Appeal of the Independent Democrats,'" *Old Northwest* 4 (1978): 119–42, esp. 123–24.

58. Kathleen Diffley, "'Erecting Anew the Standard of Freedom': Salmon P. Chase's 'Appeal of the Independent Democrats' and the Rise of the Republican Party," *Quarterly Journal of Speech* 74 (1988): 401–15, esp. 401–3, 407–10.

59. Chase is recognized as the primary author of the *Appeal*, which was drafted by Joshua Giddings, extensively rewritten by Chase, and polished by Charles Sumner. See Niven, *Chase*, 149.

60. While the text of the *Appeal* would appear in the *Congressional Globe* as well as in countless periodicals and pamphlets, I rely upon an 1854 pamphlet version, Salmon P. Chase, *Appeal of the Independent Democrats in Congress, to the People of the United States. Shall Slavery be Permitted in Nebraska?* (Washington, D.C.: Towers' Printers, 1854), 1.

61. On the nexus between the fragility of the Republic and the necessity for vigilance against conspiracies in the context of nineteenth-century American republicanism, see Holt, *Political Crisis*, 134; Jean H. Baker, *Affairs of Party: The Political Culture of Northern Democrats in the Mid-Nineteenth Century* (Ithaca, N.Y.: Cornell University Press, 1983), 147; Ericson, *Shaping of American Liberalism*, 12, 17–18; Morrison, *Slavery*, 170–71.

62. Chase, *Appeal*, 1.

63. Robert A. Kraig, "The Anatomy of Conspiracy: Salmon P. Chase's *Appeal of the Independent Democrats*," (paper presented at the annual meeting of the National Communication Association, Chicago, November 1999), 11.

64. Kraig, "Anatomy," 11.

65. Chase, *Appeal*, 2.

66. Chase, *Appeal*, 3.

67. Hofstadter, "Paranoid Style," 6, 29, 37–38.

68. Niven, *Chase*, 151.

69. Chase, *Appeal*, 5. Four years later Lincoln, too, would seek the mantle of compromiser Henry Clay as he sought to position himself less radically. See Zarefsky, *Lincoln, Douglas and Slavery*, 65, 155, 227–28.

70. On the nexus of plot, frame, and action, see O'Leary, "Reading the Signs of the Times," 196, 254, 263. O'Leary relies on Burke for the notion of tragic and comic frames. See Burke, *Attitudes toward History*. On the abolitionists' increasingly tragic resignation toward the necessity of violence, see Demos, "Anti-slavery Movement," 115–40, esp. 116–17, 136–37. On the rhetorical narrative, see Lucaites and Condit, "Reconstructing Narrative Theory," 100.

71. Chase, *Appeal*, 3–4.

72. Kraig, "Anatomy," 10, 14.

73. Chase, *Appeal*, 5.

74. Chase, *Appeal*, 6.

75. Chase, *Appeal*, 6–7.

76. Chase, *Appeal*, 7.

77. Two of the most prominent proponents of understanding republicanism in its ancient sense as a return to first principles in response to the decay and corruption of the recent past are Hannah Arendt, *On Revolution* (New York: Viking Press, 1963); and Pocock, *Machiavellian Moment*. Daniel Sisson's *American Revolution* examines the Jeffersonian persuasion in this light. On Lincoln and the civic humanist understanding of political time, see William Corlett, "The Availability of Lincoln's Political Religion," *Political Theory* 10 (November 1982), 520–40. On the link between organic imagery and the comic frame, see Burke, *Attitudes toward History*, 285.

78. Salmon P. Chase, "Maintain Plighted Faith. Speech of Hon. S. P. Chase, of Ohio, in the Senate, February 3, 1854, against the repeal of the Missouri prohibition of slavery north of 36°30" (Washington, D.C.: John T. and Lem Towers, 1954), 29. For an excellent reading of this speech, see Kraig, "Narration of Essence," 234–53, esp. 236.

79. Kruman, "Second American Party System," 536.

80. Holt, *Political Parties*, 261.

81. Holt, *Political Crisis*, 151–52.

82. Foner, *Free Soil*, 126–29.

3. Charles Sumner's "Crime Against Kansas": Conspiracy Rhetoric in the Oratorical Mold

1. David Herbert Donald, *Charles Sumner and the Coming of the Civil War* (New York: Alfred and Knopf, 1960), 109, 130–35. Sumner's reform causes included prison reform, pacifism, and antislavery, and he was not alone in eventually focusing his reform efforts exclusively on the slavery issue. By 1845 many Massachusetts reformers had come to believe that slavery and the slave power were the primary obstacles to all kinds of reform. See Brock, *Parties and Political Conscience*, 189. On Sumner's hopes to use the Whig Party as an instrument to oppose slavery, see Donald, *Sumner*, 135; Carl Schurz, *Charles Sumner: An Essay* (Urbana: University of Illinois Press, 1951), 29.

2. On the divide generally, see Brock, *Parties and Political Conscience*, 191; Formisano, *Political Culture*, 330; Donald, *Sumner*, 137; Schurz, *Sumner*, 31–32. According to Michael Holt, Conscience Whigs suspected their cotton comrades of being more concerned with ensuring the continued flow of cotton and political office than with antislavery reform. See Holt, *Whig Party*, 227–32; Formisano, *Political Culture*, 330. On alliance with Garrisonians, see Richard H. Sewell, "Slavery, Race and the Free Soil Party, 1848–1854," in Kraut, *Crusaders and Compromisers*, 101–24, esp. 118. Regarding Sumner's distaste for abolitionist methods and his moderate position, see Brock, *Parties and Political Conscience*, 198–99; Donald, *Sumner*, 132–33, 138. On the feud with Winthrop, see Brock, *Parties and Political Conscience*, 198–99; Schurz, *Sumner*, 31–32; Donald, *Sumner*, 141–44.

3. Regarding Sumner's strategy, see Brock, *Parties and Political Conscience*, 195. On the Worcester convention, see Donald, *Sumner*, 147–48.

4. Sumner to Salmon P. Chase, December 12, 1846, in *The Selected Letters of Charles Sumner*, ed. Beverly Wilson Palmer, 1:180 (Boston: Northeastern University Press, 1990).

5. Charles Sumner, "Speech for Political Action Against the Slave Power and the Extension of Slavery, in the Whig State Convention of Massachusetts, at Springfield, 29 September 1847," in *Orations and Speeches by*

Charles Sumner (Boston: Ticknor, Reed, and Fields, 1850), 2:243–45, 247, 256–57.

6. Donald, *Sumner,* 159. While the split was a loss for Massachusetts Whigs, few within the Whig leadership actually defected. See Holt, *American Whig Party,* 341.

7. Donald, *Sumner,* 164.

8. Charles Sumner, "Speech for Union Among Men of All Parties Against the Slave Power, and the Extensions of Slavery, in a Mass Convention at Worcester, June 28, 1848," in *Orations and Speeches,* 2:252, 259–60.

9. Sumner, "Speech for Union Among Men," 2:255.

10. Sumner, "Speech for Union Among Men," 2:256–57.

11. Donald, *Sumner,* 177–81. Many Conscience Whigs were unable to think of their traditional enemies—the Democrats—as potential allies. See John R. Mulkern, *The Know-Nothing Party in Massachusetts: The Rise and Fall of a People's Movement* (Boston: Northeastern University Press, 1990), 31. During this period, Sumner's Democratically tilted public utterances acquired an "equalitarian mood" that was branded as Locofoco by many who resented appeals to class prejudices. See Donald, *Sumner,* 180–82.

12. Charles Sumner, "Address to the People of Massachusetts, Explaining and Vindicating the Free Soil Movement; Reported to the Free Soil State Convention, and Adopted by that Convention, at Worcester, Sept. 12, 1849," in *Orations and Speeches,* 2:296–99, 305–7, 328–29.

13. On Free Soil successes at drawing Massachusetts Whig voters, see Holt, *American Whig Party,* 380. On Sumner's rise to the Senate, see Donald, *Sumner,* 187–97.

14. Donald, *Sumner,* 221–24. Donald notes Sumner's apparently contradictory political positions—an extremely radical "jacobinal" streak alongside a Burkean conservatism. See Donald, *Sumner,* 228. Kirt Wilson's account of Sumner's mode of political judgment leans toward the radical side. Wilson argues that Sumner practiced a radical form of prudence—a "transcendental prudence"—that had little in common with the more conservative version of prudence as accommodation to circumstances. See Kirt Wilson, "Emerson, Transcendental Prudence, and the Legacy of Senator Charles Sumner," *Rhetoric and Public Affairs* 2 (1999): 453–79. As Sumner's correspondence illustrates, however, he understood prudence in the conventional sense. Sumner to John Greenleaf Whittier, May 4, 1851, in *Selected Letters,* 1:333; Sumner to Charles Francis Adams, February 1, 1852, in *Selected Letters,* 1:350; Sumner to Samuel Gridley Howe, April 5, 1852, in *Selected Letters,*

1:356–57. The moderate tone of "Freedom National, Slavery Sectional" was said to have angered Boston's Garrisonians. See Donald, *Sumner,* 233, 241.

15. Sumner to Lord Wharncliffe, December 19, 1852, in *Selected Letters,* 1:379–80.

16. On Sumner's revision of the *Appeal,* see Donald, *Sumner,* 252. On Massachusetts anti-Nebraska meetings, see Donald, *Sumner,* 257; Sumner to Amasa Walker, April 26, 1854, in *Selected Letters,* 1:407; Sumner to James Freeman Clarke, June 10, 1854, in *Selected Letters,* 1:412; Sumner to Ralph Waldo Emerson, June 12, 1854, in *Selected Letters,* 1:412.

17. Mulkern, *Know-Nothing Party.* On the American victory at the polls in 1854, see 61–86. On failed Republican attempts to fuse with the Know-Nothings and Know-Nothing attempts to court Conscience Whigs, see 71–73. On Republican gains, see 99, 105, 116, 132.

18. Donald, *Sumner,* 282; Michael D. Pierson, "'All Southern Society Is Assailed by the Foulest Charges': Charles Sumner's 'The Crime Against Kansas' and the Escalation of Republican Anti-slavery Rhetoric," *New England Quarterly* 68 (1995): 526–27. On Whig disintegration and conspiratorial perceptions of the Democratic Party, see Holt, *Political Crisis,* 4, 238; Holt, *Political Parties,* 118, 146, 150, 272, 279. On events in Kansas and the plausibility of the slave power conspiracy, see William Gienapp, "The Crime against Sumner: The Caning of Charles Sumner and the Rise of the Republican Party," *Civil War History* 25 (1979): 229, 231–33.

19. James A. Rawley, *Race and Politics, "Bleeding Kansas" and the Coming of the Civil War* (Philadelphia and New York: J. B. Lippincott, 1969), 126–27.

20. Donald's biography of Sumner, for instance, dedicates four to five pages summarizing the speech (and, of this, three to four pages focus exclusively on Sumner's use of epithet and insult) and more than twenty-four pages tracing its reception in terms of the Brooks assault and its aftermath. See Donald, *Sumner,* 281–310. Similarly, Carl Schurz dedicates one and a half pages to considering the speech and roughly ten to its subsequent fallout. See Schurz, *Sumner,* 59–70. Rawley also dedicates approximately half a page to the "coarse tirade" and over three and a half pages to the reception of the speech. See Rawley, *Race and Politics,* 125–29. Other accounts also focus on the insult theme. Andrew Robertson views the speech as part of a new strategy of oratorical rhetoric enabled by the telegraph in which members of Congress began addressing their speeches predominantly to the public rather than to their fellow deliberators. Because Sumner was primarily concerned with the reading rather than the listening audience, Robertson suggests that

Sumner's vehemence and sexual imagery inadvertently violated older
congressional standards of decorum, precipitating Brooks's attack. See
Andrew W. Robertson, *The Language of Democracy: Political Rhetoric in the
United States and Britain, 1790–1900* (Ithaca, N.Y.: Cornell University
Press, 1995), 83–84.

21. On the speech's organization, see R. Elaine Pagel and Carl Dallinger,
"Charles Sumner," in *A History and Criticism of American Public Address,* 3
vols., ed. William Norwood Brigance (New York: Russell and Russell,
1943–55), 2:756, 762–63. Sumner is said to have been criticized for allowing the "skeleton" of his organizational scheme to be so readily visible (2:758). On the use of epithet and the digression in Sumner's
"Crime," see 2:756, 760–64; Glenn Stocker, "Charles Sumner's
Rhetoric of Insult," *Southern Speech Communication Journal* 38 (1973):
223–34.

22. Pierson, "Foulest Charges," 544–45,

23. Pierson, "Foulest Charges," 547–50.

24. Cecil W. Wooten, *Cicero's Philippics: The Rhetoric of Crisis* (Chapel Hill:
University of North Carolina Press, 1983), 46; Michael Leff, "The Idea
of Rhetoric as Interpretive Practice: A Humanist's Response to
Gaonkar," in Gross and Keith, *Rhetorical Hermeneutics,* 97–98.

25. On imitation as hermeneutic strategy, see Leff, "Idea of Rhetoric." Cecil
Wooten identifies the manner in which Cicero imitated Demosthenes
in his *Philippics.* For Wooten, imitation takes place on a number of levels. Cicero is said to have imitated the performative role, style, literary
devices, argumentative strategies, and themes of Demosthenes' rhetorical practice. See Wooten, *Cicero's Philippics,* 66, 91, 169–71. James Farrell also utilizes imitation in order to elucidate John Adams's choice of
forensic argumentative strategies in terms of those of Cicero. See Farrell, "*Pro Militibus Oratio,*" 233–49; Farrell, "John Adams." According to
Robert Hariman, "The individual active in public life studies classical
rhetorical texts to discern the model of the ideal orator in order to become such a figure in one's own time." Orators such as John Adams,
for instance, sought to secure a "reputation in his own republic similar
to what Cicero had achieved in Rome." See Robert Hariman, "After-
word: Relocating the Art of Public Address," in *Rhetoric and Political Culture in Nineteenth-Century America,* ed. Thomas Benson, 173 (East
Lansing: Michigan State University Press, 1997). Daniel Walker Howe
testifies to the prevalence of imitation within nineteenth-century Whig
oratorical culture and "the influence of the classics in providing role
models for orators." See Howe, *American Whigs,* 26–27.

26. Wood, "Conspiracy and the Paranoid Style," 409–10; Wooten, *Rhetoric of Crisis*, 66, 169, 171.

27. Pocock, *Machiavellian Moment*, 75–76. On the problem of time in its application to nineteenth-century American rhetoric, see also Corlett, "Availability of Lincoln's Political Religion," 520–40. On Cicero's civic republican predispositions, see Thomas N. Mitchell, *Cicero the Senior Statesman* (New Haven, Conn.: Yale University Press, 1991), 9–62.

28. Pocock, *Machiavellian Moment*, 3, 37–41, 49, 67. According to Pocock, the concept of contingency was frequently expressed within the term *"fortuna."*

29. Aristotle, *The Rhetoric*, trans. George Kennedy (New York: Oxford University Press, 1991), 141–43; Aristotle, *The Nicomachean Ethics*, trans. David Ross (New York: Oxford University Press, 1991), 55–65.

30. In his *Third Philippic*, Demosthenes sought to guide citizens toward a middling fear of the threat posed by Philip by attacking the "self-complacency" that made them refuse to hear anything "but pleasant speeches." Demosthenes labeled such unwarranted confidence as "folly and cowardice" and sought to overturn this confidence by telling the Athenians "the grounds for my alarm about our condition." Demosthenes' speech also recognized the attitude of those Athenians who suffered from overpowering fear: "They seem to watch him just as they would watch a hailstorm, each praying that it may not come their way, but none making any effort to stay its course." To these citizens suffering from overpowering fear, Demosthenes insists that effective action against Philip and his minions in Athens is still possible. Demosthenes, "Third Philippic," in *Demosthenes: Olynthiacs, Philippics, Minor Public Speeches and Speech against Leptines*, trans. J. H. Vince (New York: G. P. Putnam, 1930), 227, 236–37, 243, 261. Cicero, too, recognized that excesses and deficits of fear in regards to Catiline's conspiracy discouraged both deliberation and the proper action necessary to protect the state: "Some senators were disinclined to take firm measures because they saw nothing to fear, others because they were afraid of everything. Catiline dashed from the Senate in triumphant delight although he should never have left alive." Cicero, "Pro Murena," in *In Catilinum I-IV, Pro Murena, Pro Sulla, Pro Flacco*, trans. C. MacDonald (Cambridge, Mass.: Harvard University Press, 1977), 253.

31. Niccolo Machiavelli, "The Discourses on the First Ten Books of Titus Livius," in *The Prince and the Discourses*, trans. M Lerner (New York: Modern Library, 1950), 397. On the return to first principles in the

context of the American Revolution, see also Arendt, *On Revolution*, esp. 36–37; Sisson, *American Revolution*, 74–76.

32. On Sumner's education and admiration for Adams, see Donald, *Sumner*, 152, 215. In the *Lectures*, Adams advocates the imitation or emulation of Demosthenes and especially Cicero: "[I]t must be rather by the contemplation of examples, than from the abstraction of precepts, I shall . . . invite your attention to some of these imperishable models, which have commanded the admiration of the ages, . . . which may teach you what to do, by showing you what has been done." As he guided his students through the key rhetorical topics, his examples invariably centered on Cicero, Demosthenes, and, to a lesser extent, Burke. Adams also partook of the corollary of imitation—that history was cyclical and therefore provided a storehouse of precepts for addressing the problems of the present: "There is nothing new under the sun. The future is little more than a copy of the past. What hath been shall be again. And to exhibit an image of the past is often to present the clearest prospect of the future." See John Quincy Adams, *Lectures on Rhetoric and Oratory*, 2 vols. (1810; reprint, New York: Russell and Russell, 1962), 1:113, 271, 431, 2:57–61, 239–40, 245–46. On the Whig fondness for the oratorical canon, see Howe, *American Whigs*, 25–26. On Sumner's fondness for Burke, see Donald, *Sumner*, 215. On Sumner's admiration for Cicero, see Sumner to William Wetmore Story, July 6, 1839, in *Selected Letters*, 1:64; Sumner to William H. Seward, October 22, 1851, in *Selected Letters*, 1:340.

33. On the classical organizational structure of Sumner's "Crime," see Pagel and Dallinger, "Charles Sumner," 756. Pagel and Dallinger also note that Sumner was criticized for allowing the organizational "skeleton" of his speeches to be too prominently visible. See 758. This chapter relies on the version of the speech prepared by Sumner himself. See Charles Sumner, "The Crime Against Kansas: The Apologies for the Crime; the True Remedy," speech delivered in the Senate May 19 and 20, 1856, in *Charles Sumner: His Complete Works*, vol. 5 (New York: Negro University Press, 1969), 125–56. Pagel and Dallinger note that the Sumner corpus is filled with "unreliable texts," revealing "extensive and important inconsistencies in both style and content." See Pagel and Dallinger, "Charles Sumner," 2:756. But this is to be expected in the nineteenth-century culture of "oral literature" in which speeches were often extensively revised and edited for publication. On oral literature, see Howe, *American Whigs*, 25–26, 212–14; Leff, "Oratory and Oral Literature," unpublished manuscript. The version of the text utilized for the purposes of this reading is the version Sumner prepared and edited in

the 1860s and 1870s for inclusion in his *Complete Works*. Though it was surely edited and polished, this version remains substantively similar to the version of the speech that appears in the *Congressional Globe*. See Charles Sumner, Speech to the Senate, May 19, 1856, *Congressional Globe Appendix*, 34th Cong., 1st sess., 529–47. In at least one place, the *Globe* misplaces several paragraphs of the speech. See 536. In any event, the question of the so-called unreliable texts is endemic to the related practices of imitation and oral literature.

34. Leff's approach to the temporality of oratorical texts is perhaps an especially appropriate way to approach Sumner's text. Leff's goal is to attend to "the action within the text, the way the elements condition one another within the life cycle of the performance," and to understand how "the meaning of the speech progresses through time to reconfigure the audience's perception of both space and time relative to public events." See Leff, "Rhetorical Timing," 7. His emphasis on the life cycle of the text and the reconfiguration of audiences' understandings of space and time is especially salient to the text of "The Crime Against Kansas." The speech, after all, is itself intimately concerned with the life cycle of republics and the means by which audiences may be encouraged, through textual/aural movements through time and space, to renew their republic despite the limitations of time and space.

35. Sumner, "Crime," 137–38.

36. Sumner, "Crime," 138–39. This parallel with Verres is emphasized in Pierson, "Foulest Charges," 544–45. Alluding to Burke, Sumner writes: "The cry, 'I am an American citizen,' is interposed in vain against outrage of every kind, even upon life itself. Are you against robbery? I hold it up to your scorn. Are you against sacrilege? I present it for your execration. Are you for the protection of American citizens? I show you how their dearest rights are cloven down, while a Tyrannical Usurpation seeks to install itself on their very necks." Sumner, "Crime," 139–40. The relevant passage from Burke is "Do we want a cause, my Lords? You have the cause of oppressed Princes, of undone women of the first rank, of desolated Provinces and of wasted Kingdoms. Do you want a criminal, my Lords? When was there so much iniquity ever laid to the charge of any one? . . . My Lords, is it a Prosecutor that you want? You have before you the Commons of Great Britain as Prosecutors. . . . Do you want a Tribunal? My Lords, no example of antiquity, nothing in the modern world, nothing in the range of human imagination can supply us with a Tribunal like this." See Edmund Burke, "Speech on Opening of Impeachment," February 15, 16, 18, 19, 1788,

in *The Writings and Speeches of Edmund Burke,* ed. Paul Langford, P. J. Marshall, and William B. Todd (Oxford: Clarendon Press, 1991), 6:457–58. Thanks to James Farrell for pointing out this parallel between Sumner and Hastings.

37. According to James Farrell, not only did John Adams imitate particular strategies of Cicero's forensic speeches, but he also is said to have been inspired to defend the British officers involved in the Boston massacres, in part, by Cicero's choices in such famous cases as the trial of Roscius. In this respect, Adams imitated not Cicero's rhetorical practices but rather his role. See Farrell, *"Pro Militibus Oratio,"* 233–49, esp. 237.

38. Sumner, "Crime," 140. While this sexual imagery is undoubtedly important for the purposes of Sumner's well-discussed personal attacks, it may be equally important in its organic implications. The imagery of sexual violation encompasses not just the crime itself but also the product. Sumner may also be gesturing toward organic imagery of the state—in this act of rape, the slave power aims at the birth of a monstrous new state in Kansas. See Sumner, "Crime," 141–42, on the perpetrator of the crime.

39. Sumner, "Crime," 142–43.

40. Sumner, "Crime," 144–45. Although this section is identified as a digression in Pagel and Dallinger, "Charles Sumner," 2:756, 762–63, this reading will suggest that it is an essential component of Sumner's imitation of Cicero and Demosthenes.

41. George Campbell, *Philosophy of Rhetoric,* ed. Lloyd F. Bitzer (1776; reprint, Carbondale: Southern Illinois University Press, 1963), 105–6.

42. On the paranoid style and lurid exaggeration, see Creps, "Conspiracy Argument," 60, 96–97. A number of scholars have speculated about Sumner's motive for the lewd insults. For instance, Stocker asks why Sumner resorted to a rhetoric of "insult and invective." See Stocker, "Rhetoric of Insult," 223. Similarly, Pierson recognizes that "The Crime Against Kansas" was far more strident than Sumner's previous Senate speeches, representing an "escalation" of antislavery rhetoric that attacked the morality of slavery. See Pierson, "Foulest Charges," 533. Finally, Robertson provides one answer to the question, suggesting that Sumner's vehemence and sexual imagery were designed more to inflame the popular mind in the daily newspapers than to contribute to senatorial deliberation. See Robertson, *Language of Democracy,* 83–84.

43. Sumner, "Crime," 151–53, 157–58. In discussing the Nebraska bill, Sumner makes two moves important to understanding his rhetoric of conspiracy. First, he hints at a larger conspiracy, involving the possibility that

"vast regions" might be opened to slavery, though he insists that "my purpose is with the Crime against Kansas, and I shall not stop to expose the conspiracy beyond." Sumner, "Crime," 158. Second, in summarily interpreting the Nebraska bill as part of a conspiracy, Sumner lays down a general axiom for interpreting actions: "men are wisely presumed to intend the natural consequences of their conduct, and to seek what their acts seem to promote. Now the Nebraska Bill, on its very face, openly clears the way for Slavery, and it is not wrong to presume that its originators intended the natural consequences of such an act, and sought in this way to extend Slavery. Of course they did. And this is the first stage of the Crime against Kansas." Sumner, "Crime," 158. "Natural consequences" of acts signify underlying motives.

44. Sumner, "Crime," 153, 158–60.
45. Sumner, "Crime," 160–61.
46. Wooten, *Rhetoric of Crisis,* 170; Adams, *Lectures,* 1:271.
47. On the one-sided nature of some of the evidence, see Donald, *Sumner,* 279; Sumner, "Crime," 161. Sumner's antislavery opinions undoubtedly bias his account to some degree, but his account is not too far removed from that of historians. See Alice Nichols, *Bleeding Kansas* (New York: Oxford University Press, 1954); Rawley, *Race and Politics.* Nichols points out that due to the proslavery majority, the result of the earlier elections would probably have been the same even without Missouri invasions. See Nichols, *Bleeding Kansas,* 29.
48. Sumner, "Crime," 163–64, 165–69. For historical accounts of the invasions and associated violence, see Nichols, *Bleeding Kansas,* 29–70; Rawley, *Race and Politics,* 79–99.
49. Sumner, "Crime," 171–74. Other kinds of evidence from proslavery forces buttress the text's claim as to the motive for the conspiracy. Another proslavery paper, the *New York Herald,* also recounted the success of the Missourians in asserting themselves in the Kansas election. See Sumner, "Crime," 175. A circular from a Missouri emigration society speaks of the immense monetary sacrifices that western Missouri counties had made in order to ensure that Free-Soil would not prevail in Kansas. Other sources not related to the conspiracy—a St. Louis paper, Governor Reeder, and resolutions from the people of Kansas—all concur in the determination that Missourians had managed to usurp the election for slavery. See Sumner, "Crime," 176–77.
50. Sumner, "Crime," 178. Translated passage from Cicero, *In Catilinum,* 63.
51. Sumner, "Crime," 178–79. Among those legislative acts violating the rights of Free-Soilers, Sumner singles out three in particular for his

condemnation. First is the act making it a crime to speak or write in terms that question or deny the right to hold slave property. Second is the act requiring attorneys at law to obtain a license, obtainable only by swearing an oath to uphold the fugitive slave bill. The third act excludes from jury duty all those unwilling to admit of the right to hold slaves. By these means, Sumner indicates, are citizens of Free-Soil sympathies excluded from both the political and legal processes of the territory entirely. See Sumner, "Crime," 180–82.

52. Sumner, "Crime," 182–83.

53. Sumner, "Crime," 184–85.

54. Sumner, "Crime," 187.

55. The absurdity of the "Apology imbecile" is underscored by the citation of several incidents around the world in which the president had intervened to protect the rights of U.S. citizens. Sumner, "Crime," 187–89. The passivity of the president is further questioned by a contrast with presidential action in favor of the slave power: "Kansas is left a prey to the Propagandists of Slavery, while the whole Treasury, the Army, and Navy of the United States are lavished to hunt a single slave through the streets of Boston." Sumner, "Crime," 189. The document inspiring the "Apology absurd," retrieved as a member attempted to eat the evidence, is observed to require that members exert all influence to make Kansas a free state in any way "which will not conflict with the laws of the country and the Constitution of the United States." Sumner, "Crime," 192–94. On the "Apology infamous," see Sumner, "Crime," 194–205.

56. Sumner, "Crime," 205–6. According to Michael Holt, notions of preserving the Revolutionary heritage and refighting the Revolution had become a staple of nineteenth-century partisan rhetoric. See Holt, *Political Parties,* 261; Holt, *Political Crisis,* 151–52.

57. Sumner, "Crime," 207–8.

58. Sumner, "Crime," 208–10.

59. Sumner, "Crime," 211–12, 214–15.

60. For Sumner's refutation of the legal objections to the plan, see Sumner, "Crime," 218–32. On the Declaration as precedent for Seward's plan, see Sumner, "Crime," 232. This principle, Sumner continues, is supported by Virginians Madison and George Tucker, as well as by John Calhoun himself. According to Calhoun, this right meant that "'a majority . . . can alter or change their fundamental laws at pleasure.'" See Sumner, "Crime," 233–35. On the appeal to the Republic's first principles, see Sumner, "Crime," 236.

61. Sumner, "Crime," 236–37. Sumner explicated his own conclusion in a letter. Sumner to Samuel Gridley Howe, March 31, 1856, in *Selected Letters*, 1:455.

62. Sumner, "Crime," 237–39.

63. Sumner, "Crime," 241–42. Turning to Douglas, the text identifies him, along with the slave power, as responsible for the degeneration of the Republic—one of "those mad spirits who would endanger and degrade the Republic, while they betray all the cherished sentiments of the Fathers and the spirit of the Constitution, that slavery may have new spread." Sumner, "Crime," 243. Senator James Mason of Virginia also receives condemnation in terms of the dimension of time: "he does not represent that early Virginia, so dear to our hearts, which gave to us the pen of Jefferson, by which the equality of men was declared, and the sword of Washington, by which Independence was secured: he represents that other Virginia, from which Washington and Jefferson avert their faces." In sum, Butler, Douglas, and Mason are the "natural enemies of Kansas," mad for power and slavery, degraded, corrupted, and hopelessly cut off from the nourishing first principles of the Republic. See Sumner, "Crime," 244.

64. Sumner, "Crime," 242. Sumner relies here on Massachusetts historian Lorenzo Sabine's 1847 work, *The American Loyalist or Biographical Sketches of Adherents to the British Crown in the War of Revolution*. This text was extremely anti-Southern, concluding that slavery made Southern colonies—especially South Carolina—hesitant to resist the Crown. Such action, South Carolinians feared, would cause the British to foment slave insurrections in the Slave Belt of the Deep South. See John Hope Franklin, "The North, the South, and the American Revolution," in *Race and History: Selected Essays* (Baton Rouge: Louisiana State University Press, 1989), 367–83, esp. 370–72, 376.

65. Sumner, "Crime," 243–44, 247.

66. On "Harvard republicanism" versus "St. Louis republicanism" (which holds that republican ideology remained influential well into the nineteenth or perhaps even twentieth century), see Rodgers, "Republicanism," 18–20. Gordon S. Wood identifies the debate over the Constitution as the "hinge" between a premodern republican political thought and more modern liberal sensibilities. See Wood, *Creation of the American Republic*. According to Wood, "classical and Renaissance accounts of plots differed from most of the conspiratorial interpretations of the eighteenth century. They usually described actions by which ambitious politicians gained control of governments: conspiracy was taken

for granted as a normal means by which rulers were deposed. . . . By the eighteenth century conspiracy . . . had become a common means of explaining how rulers and others directing political events really operated." See Wood, "Conspiracy and the Paranoid Style," 409–10, 412–13.

67. Pocock, *Machiavellian Moment*, 79. Recall Wooten's recognition that "the orator is prone to assume role-models and to see the crisis that he faces in terms of patterns that have appeared in the past. Demosthenes surely was inspired by the model of Pericles. . . . Likewise Cicero . . . modeled his own actions on those of a whole series of earlier Romans and was always prone to interpret each crisis in which he was involved in light of an earlier pattern." Wooten, *Cicero's Philippics*, 170. Recall also John Quincy Adams's enunciation of the same doctrine: "There is nothing new under the sun. The future is little more than a copy of the past. What hath been shall be again. And to exhibit an image of the past is often to present the clearest prospect of the future." Adams, *Lectures*, 1:271.

68. See note 20 for a brief summary of scholars interested in this question.

69. Gienapp, "Crime against Sumner," 218–19; Pierson, "Foulest Charges," 526–27; Holt, *Political Crisis*, 4, 238; Holt, *Political Parties*, 272.

70. Gienapp, "Crime against Sumner," 229, 231–33.

71. Recall Campbell's passage: "It would have been impossible even for Cicero to inflame the minds of the people to so high a pitch against oppression, considered in the abstract, as he actually did inflame them against Verres the *oppressor*. Nor could he have incensed them so much against *treason* and *conspiracy* as he did against Catiline the *traitor* and *conspirator*." Campbell, *Philosophy of Rhetoric*, 105–6.

4. Lincoln, Conspiracy Rhetoric, and the "House Divided": Assessing the Judgment of History

1. Don E. Fehrenbacher, *Prelude to Greatness: Lincoln in the 1850's* (Stanford, Calif.: Stanford University Press, 1962), 154–59.

2. For a reception history of Lincoln in the United States, see Merrill D. Peterson, *Lincoln in American Memory* (New York: Oxford University Press, 1994); Michael C. Leff, "Lincoln among the Nineteenth Century Orators," in *Rhetoric and Political Culture in Nineteenth-Century America*, ed. T. Benson, 131–55 (East Lansing: Michigan State University Press, 1997). The concept of interpretive context is derived from Michael

Leff's reading of Steven Mailloux, *Rhetorical Power* (Ithaca, N.Y.: Cornell University Press, 1989), esp. 3–18.

3. On Lincoln's adherence to the Whig economic program, see Gabor S. Boritt, *Lincoln and the Economics of the American Dream* (Urbana: University of Illinois Press, 1978); Joel H. Silbey, "'Always a Whig in Politics': The Partisan Life of Abraham Lincoln," *Papers of the Abraham Lincoln Association* 8 (1986): 21–42. Regarding Lincoln's important role in the Whig Party, see Silbey, "'Always a Whig,'" 24–25, 28. Harry Jaffa also notes Lincoln's skill as a party politician and his loyalty to the Whigs and advocacy of their issues. See Harry Jaffa, *Crisis of the "House Divided": An Interpretation of the Issues in the Lincoln-Douglas Debates* (Garden City, N.Y.: Doubleday, 1959), 184–85. Robert W. Johannsen also notes Lincoln's "single minded partisanship" and his insistence that party loyalty and regularity were moral obligations. See Robert W. Johannsen, *Lincoln, the South and Slavery: The Political Dimension* (Baton Rogue: Louisiana State University Press, 1991), 6–7. On Lincoln's pragmatic orientation and commitment to party organization, see Silbey, "'Always a Whig,'" 28.

4. Abraham Lincoln, Circular Letter from Whig Committee, March 4, 1843, in *The Collected Works of Abraham Lincoln*, ed. Roy P. Basler, Marion Dolores Pratt, and Lloyd A. Dunlap (New Brunswick, N.J.: Rutgers University Press, 1953), 1:315. This was Lincoln's first recorded reference to the house divided passage. David Herbert Donald, *Lincoln* (New York: Simon and Schuster, 1995), 206; Zarefsky, *Lincoln, Douglas and Slavery*, 44.

5. Donald, *Lincoln*, 114; Johannsen, *Lincoln*, 41.

6. Donald, *Lincoln*, 119. According to Fehrenbacher, the "passing of the Whig party and the rise of the Republicans was like a motion picture 'dissolve' in which one scene slowly fades from view while another gradually takes its place." See Fehrenbacher, *Prelude to Greatness*, 25, 31. Lincoln's loyal Whiggery until 1855–56 is attested to in Johannsen, *Lincoln*, 44–45; and Donald, *Lincoln*, 171. Lincoln objected to the actions of members of a radical party calling themselves Republican which had affixed Lincoln's name to their committee. See Lincoln to Ichabod Codding, November 27, 1854, in *Collected Works*, 2:288.

7. M. E. Bradford identifies three phases in Lincoln's political career—the Whig years prior to 1854, 1854–60, and 1860–65. See M. E. Bradford, "Dividing the House: The Gnosticism of Lincoln's Rhetoric," *Modern Age* 23 (1979): 20–21. Johannsen speaks of 1854 as the beginning of Lincoln's "second political career." See Johannsen, *Lincoln*, 8. Lincoln

condemned Douglas as early as his "Speech at Peoria, IL," October 16, 1854, in *Collected Works*, 2:255. Regarding Douglas's "lullaby" arguments, see Abraham Lincoln, "Speech at Peoria, IL," October 16, 1854, in *Collected Works*, 2:261–64. On Lincoln's numerous conspiracy charges, see M. E. Bradford, "Lincoln's Republican Rhetoric: The Development of a Political Idiom," *Old Northwest* 14 (1988): 186–87.

8. On the revisionists, see Peterson, *American Memory*, 302–8; Johnson, "Along the Twisted Road," 119–41, esp. 124; Avery Craven, *The Repressible Conflict, 1830–1861* (Baton Rogue: Louisiana State University Press, 1939), 63–64, 95–96, and, more generally, 63–96. Craven, of course, also recognizes the corresponding conspiracy alleged to have been in control of Northern affairs—the "black republicans." While Craven's work has been accused of a romantic pro-Southern bias, more moderate revisionists followed his general thesis that emotional rhetoric had served to polarize the nation. See J. G. Randall, *Lincoln the Liberal Statesman* (New York: Dodd, Mead, 1947), 26, 39, 46, 50; J. G. Randall, *Mr. Lincoln* (New York: Dodd, Mead, 1945), 50.

9. Allan Nevins, *The Emergence of Lincoln*, 2 vols. (New York: Charles Scribner's Sons, 1950), 1:14–15; Forgie, *Patricide*, 243–44; Bradford, "Lincoln's Republican Rhetoric," 187, 206. The similarity of this position to the revisionists is indicated by Peterson, *American Memory*, 390–91; Bradford, "Dividing the House," 10–24, esp. 21; Bradford, "Lincoln's Republican Rhetoric," 185–211.

10. Roy Basler, "Abraham Lincoln's Rhetoric," *American Literature* 11 (1939): 165–82, quote on 180; Avery Craven, *The Coming of the Civil War* (New York: Charles Scribner's Sons, 1942), 392–93; Randall, *Liberal Statesman*, 21; Randall, *Mr. Lincoln*, 102–3; Nevins, *Emergence*, 1:362; Bradford, "Dividing the House," 18; Bradford, "Republican Rhetoric," 187, 204; Johannsen, *Lincoln*, 75, 86, 89. Johannsen is less condemnatory than others, recognizing the general pervasiveness of conspiracy rhetoric and the slave power conspiracy charge in particular in the mid-nineteenth century (see 85).

11. Jaffa, *Crisis*, 10, 27, and, more generally, 275–93 and 294–301. Leff identifies the contrast between the extremely overstated and paranoid Conspiracy section and the understated Living Dog section, as an example of hyperbole, making the final section (discrediting Douglas) appear even more probable by virtue of the relative improbability of Douglas's role in the Conspiracy section. Leff explains, "We might call this a recoil effect, where an exaggerated preparatory stretching of a spring loosens it for a more practical purpose." Leff, in other words,

assumes the conspiracy argument to be a "stretch" not relating to Lincoln's "more practical purpose." See Leff, "Rhetorical Timing," 15–18. Don E. Fehrenbacher defends Lincoln's use of the conspiracy claim by pointing out that politicians ought to be held to different standards than historians, that "political rhetoric is a response to historical developments, not a record of them, and circumstances can sometimes make the most erroneous statements credible, even justifiable, thus giving it a kind of temporal validity." See Don E. Fehrenbacher, "The Origins and Purpose of Lincoln's 'House Divided' Speech," *Mississippi Valley Historical Review* 46 (1960): 615–43, quote on 628. On the prevalence of conspiracy theories in the nineteenth century, see Zarefsky, *Lincoln, Douglas and Slavery,* 68–69 and, more generally, 68–110. On the importance of conspiracy rhetoric to political parties, in particular, the Illinois Republicans in 1858, see Pfau, "House That Abe Built," 625–51, esp. 637–42 and 649–51.

12. Fehrenbacher, *Prelude to Greatness,* 19, 44–46; Donald, *Lincoln,* 189–91. The speech was lost in the sense that the person responsible for its recording was said to have been so enthralled as to be unable to carry out his recording task.

13. Fehrenbacher, "House Divided," 627, 631–32. Fehrenbacher also cites older readings of the speech that portray it as the work of an impassioned prophet or as a radical gamble designed to further future presidential aspirations. See Fehrenbacher, "House Divided," 619–20.

14. *Collected Works,* 2:461. All references to the "A House Divided" speech at Springfield, Illinois, on June 16, 1858, refer to the version contained in *Collected Works,* 2:461–69.

15. For a full explication of this interpretation (of the House Divided and Conspiracy sections), see Pfau, "House That Abe Built," esp. 632–37.

16. On the relationship of the Conspiracy section to strategies of mobilization and unification, see Pfau, "House That Abe Built," 625–51, esp. 637–42 and 649–51. On the keynoter's dilemma, see Thompson, "Barbara Jordan's Keynote Address," 272. Thompson cites Smith, "Keynoter's Dilemma." Linda Horwitz's work on Barbara Jordan's keynote address utilizes the concept of the keynoter's dilemma. Linda Diane Horwitz, "Transforming Appearance into Rhetorical Argument: Rhetorical Criticism of Public Speeches of Barbara Jordan, Lucy Parsons, and Angela Y. Davis" (Ph.D. diss., Northwestern University, 1998), 28–66.

17. *Collected Works,* 2:462. Fehrenbacher discusses the relative proportions of the speech's sections in "House Divided," 631.

18. Hofstadter, "Paranoid Style," 36–38.

19. C. H. Perelman and L. Olbrechts-Tyteca, *The New Rhetoric: A Treatise on Argumentation* (Notre Dame, Ind.: Notre Dame University Press, 1969), 193–95. On the connection between Hofstadter's insights and the quasi-logical argument, see Young, Launer, and Austin, "Need for Evaluative Criteria," 89–107; Hasian, "Conspiratorial Rhetoric," 195–214; Creps, "Conspiracy Argument," 45–48.

20. *Collected Works*, 2:466. Zarefsky explains Lincoln's professed uncertainty as a strategy for minimizing his own burden of proof in the debates. See Zarefsky, *Lincoln, Douglas and Slavery*, 87, 106–7. Whatever the motive for such a move, what is important here is the contrast with the avowed certainty said to be associated with the paranoid style.

21. Abraham Lincoln, "Speech at Springfield, Illinois," July 17, 1858, in *Collected Works*, 2:521; Abraham Lincoln, "Fragment: Notes for Speeches," August 21, 1858, in *Collected Works*, 2:548–50.

22. [Cicero], *Ad Herrenium*, trans. H Caplan (Cambridge, Mass.: Harvard University Press, 1954), 362–63.

23. Trudy Govier, "Two Unreceived Views About Reasoning and Argumentation," in *Problems in Argument Analysis and Evaluation* (Providence, R.I.: Foris, 1987), 66–69. Govier makes the distinction between conductive arguments and inductive arguments in this way: "The conclusion is not a generalization from cases, as it would be in an enumerative induction. Nor does it presume empirical regularities among considered cases or the kind of background empirical knowledge needed for explanatory or causal inductive reasoning" (70). See also Trudy Govier, *A Practical Study of Argument* (Belmont, Calif.: Wadsworth, 1997), 388–90.

24. *Collected Works*, 2:465. The scaffolding for the house, according to Lincoln, was provided by Douglas: "Under the Dred Scott decision, 'squatter sovereignty' squatted out of existence, tumbled down like temporary scaffolding—like the mould at the foundry served through one blast and fell back into loose sand—helped to carry an election, and then was kicked to the winds." *Collected Works*, 2:464.

25. Leff, "Rhetorical Timing," 7. On the importance of narrative in conspiracy discourse, see Hofstadter, "Paranoid Style," 6; Zarefsky, *Lincoln, Douglas and Slavery*, 103; Leff "Rhetorical Timing," 10–11; Browne, *Edmund Burke*, 19. I rely on Leff's account of the text's narrative configuration. Extensive quotation of Leff's interpretation is warranted given its importance as well as the relative difficulty of obtaining Leff's text.

26. Paul Ricoeur, *Time and Narrative*, 3 vols., trans. Kathleen McLaughlin and David Pellauer (Chicago: University of Chicago Press, 1983), 1:53, 56–57, 64, 76, 80. For Ricoeur, a narrative configuration reconfigures or resignifies "our preunderstanding of the world of action . . . characterized by the mastering of a network of intersignifications constitutive of the semantics of action, by familiarity with the symbolic resources and the prenarrative sources of human acting." Ricoeur, *Time and Narrative*, 1:81. On mimesis$_1$ generally, see 1:55–64. On mimesis$_3$ generally, see 1:70–82

27. The concept of "narrative preunderstandings" expressed within mimesis$_1$ closely resembles Walter Fisher's observation that the acceptance of a particular narrative by an audience will depend in part on the story's fidelity to stories the audience members know or experiences they have had. See Walter R. Fisher, *Human Communication as Narration: Toward a Philosophy of Reason, Value and Action* (Columbia: University of South Carolina Press, 1987), 47–48, 75–76. While Fisher's concept of narrative fidelity appears to serve primarily an evaluative rather than interpretive function, other studies have used the more elastic concept of narrative preunderstandings as an illuminating interpretive strategy. Robert Kraig's work on Salmon P. Chase's oration against the Kansas-Nebraska Act, "Maintain Plighted Faith," interprets Chase's narrative practices in terms of the preunderstandings of historically situated audiences. See Kraig, "Narration of Essence," 234–53, esp. 236.

28. Leff, "Rhetorical Timing," 10.

29. *Collected Works*, 2:462–63.

30. *Collected Works*, 2:464–65.

31. Leff, "Rhetorical Timing," 11, 14; *Collected Works*, 2:465.

32. Leff, "Rhetorical Timing," 14.

33. *Collected Works*, 2:466–67.

34. Zarefsky, *Lincoln, Douglas and Slavery*, 69.

35. Ricoeur, *Time and Narrative*, 1:56–57 (on mimesis$_1$ generally, see 1:55–64).

36. Forgie, *Patricide*, 258; Holt, *Political Crisis*, 4, 238; Holt, *Political Parties*, 272.

37. Lincoln to Joshua F. Speed, August 24, 1855, in *Collected Works*, 2:322.

38. Lincoln, "Speech at Springfield, Illinois," July 17, 1858, in *Collected Works*, 2:502–21, esp. 506.

39. Leff, "Rhetorical Timing," 9–10. Holt cites mid-1850s sources condemning the "machinery of party" and political machines in general. See Holt, *Political Parties*, 276. On the Whig suspicion of political

machines and their demagogic bosses, see Howe, *American Whigs,*
30–32; Brown, *Politics and Statesmanship,* 7, 216. Holt has indicated the
extent to which the 1850s was a decade of cynicism and disillusionment, with party machines that seemed to stand for nothing but the
maintenance of their own power. Holt notes that many "felt the need
to reform . . . expressed as a desire to change the old party machinery"
and that "in 1852 and 1853, complaints about politicians and parties
that . . . identified them as anti-republican reached a crescendo." See
Holt, *Political Crisis,* 136–37; Holt, *Political Parties,* 272–76.

40. Leff, "Rhetorical Timing," 10.
41. Howe, *American Whigs,* 79–81.
42. Mailloux, *Rhetorical Power,* 17, 52.
43. Ericson, *American Liberalism,* 21–24. One of the seminal works on plu-
    ralism is Robert A. Dahl, *Who Governs? Democracy and Power in an Ameri-
    can City* (New Haven, Conn.: Yale University Press, 1961). See also
    Robert A. Dahl, *A Preface to Democratic Theory* (Chicago: University of
    Chicago Press, 1956).
44. The complexities of bargaining and negotiation required to maintain
    the Democratic coalition, as well as Douglas's abilities along these lines,
    are noted in Douglas Jaenicke's account of the eventual break-up of
    the Democratic coalition in the 1860s. See Douglas W. Jaenicke, "The
    Rupture of the Antebellum Democratic Party: Prelude to Secession
    from the Union," *Party Politics* 3 (1995): 347–67. On Douglas's hopes to
    occupy the middle ground, see Jaffa, *Crisis,* 50; Nevins, *Emergence,*
    366–68. On the pluralist imperative to satisfy multiple competing pref-
    erences, see Ericson, *American Liberalism,* esp. 117–35. For Douglas on
    the need for compromise and practical agreement, see Jaffa, *Crisis,* 41,
    169. Ericson goes so far as to suggest that to Douglas, silence was the
    best way to solve the most divisive moral controversies. See Ericson,
    American Liberalism, 118, 126–27.
45. Nevins, *Emergence,* 365; Zarefsky, *Lincoln, Douglas and Slavery,* 69.
46. "Douglas's Opening Speech at Ottawa," August 21, 1858, in *The Com-
    plete Lincoln-Douglas Debates of 1858,* ed. Paul M. Angle, 105, see also
    108, 162 (Chicago: University of Chicago Press, 1991) (hereafter cited
    as *Debates*).
47. Craven, *Repressible Conflict,* 95. On the Compromises of 1820 and 1850,
    see Craven, *Civil War,* 123, 272; Randall, *Liberal Statesman,* 12. On the
    prediction that a Douglas administration could have prevented civil
    war, see Saul Sigelschiffer, *The American Conscience: The Drama of the Lin-
    coln-Douglas Debates* (New York: Horizon Press, 1979), 418–19, 427.

48. Rodgers, "Republicanism," 15; Hartz, *Liberal Tradition.*
49. Fenster, *Conspiracy Theories,* 4–13, and, more generally, 3–21; Richard Hofstadter, "Goldwater and Pseudo-Conservative Politics," in *Paranoid Style,* 103.
50. Fenster, *Conspiracy Theories,* 5, 8, 10, 15.
51. Howe, *American Whigs,* 329, note 50.
52. Ericson, *American Liberalism,* 7–9.
53. Andrew Robertson, *The Language of Democracy: Political Rhetoric in the United States and Britain, 1790–1900* (Ithaca, N.Y.: Cornell University Press, 1995), 11–15, 28–35. On the House Divided speech, see 90. On the transition from hortatory to admonitory rhetoric, see 16–17, 117.
54. For a discussion and refutation of "republican revisionism" as applied to Lincoln, see Ericson, *American Liberalism,* 140–41, 157. On Lincoln's pluralism, see Ericson, *American Liberalism,* 138. For a thorough consideration of Lincoln's materialist liberalism, see Boritt, *American Dream.*
55. While Lincoln consistently speaks of a conspiracy to nationalize slavery, there are also a great number of references that characterize the "conspiracy" in the "House Divided" as the work of a mere interest group or faction. In the Peoria speech, we find Lincoln speaking of those interested in expanding slavery as "a mere handful of men, bent only on temporary self-interest," who in their "greedy chase to make profit of the negro," were willing to abandon the antiextension slavery policy of the founders. See Lincoln, "Speech at Peoria, IL," October 16, 1854, in *Collected Works,* 2:270, 276. One month after the "House Divided" speech, Lincoln continued to speak of a conspiracy to nationalize slavery, but he also described the motives of the conspirators in terms better befitting a faction: "the men of the present age . . . have become wiser than the framers of the Constitution; and the invention of the cotton gin had made the perpetuity of slavery a necessity in this country." See Lincoln, "Speech at Springfield, Illinois," July 17, 1858, in *Collected Works,* 2:514–15. Not long after, Lincoln is reported to have said in a speech at Lewiston that the founders were well aware "of the tendency of prosperity to breed tyrants" and that they provided the Declaration's words because they anticipated that "in the distant future some man, some faction, some interest, should set up the doctrine that none but rich white men . . . were entitled to life, liberty and pursuit of happiness." See Abraham Lincoln, "Speech at Lewiston," August 17, 1858, in *Debates,* 101. In the debate at Alton, Lincoln again seems to link Douglas to a faction or interest rather than conspiracy: "willingly or unwillingly, purposely or without purpose, Judge Douglas has been

the most prominent instrument in changing the position of the institution of slavery which the fathers of the government expected to come
to an end ere this—and putting it upon Brooks' cotton gin basis,—
placing it where he openly confesses he has no desire there shall ever
be an end of it." See "Lincoln's Reply at Alton," October 15, 1858, in
Debates, 394. See also "Lincoln's Rejoinder at Quincy," October 8, 1858,
in *Debates,* 354. At Cooper Union, Lincoln speaks of the "Southern people" as a faction that, having discarded the founders' policy, seeks to
advance its interests through unreasonable demands backed up by
threats of disunion. See "Address at Cooper Institute," February 27,
1860, in *Collected Works,* 3:535–47.

56. That Lincoln's speech was intended to have such practical effects is not
a novel claim (see, for instance, Fehrenbacher, "House Divided"). But
given the assumption of the paranoid style approach, that conspiracy
rhetoric is an ineffective means of political engagement, the point is
worth emphasizing here.

57. Abraham Lincoln, "Lincoln's Reply at Jonesboro," September 15, 1858,
in *Debates,* 209; see also Lincoln, "Lincoln's Reply at Alton," in *Debates,*
384.

58. *Collected Works,* 2:468.

5. Lessons of the Slave Power Conspiracy: Conspiracy Rhetoric at the Center and Fringe

1. For a few examples of scholars who remain paranoid about conspiracy
rhetoric, see George Johnson, *Architects of Fear: Conspiracy Theories and
Paranoia in American Culture* (Los Angeles: Jeremy P. Tareher, 1983);
Pipes, *Conspiracy;* Goldberg, *Enemies Within.* A number of historians, political scientists, and rhetorical scholars, among others, have questioned
several of Hofstadter's assumptions—most notably his assumption that
conspiracy discourse is the practice of the fringe of society. See, for instance, Howe, *American Whigs;* Zarefsky, *Lincoln, Douglas and Slavery;*
Holt, *Political Crisis;* Holt, *Political Parties;* Fenster, *Conspiracy Theories;*
Richards, *Slave Power.* With the exceptions of Zarefsky and Fenster, none
of these scholars exhibits a concern with textual form or rhetorical criticism, and even Zarefsky and Fenster explore this issue only tangen-
tially. Most rhetorical studies of conspiracy have relied on the
assumptions of the paranoid style. Earl Creps relies heavily on assumptions of the paranoid style and its characteristic texts. See Creps, "Conspiracy Argument." Goodnight and Poulakos gesture toward the

occasional importance of conspiracy rhetoric in mainstream politics, but they also rely upon several of Hofstadter's presumptions about conspiracy discourse. See Goodnight and Poulakos, "Conspiracy Rhetoric," 299–316, esp. 310–11. Charles Griffin utilizes the paranoid style in combination with the jeremiad to read Morse's conspiracy texts. See Griffin, "Jedediah Morse," 293–303. Marouf Hasian interprets the very kind of Right Wing anti-Semitic conspiracy rhetoric from which the paranoid style was developed. See Hasian, "Understanding the Power," 195–214.

2. See Creps, "Conspiracy Argument," 58, 211; Zarefsky, *Lincoln, Douglas and Slavery,* 103–6. Though they rely on many of the assumptions of the paranoid style, Goodnight and Poulakos also consider the possibility that conspiracy rhetoric is occasionally "mainstreamed." See Goodnight and Poulakos, "Conspiracy Rhetoric," 302.

3. Hofstadter, "Paranoid Style," 29.

4. Leff, "Rhetorical Timing."

5. On the jeremiad, see Bercovitch, *American Jeremiad.* On millennialism and eschatology, see O'Leary, "Reading the Signs of the Times."

6. Pocock, for instance, shows how the rhetoric of Jacksonian Democrats was based on republican ideology. See Pocock, *Machiavellian Moment,* 506–52. Similarly, Howe indicates the republican basis of Whig Party ideology. See Howe, *American Whigs,* 77–79.

7. Howe, *American Whigs,* 79–82.

8. On the nexus between the Revolution and conspiracy rhetoric, see Bailyn, *Ideological Origins.* For a rhetorical account of conspiracy and the Revolution, see Burnett, "Impetus for Rebellion."

9. Pocock, *Machiavellian Moment,* 3–80.

10. On Hofstadter's method, see Fenster, *Conspiracy Theories,* esp. 3–21. On the tradition of mainstream conspiracy rhetoric, Burnett's study of conspiracy rhetoric during the Revolution finds English commonwealth (republican) ideology, actual English conspiracies, and English millennialism and anti-Catholicism to be primary sources of the American revolutionaries' preoccupation with conspiracies against liberties. See Burnett, "Impetus," 66–80. Howe (*American Whigs*) and Holt (*Political Crisis* and *Political Parties*) each testify to the predominance of conspiracy rhetoric in the early party systems.

11. Kenneth Burke strongly links organic imagery to the comic frame, suggesting an additional connection between republican ideology and narrative practices of conspiracy. He characterizes such organic imagery of decay, degeneration, and rebirth as a transcendent mode of purification. Burke, however, does not make the connection between organic

imagery and civic republicanism. See Burke, *Attitudes toward History*, 285.

12. On the "republican drama" and "enduring republican crisis," see Kruman, "Second American Party System," 261; Holt, *Political Crisis*, 151–52.

13. Hofstadter, "Paranoid Style," 7; Fenster, *Conspiracy Theories*, xv.

14. McCormick, *Second American Party System*, 95, 348–49; McCormick "Political Development," 90–116, esp. 105. On the issue of intraparty democracy and deliberation and the trade-off between intraparty democracy and interparty competition, see Teorell, "Deliberative Defence," 363–82.

15. While Chase's *Address* was not technically a keynote speech, it nevertheless needed to negotiate the tension between inside and outside audiences that is at the core of the keynoter's dilemma. On the keynoter's dilemma, see Thompson, "Barbara Jordan's Keynote Address," 272. Thompson cites Smith, "Keynoter's Dilemma." This concept is also utilized by Pfau, "House That Abe Built," 635–51. On Douglas's exploitation of the "House Divided" speech, see David Zarefsky, "Four Senses of Rhetorical History," in *Doing Rhetorical History: Concepts and Cases,* ed. Kathleen J. Turner (Tuscaloosa: University of Alabama Press, 1998), 21; Pfau, "House That Abe Built," 642–43.

16. Thomas Brown, "The Image of the Beast: Anti-Papal Rhetoric in Colonial America," in *Conspiracy: The Fear of Subversion in American History*, ed. Richard O. Curry and Thomas Brown (New York: Holt, Rinehart and Winston, 1972), 18–19. Brown suggests that the Reformation strain was the more extreme and eschatological version and was modified into a more secular strain by the Enlightenment.

17. Wooten, *Cicero's Philippics*.

18. Aristotle, *The Politics*, trans. Carnes Lord (Chicago: University of Chicago Press, 1984), 163.

19. Aristotle, *Rhetoric*, 141; Aristotle, *Nicomachean Ethics*, 55, 57 (III, 3).

20. On the marginalization of conspiracy discourse in an increasingly liberal-pluralist age, see Howe, *American Whigs*, 329 (note 50); Fenster, *Conspiracy Theories*, 5, 8, 10, 15. On the transition from civic republicanism to liberal-pluralism following the Civil War, see Ericson, *American Liberalism*, 7–9; on the associated transition from hortatory to admonitory rhetoric, see Robertson, *Language of Democracy*, 11–15, 28–35. Robert Goldberg contends that conspiracy theories are increasingly appearing within the political mainstream. See Goldberg, *Enemies Within*.

21. See Wood, "Conspiracy and the Paranoid Style," 408–11; Howe, *American Whigs*, 79; Timothy Melley, *Empire of Conspiracy: The Culture of Paranoia in Postwar America* (Ithaca, N.Y.: Cornell University Press, 2000), 3–8, 11–14. On conspiracy theories as oversimplifications of the modern world, see Fenster, *Conspiracy Theories*, 58, 63, 67.

22. Dahl's initial work is largely descriptive, positing pluralism as the most accurate description of how politics actually works. See Dahl, *Who Governs?* Some of Dahl's work also positions pluralism as a normatively preferable way of conducting politics. See, for example, Dahl, *Preface to Democratic Theory.*

23. Goldberg, *Enemies Within.* Goodnight and Poulakos, for instance, assume that the mechanism by which conspiracy rhetoric enters the mainstream is one of invasion, postulating that the assumptions of the paranoid style hold (the all-powerful demonic conspiracy, etc.) as conspiracy rhetoric enters the mainstream, ultimately having the effect of eroding the "pragmatic frame" of normal political discussion and replacing it with a conspiratorial frame driven by fantastic assumptions. See Goodnight and Poulakos, "Conspiracy Rhetoric," 302, 307–8, 310–11. Goldberg begins with what are traditionally taken to be paranoid conspiracy theories and documents their occasional entrance into the mainstream. See Goldberg, *Enemies Within*, esp. xii.

24. Fenster, *Conspiracy Theories*, xiii–xiv, 69–72, and, more generally, 52–74. On the special appeal of conspiracy theories to subaltern identities, see Fenster, *Conspiracy Theories*, 55–59, 72. In terms of the black public sphere, Fenster mentions the paranoid conspiracy theory that KKK-controlled Church's fried chicken franchises aimed at sterilizing African American males, as well as more believable conspiracies revolving around the assassination of Martin Luther King Jr. To this might be added recent allegations that the CIA conspired to finance its secret war in Central America by selling crack to African Americans in Los Angeles.

25. Fenster, *Conspiracy Theories*, xv–xvi, 63, 67.

26. See, for instance, Ralph Nader, "Acceptance Speech at the Greens' National Convention," August 19, 1996, UCLA Campus (http://www.nader2k.org/speech.html); Michael Moore, *Stupid White Men . . . and Other Sorry Excuses for the State of the Nation* (New York: Regan Books, 2001), 1–12, and, more generally, 1–28.

27. Goldberg, *Enemies Within*, 260; Burke, *Philosophy of Literary Form*, 191–220. Among the most recent work on conspiracy, Daniel Pipes insists on the maliciousness and violent tendencies of conspiracy in the

paranoid style. See Pipes, *Conspiracy,* esp. 178–79. Hofstadter critic Mark Fenster also speaks of the fascism, racism, and scapegoating associated with conspiracy theories. See Fenster, *Conspiracy Theories,* xvi.

28. On the connection between Hofstadter's insights and the irrationality of conspiracy rhetoric, see Young, Launer, and Austin, "Need for Evaluative Criteria," 89–107; Hasian, "Conspiratorial Rhetoric," 195–214. On conspiracy arguments as quasi-logical, see Young, Launer, and Austin, "Need for Evaluative Criteria," 102.

29. Young, Launer, and Austin, "Need for Evaluative Criteria," 89–90, 93, 98, 102.

30. On the evaluation of conductive arguments, see Govier, "Two Unreceived Views," 70; Govier, *Practical Study of Argument,* 393–94, 397. Michael Billig's work in argument theory and conspiracy has highlighted the importance of "argumentative context," the recognition that "any attitude is more than an expression in favor of a position: it is also implicitly or explicitly an argument against a counter-position." See Michael Billig, "Rhetoric of Conspiracy Theory," *Patterns of Prejudice* 22 (1988): 23–34, esp. 27.

31. Michael William Pfau and David Zarefsky, "Evaluating Conspiracy Arguments: The Case of the Texas Annexation Controversy," in *Argument at Century's End: Reflecting on the Past and Envisioning the Future, Selected Papers from the Eleventh NCA/AFA Conference on Argumentation,* ed. Thomas A. Hollihan, 427–35 (Annandale, Va.: NCA, 2000). Other scholars have emphasized the importance of applying common sense and knowledge of history to the issue of evaluating conspiracy theories. See Pipes, *Conspiracy,* 38. The primary difficulty with this comparative and contextual approach to evaluation is that it requires an extensive familiarity with the historical context of conspiracy claims.

32. Burke, "Rhetoric of Hitler's Battle," 191–220. On the perfecting of the scapegoat, see Burke, *Permanence and Change* 284–94. For a more recent expression of assumptions regarding the danger of conspiracy theory, see Pipes, *Conspiracy,* 178–79.

33. Melley has gone so far as to suggest that some interpretive theories, such as those founded on a hermeneutic of suspicion or the assumption of Straussians that reading involves the unearthing of secret messages or codes, are themselves paranoid. See Melley, *Empire of Conspiracy,* 16, 22–25.

Bibliography

Adams, John Quincy. Lectures on Rhetoric and Oratory. 2 vols. 1810. Reprint. New York: Russell and Russell, 1962.

———. "Speech of John Quincy Adams of Massachusetts, upon the Right of the People, Men and Women, to Petition on the Freedom of Speech and of Debate in the House of Representatives of the United States; on the Resolution of Seven State Legislatures, and the Petitions of more than one hundred thousand Petitioners, relating to the Annexation of Texas to the Union. Delivered in the House of Representatives of the United States, in fragments of the morning hour, from the 16th of June to the 7th of July 1838, inclusive." Washington D.C.: Gales and Seaton, 1838.

Ambrosius, Lloyd, ed. A Crisis of Republicanism: American Politics in the Civil War Era. Lincoln: University of Nebraska Press, 1990.

Ames, Fisher. The Works of Fisher Ames as published by Seth Ames. 2 vols. Edited by W. B. Allen. 1809. Reprint. Indianapolis, Ind.: Liberty Press, 1983.

Angle, Paul M., ed. The Complete Lincoln-Douglas Debates of 1858. Chicago: University of Chicago Press.

Appleby, Joyce. Capitalism and a New Social Order. New York: New York University Press, 1984.

———. "Republicanism in Old and New Contexts." William and Mary Quarterly 43 (1986): 20–34.

Arendt, Hannah. On Revolution. New York: Viking Press, 1963.

Aristotle. The Nicomachean Ethics. Translated by David Ross. New York: Oxford University Press, 1991.

———. The Politics. Translated by Carnes Lord. Chicago: University of Chicago Press, 1984.

———. The Rhetoric. Translated by George Kennedy. New York: Oxford University Press, 1991.

Ashworth, John. "Agrarians" and "Aristocrats": Party Political Ideology in the United States, 1837–1846. Atlantic Highlands, N.J.: Humanities Press, 1983.

Bailyn, Bernard. *Ideological Origins of the American Revolution*. Cambridge, Mass.: Belknap Press of Harvard University Press, 1967.

Baker, Jean H. *Affairs of Party: The Political Culture of Northern Democrats in the Mid-Nineteenth Century*. Ithaca, N.Y.: Cornell University Press, 1983.

Banning, Lance. *The Jeffersonian Persuasion*. Ithaca, N.Y.: Cornell University Press, 1978.

Barker, Joseph. *Proceedings of the American Anti-Slavery Society at Its Second Decade*. 1854. Reprint, Westport, Conn.: Negro University Press, 1970.

Barthes, Roland. "An Introduction to the Structural Analysis of Narrative." *New Literary History* 6 (1975): 237–72.

Basler, Roy. "Abraham Lincoln's Rhetoric." *American Literature* 11 (1939): 165–82.

Beck, Paul Allen, and Frank J. Sorauf. *Party Politics in America*. New York: HarperCollins, 1992.

Benson, Thomas, ed. *Rhetoric and Political Culture in Nineteenth-Century America*. East Lansing: Michigan State University Press, 1997.

Bercovitch, Sacvan. *The American Jeremiad*. Madison: University of Wisconsin Press, 1978.

Berkhofer, Robert F. *Beyond the Great Story: History as Text and Discourse*. Cambridge, Mass.: Belknap Press of Harvard University Press, 1995.

Berwanger, Eugene H. *The Frontier against Slavery: Western Anti-Negro Prejudice and the Slavery Extension Controversy*. Urbana: University of Illinois Press, 1967.

Billig, Michael. "Rhetoric of Conspiracy Theory." *Patterns of Prejudice* 22 (1988): 23–34.

Bitzer, Lloyd. "The Rhetorical Situation." *Philosophy and Rhetoric* 1 (1968): 1–14.

Blue, Frederick J. *Salmon P. Chase: A Life in Politics*. Kent, Ohio: Kent State University Press, 1987.

Boritt, Gabor S. *Lincoln and the Economics of the American Dream*. Urbana and Chicago: University of Illinois Press, 1978.

Bradford, M. E. "Dividing the House: The Gnosticism of Lincoln's Rhetoric." *Modern Age* 23 (1979): 10–24.

———. "Lincoln's Republican Rhetoric: The Development of a Political Idiom." *Old Northwest* 14 (1988): 185–211.

Brigance, William Norwood, ed. *A History and Criticism of American Public Address*. 3 vols. New York: Russell and Russell, 1943–55.

Brock, William R. *Parties and Political Conscience: American Dilemmas, 1840–1850*. Millwood, N.Y.: KTO Press, 1979.

Brown, Thomas. *Politics and Statesmanship: Essays on the American Whig Party.* New York: Columbia University Press, 1985.

Browne, Stephen. *Edmund Burke and the Discourse of Virtue.* Tuscaloosa: University of Alabama Press, 1993.

Burke, Edmund. *The Writings and Speeches of Edmund Burke,* vol. 6. Edited by Paul Langford, P. J. Marshall, and William B. Todd. Oxford: Clarendon Press, 1991.

Burke, Kenneth. *Attitudes toward History.* Berkeley: University of California Press, 1937.

———. *A Grammar of Motives.* Berkeley: University of California Press, 1969.

———. *On Symbols and Society.* Edited by Joseph R. Gusfield. Chicago: University of Chicago Press, 1989.

———. *Permanence and Change.* Indianapolis, Ind.: Bobbs-Merrill, 1965.

———. *The Philosophy of Literary Form: Studies in Symbolic Action.* Berkeley: University of California Press, 1973.

Burnett, Nicholas. "The Impetus for Rebellion: A Rhetorical Analysis of the Conditions, Structures, and Functions of Conspiracy Argumentation during the American Revolution." Ph.D. diss., University of Pittsburgh, 1989.

Campbell, George. *Philosophy of Rhetoric.* Edited by Lloyd F. Bitzer. 1776. Reprint. Carbondale: Southern Illinois University Press, 1963.

Campbell, John Angus. "Between the Fragment and the Icon: Prospect for a Rhetorical House of the Middle Way." *Western Journal of Speech Communication* 54 (1990): 346–76.

Campbell, Karlyn Kohrs, and Kathleen Hall Jamieson. *Deeds Done in Words: Presidential Rhetoric and the Genres of Governance.* Chicago: University of Chicago Press, 1990.

Chambers, William Nisbet. *Political Parties in a New Nation.* New York: Oxford University Press, 1963.

Chambers, William Nisbet, and Walter Dean Burnham, eds. *The American Party Systems: Stages of Political Development.* New York: Oxford University Press, 1967.

Chase, Salmon P. *The Address of the Southern and Western Liberty Convention held at Cincinnati, June 11 & 12, 1845, to the People of the United States, with Notes by a Citizen of Pennsylvania.* Philadelphia: Office of the American Citizen, 1845.

———. *Appeal of the Independent Democrats in Congress, to the People of the United States. Shall Slavery be Permitted in Nebraska?* Washington, D.C.: Towers' Printers, 1854.

_____. "Maintain Plighted Faith. Speech of Hon. S. P. Chase, of Ohio, in the Senate, February 3, 1854, against the repeal of the Missouri prohibition of slavery north of 36°30". Washington, D.C.: John T. and Lem Towers, 1954.

_____. *The Salmon P. Chase Papers.* 3 vols. Edited by John Niven. Kent, Ohio: Kent State University Press, 1994.

_____. "Union and Freedom, Without Compromise, Speech of Hon. S. P. Chase of Ohio, on Mr. Clay's Compromise Resolutions delivered to the United States Senate March 26 & 27, 1850." Boston, Mass.: Redding, 1850.

[Cicero]. *Ad Herrenium.* Translated by H. Caplan. Cambridge, Mass: Harvard University Press, 1954.

_____. *In Catilinum I–IV, Pro Murena, Pro Sulla, Pro Flacco.* Translated by C. MacDonald. Cambridge, Mass.: Harvard University Press, 1977.

Clubb, Jerome, William H. Flanigan, and Nancy H. Zingale. *Partisan Realignment: Voters, Parties, and Government in American History.* Boulder, Colo.: Westview Press, 1990.

Congressional Globe Appendix, 25th Cong., 3rd sess., 1838.

Congressional Globe Appendix, 28th Cong., 1st sess., 1844.

Congressional Globe Appendix, 28th Cong., 2nd sess., 1845.

Congressional Globe Appendix, 34th Cong., 1st sess., 1856.

Corlett, William. "The Availability of Lincoln's Political Religion." *Political Theory* 10 (1982): 520–40.

Craven, Avery. *The Coming of the Civil War.* New York: Charles Scribner's Sons, 1942.

_____. *The Repressible Conflict, 1830–1861.* Baton Rogue: Louisiana State University Press, 1939.

Creps, Earl. "Conspiracy Argument as Rhetorical Genre." Ph.D. diss., Northwestern University, 1981.

Curry, Richard O., and Thomas Brown, eds. *Conspiracy: The Fear of Subversion in American History.* New York: Holt, Rinehart and Winston, 1972.

Dahl, Robert A. *A Preface to Democratic Theory.* Chicago: University of Chicago Press, 1956.

_____. *Who Governs? Democracy and Power in an American City.* New Haven, Conn.: Yale University Press, 1961.

Darsey, James. *The Prophetic Tradition and Radical Rhetoric in America.* New York: New York University Press, 1997.

Davis, David Brion. *The Fear of Conspiracy: Images of Un-American Subversion from the Revolution to the Present.* Ithaca, N.Y.: Cornell University Press, 1971.

———. *The Slave Power Conspiracy and the Paranoid Style.* Baton Rouge: Louisiana State University Press, 1969.

———. "Some Themes of Counter-Subversion: An Analysis of Anti-Masonic, Anti-Catholic, and Anti-Mormonic Literature." *Mississippi Valley Historical Review* 47 (1960): 205–24.

Demosthenes. *Demosthenes: Olynthiacs, Phillipics, Minor Public Speeches and Speech against Leptines.* Translated by J. H. Vince. New York: G. P. Putnam, 1930.

Diffley, Kathleen. "'Erecting Anew the Standard of Freedom': Salmon P. Chase's 'Appeal of the Independent Democrats' and the Rise of the Republican Party." *Quarterly Journal of Speech* 74 (1988): 401–15.

Diggins, Patrick. *The Lost Soul of American Politics.* New York: Basic Books, 1984.

Donald, David Herbert. *Charles Sumner and the Coming of the Civil War.* New York: Alfred and Knopf, 1960.

———. *Lincoln.* New York: Simon and Schuster, 1995.

Eagleton, Terry. *Ideology: An Introduction.* New York: Verso, 1991.

Ericson, David. *The Shaping of American Liberalism: The Debates Over Ratification, Nullification and Slavery.* Chicago: University of Chicago Press, 1993.

Farrell, James M. "John Adams and the Ciceronian Paradigm." Ph.D. diss., University of Wisconsin, 1988.

———. "*Pro Militibus Oratio:* John Adams's Imitation of Cicero in the Boston Massacre Trial." *Rhetorica* 9 (1991): 233–49.

Farrell, Thomas. *The Norms of Rhetorical Culture.* New Haven, Conn.: Yale University Press, 1993.

Fehrenbacher, Don E. *The Dred Scott Case: Its Significance in American Law and Politics.* New York: Oxford University Press, 1978.

———. "The Origins and Purpose of Lincoln's 'House Divided' Speech." *Mississippi Valley Historical Review* 46 (1960): 615–43.

———. *Prelude to Greatness: Lincoln in the 1850's.* Stanford, Calif.: Stanford University Press, 1962.

———. *Slavery, Law, and Politics: The Dred Scott Case in Historical Perspective.* New York: Oxford University Press, 1981.

Fenster, Mark. *Conspiracy Theories: Secrecy and Power in American Culture.* Minneapolis: University of Minnesota Press, 1999.

Finkelman, Paul, ed. *Articles on American Slavery: Antislavery.* New York: Garland, 1989.

Fisher, Walter R. *Human Communication as Narration: Toward a Philosophy of Reason, Value and Action.* Columbia: University of South Carolina Press, 1987.

Fleishman, Joel L., ed. *The Future of American Political Parties: The Challenge of Governance.* Englewood Cliffs, N.J.: Prentice-Hall, 1982.

Foner, Eric. *Free Soil, Free Labor, Free Men: The Ideology of the Republican Party before the Civil War.* New York: Oxford University Press, 1970.

Forgie, George. *Patricide in the House Divided: A Psychological Interpretation of Lincoln and His Age.* New York: W. W. Norton, 1979.

Formisano, Ronald P. *The Transformation of Political Culture: Massachusetts Parties, 1790s-1840s.* New York: Oxford University Press, 1983.

Franklin, John Hope. *Race and History: Selected Essays.* Baton Rouge: Louisiana State University Press, 1989.

Freehling, William. *The Road to Disunion: Secessionists at Bay, 1776–1854.* New York: Oxford University Press, 1990.

Gara, Larry. "Slavery and the Slave Power: A Crucial Distinction." *Civil War History* 15 (1969): 5–18.

Garrison, William Lloyd. *Selections from the Writings and Speeches of William Lloyd Garrison.* 1852. Reprint. New York: Negro University Press, 1969.

Geertz, Clifford. *The Interpretation of Cultures.* New York: Basic Books, 1973.

Gerring, John. *Party Ideologies in America: 1828–1996.* New York: Cambridge University Press, 1998.

Gienapp, William. "The Crime against Sumner: The Caning of Charles Sumner and the Rise of the Republican Party." *Civil War History* 25 (1979): 218–45.

———. *The Origins of the Republican Party 1852–1856.* New York: Oxford University Press, 1987.

Goldberg, Robert. *Enemies Within: The Culture of Conspiracy in Modern America.* New Haven, Conn.: Yale University Press, 2001.

Goodell, William. *Slavery and Anti-Slavery: A History of the Great Struggle in both Hemispheres; with a view of the Slavery Question in the U.S.* 1852. Reprint. New York: Negro University Press, 1968.

Goodnight, G. Thomas, and John Poulakos. "Conspiracy Rhetoric: From Pragmatism to Fantasy in Public Discourse." *Western Journal of Speech Communication* 45 (1981): 299–316.

Govier, Trudy G. *A Practical Study of Argument.* Belmont, Calif.: Wadsworth, 1997.

_____. *Problems in Argument Analysis and Evaluation.* Providence, R.I.: Foris, 1987.

Griffin, Charles. "Jedediah Morse and the Bavarian Illumaniti: An Essay in the Rhetoric of Conspiracy." *Central States Speech Journal* 39 (1988): 293–303.

Gross, Alan C., and William M. Keith, eds. *Rhetorical Hermeneutics: Invention and Interpretation in the Age of Science.* Albany, N.Y.: SUNY Press, 1997.

Hall, David D., et al., eds. *Saints and Revolutionaries: Essays on Early American History.* New York: W. W. Norton, 1984.

Hamilton, Alexander. *Papers of Alexander Hamilton,* vol. 12. Edited by Harold C. Syrett. New York: Columbia University Press, 1966.

Hart, Roderick P., and Sharon E. Jarvis. "Collective Language at the National Issues Convention." Paper presented at the annual meeting of the American Political Science Association, Boston, 1998.

Hartz, Louis. *The Liberal Tradition in America.* New York: Harcourt Brace Jovanovich, 1955.

Hasian, Marouf. "Understanding the Power of Conspiratorial Rhetoric: A Case Study of *The Protocols of the Elders of Zion.*" *Communication Studies* 48 (1997): 195–214.

Hofstadter, Richard. *The Idea of a Party System: The Rise of Legitimate Opposition in the United States, 1740–1840.* Berkeley and Los Angeles: University of California Press, 1969.

_____. *The Paranoid Style in American Politics and Other Essays.* Cambridge, Mass.: Harvard University Press, 1964.

Holt, Michael F. *The Political Crisis of the 1850s.* New York: John Wiley and Sons, 1978.

_____. *Political Parties and American Political Development.* Baton Rogue: Louisiana State University Press, 1992.

_____. *The Rise and Fall of the American Whig Party: Jacksonian Politics and the Onset of the Civil War.* New York: Oxford University Press, 1999.

Horwitz, Linda Diane. "Transforming Appearance into Rhetorical Argument: Rhetorical Criticism of Public Speeches of Barbara Jordan, Lucy Parsons, and Angela Y. Davis." Ph.D. diss., Northwestern University, 1998.

Howe, Daniel Walker. *The Political Culture of the American Whigs.* Chicago: University of Chicago Press, 1979.

Jaenicke, Douglas W. "The Rupture of the Antebellum Democratic Party: Prelude to Secession from the Union." *Party Politics* 3 (1995): 347–67.

Jaffa, Harry. *Crisis of the House Divided: An Interpretation of the Issues in the Lincoln-Douglas Debates*. Garden City, N.Y.: Doubleday, 1959.

Johannsen, Robert W. *Lincoln, the South and Slavery: The Political Dimension*. Baton Rogue: Louisiana State University Press, 1991.

_____. *Stephen A. Douglas*. New York: Oxford University Press, 1973.

Johnson, Dick. "Along the Twisted Road to Civil War: Historians and the 'Appeal of the Independent Democrats.'" *Old Northwest* 4 (1978): 119–41.

Johnson, George. *Architects of Fear: Conspiracy Theories and Paranoia in American Culture*. Los Angeles: Jeremy P. Tareher, 1983.

Jost, Walter, and Michael J. Hyde, eds. *Rhetoric and Hermeneutics in Our Time: A Reader*. New Haven, Conn.: Yale University Press, 1997.

Knox, Wendell. *Conspiracy in American Politics: 1787–1815*. New York: Arno Press, 1972.

Kraig, Robert A. "The Anatomy of Conspiracy: Salmon P. Chase's *Appeal of the Independent Democrats*." Paper presented at the annual meeting of the National Communication Association, Chicago, 1999.

_____. "The Narration of Essence: Salmon P. Chase's Senate Oration against the Kansas-Nebraska Act." *Communication Studies* 48 (1997): 234–53.

Kraut, Alan M., ed. *Crusaders and Compromisers: Essays on the Relationship of the Antislavery Struggle to the Antebellum Party System*. Westport, Conn.: Greenwood Press, 1983.

Kruman, Marc. "The Second American Party System and the Transformation of Revolutionary Republicanism." *Journal of the Early Republic* 12 (1992): 509–37.

Leff, Michael C. "Performative Traditions and the Oratorical Text." Paper presented at the annual meeting of the Southern States Speech Communication Association, 1995.

_____. "Rhetorical Timing in Lincoln's 'House Divided' Speech." Van Zelst Lecture in Communication, Northwestern University, May 19, 1983.

Leff, Michael C., and Fred J. Kauffield, eds. *Texts in Context: Critical Dialogues on Significant Episodes in American Public Address*. Davis, Calif.: Hermagoras Press, 1989.

Leff, Michael, and Andrew Sachs. "Words the Most Like Things: Iconicity and the Rhetorical Text." *Western Journal of Speech Communication* 54 (1990): 252–73.

Leonard, Gerald. "The Ironies of Partyism and Antipartyism: Origins of Partisan Political Culture in Jacksonian Illinois." *Illinois Historical Journal* 87 (1994): 21–40.

Lincoln, Abraham. *The Collected Works of Abraham Lincoln.* 8 vols. Edited by Roy P. Basler, Marion Dolores Pratt, and Lloyd A. Dunlap. New Brunswick, N.J.: Rutgers University Press, 1953.

Lucaites, John, and Celeste Condit. "Reconstructing Narrative Theory: A Functional Perspective." *Journal of Communication* 35 (1985): 90–108.

Lucas, Stephen. "The Renaissance of American Public Address: Text and Context in Rhetorical Criticism." *Quarterly Journal of Speech* 74 (1988): 241–60.

———. "The Schism in Rhetorical Scholarship." *Quarterly Journal of Speech* 67 (1981): 1–20.

Machiavelli, Niccolo. *The Prince and the Discourses.* Translated by M. Lerner. New York: Modern Library, 1950.

Mailloux, Steven. *Rhetorical Power.* Ithaca, N.Y.: Cornell University Press, 1989.

Mayfield, John. *Rehearsal for Republicanism: Free Soil and the Politics of Slavery.* Port Washington, N.Y.: Kennikat Press, 1980.

McCormick, Richard P. *The Second American Party System: Party Formation in the Jacksonian Era.* Chapel Hill: University of North Carolina Press, 1966.

McGee, Michael C. "The 'Ideograph': A Link Between Rhetoric and Ideology." *Quarterly Journal of Speech* 66 (1980): 1–16.

———. "Text, Context and the Fragmentation of Contemporary Culture." *Western Journal of Speech Communication* 54 (1990): 274–89.

McPherson, James M. *Battle Cry of Freedom: The Civil War Era.* New York: Oxford University Press, 1988.

Melley, Timothy. *Empire of Conspiracy: The Culture of Paranoia in Postwar America.* Ithaca, N.Y.: Cornell University Press, 2000.

Miller, William Lee. *Arguing about Slavery: The Great Battle in the United States Congress.* New York: Alfred A. Knopf, 1996.

Mitchell, Thomas N. *Cicero the Senior Statesman.* New Haven, Conn.: Yale University Press, 1991.

Moore, Michael. *Stupid White Men . . . and Other Sorry Excuses for the State of the Nation.* New York: Regan Books, 2002.

Morrison, Michael A. *Slavery and the American West: The Eclipse of Manifest Destiny and the Coming of the Civil War.* Chapel Hill: University of North Carolina Press, 1997.

———. "Westward the Curse of Empire: Texas Annexation and the American Whig Party." *Journal of the Early Republic* 10 (1990): 221–49.

Mulkern, John R. *The Know-Nothing Party in Massachusetts: The Rise and Fall of a People's Movement.* Boston: Northeastern University Press, 1990.

Nader, Ralph. "Acceptance Speech at the Greens' National Convention." August 19, 1996. UCLA Campus (http://www.nader2k.org/speech.html).

Nevins, Allan. *The Emergence of Lincoln.* 2 vols. New York: Charles Scribner's Sons, 1950.

Nichols, Alice. *Bleeding Kansas.* New York: Oxford University Press, 1954.

Niven, John. *Salmon P. Chase: A Biography.* New York: Oxford University Press, 1995.

Ober, Josiah. *Mass and Elite in Democratic Athens.* Princeton, N.J.: Princeton University Press, 1989.

O'Leary, Stephen. "Reading the Signs of the Times: A Topical and Dramatistic Analysis of the Logic of Apocalyptic Advocacy." Ph.D. diss., Northwestern University, 1991.

Pangle, Thomas. *The Spirit of Modern Republicanism.* Chicago: University of Chicago Press, 1988.

Perelman, C. H., and L. Olbrechts-Tyteca. *The New Rhetoric: A Treatise on Argumentation.* Notre Dame, Ind.: Notre Dame University Press, 1969.

Peterson, Merrill D. *Lincoln in American Memory.* New York: Oxford University Press, 1994.

Pfau, Michael William. "The House That Abe Built: The 'House Divided' Speech and Republican Party Politics." *Rhetoric and Public Affairs* 2 (1999): 625–51.

Pfau, Michael William, and David Zarefsky. "Evaluating Conspiracy Arguments: The Case of the Texas Annexation Controversy." In *Argument at Century's End: Reflecting on the Past and Envisioning the Future, Selected Papers from the Eleventh NCA/AFA Conference on Argumentation,* edited by Thomas A. Hollihan, 427–35. Annandale, Va.: NCA, 2000.

Phillips, Wendell. *Speeches, Lectures and Letters by Wendell Phillips.* Boston: Lothrop, Lee and Shepard, 1891.

Pierson, Michael D. "'All Southern Society Is Assailed by the Foulest Charges': Charles Sumner's 'The Crime Against Kansas' and the Escalation of Republican Anti-slavery Rhetoric." *New England Quarterly* 68 (1995): 531–57.

Pipes, Daniel. *Conspiracy: How the Paranoid Style Flourishes and Where It Comes From.* New York: Free Press, 1997.

Pocock, J. G. A. *Machiavellian Moment: Florentine Political Thought and the Atlantic Republican Tradition.* Princeton, N.J.: Princeton University Press, 1975.

_____. *Politics, Language and Time: Essays on Political Thought and History.* New York: Atheneum, 1973.

_____. *Virtue, Commerce and History: Essays on Political Thought and History, Chiefly in the Eighteenth Century.* New York: Cambridge University Press, 1985.

Rahe, Paul. *Republics Ancient and Modern.* Chapel Hill: University of North Carolina Press, 1992.

Randall, J. G. *Lincoln the Liberal Statesman.* New York: Dodd, Mead, 1947.

_____. *Mr. Lincoln.* New York: Dodd, Mead, 1945.

Rawley, James A. *Race and Politics: "Bleeding Kansas" and the Coming of the Civil War.* Philadelphia, New York: J. B. Lippincott, 1969.

Reichley, James. *The Life of the Parties: A History of American Political Parties.* New York: Free Press, 1992.

Remini, Robert. *Martin Van Buren and the Making of the Democratic Party.* New York: Columbia University Press, 1959.

Richards, Leonard L. *The Slave Power: The Free North and Southern Domination, 1780–1860.* Baton Rouge: Louisiana State University Press, 2000.

Ricoeur, Paul. *Time and Narrative.* 3 vols. Translated by Kathleen McLaughlin and David Pellauer. Chicago: University of Chicago Press, 1983.

Robertson, Andrew W. *The Language of Democracy: Political Rhetoric in the United States and Britain, 1790–1900.* Ithaca, N.Y.: Cornell University Press, 1995.

Rodgers, Daniel T. "Republicanism: The Career of a Concept." *Journal of American History* 78 (1992): 11–38.

Rosenstone, Steven J., Roy L. Behr, and Edward H. Lazarus. *Third Parties in America.* Princeton, N.J.: Princeton University Press, 1984.

Rosteck, Thomas. "Form and Cultural Context in Rhetorical Criticism." *Quarterly Journal of Speech* 84 (1988): 471–90.

Sanders, Keith R., and Robert P. Newman, "John A. Stormer and the Hofstadter Hypothesis." *Central States Speech Journal* 22 (1971): 218–27.

Schurz, Carl. *Charles Sumner: An Essay.* Urbana: University of Illinois Press, 1951.

Shafer, Byron E., ed. *The End of Realignment: Interpreting American Electoral Eras.* Madison: University of Wisconsin Press, 1991.

Shefter, Martin. *Political Parties and the State: The American Historical Experience.* Princeton, N.J.: Princeton University Press, 1994.

Sigelschiffer, Saul. *The American Conscience: The Drama of the Lincoln-Douglas Debates*. New York: Horizon Press, 1979.

Silbey, Joel H. "'Always a Whig in Politics': The Partisan Life of Abraham Lincoln." *Papers of the Abraham Lincoln Association* 8 (1986): 21–42.

_____. *The Partisan Imperative*. New York: Oxford University Press, 1985.

Sisson, Daniel. *The American Revolution of 1800*. New York: Alfred Knopf, 1974.

Smith, Craig Allen. "The Hofstadter Hypothesis Revisited: The Nature of Evidence in Politically 'Paranoid' Discourse." *Southern Speech Communication Journal* 42 (1977): 274–89.

Smith, Robert L. "The Keynoter's Dilemma: A New Dimension." *Forensic* 47 (1962): 9–11.

Spiegel, Gabrielle M. "History, Historicism, and the Social Logic of the Text in the Middle Ages." *Speculum* 65 (1990): 59–86.

Stocker, Glenn. "Charles Sumner's Rhetoric of Insult." *Southern Speech Communication Journal* 38 (1973): 223–34.

Strong, Douglas M. *Perfectionist Politics: Abolitionism and the Religious Tensions of American Democracy*. Syracuse, N.Y.: Syracuse University Press, 1999.

Sumner, Charles. *Charles Sumner: His Complete Works*. 20 vols. 1872. Reprint. New York: Negro University Press, 1969.

_____. *Orations and Speeches by Charles Sumner*. 2 vols. Boston: Ticknor, Reed, and Fields, 1850.

_____. *The Selected Letters of Charles Sumner*. 2 vols. Edited by Beverly Wilson Palmer. Boston: Northeastern University Press, 1990.

Teorell, Jan. "A Deliberative Defence of Intra-Party Democracy." *Party Politics* 5 (1999): 363–82.

Thompson, Wayne N. "Barbara Jordan's Keynote Address: Fulfilling Dual and Conflicting Purposes." *Central States Speech Journal* 30 (1979): 272–77.

Turner, Kathleen J., ed. *Doing Rhetorical History: Concepts and Cases*. Tuscaloosa: University of Alabama Press, 1998.

Van Buren, Martin. *Inquiry into the Origin and Course of Political Parties in the United States*. 1867. Reprint. New York: A. M. Kelley, 1967.

Volpe, Vernon L. *Forlorn Hope of Freedom: The Liberty Party in the Old Northwest, 1838–1848*. Kent, Ohio: Kent State University Press, 1990.

White, Hayden. *Metahistory: The Historical Imagination in Nineteenth-Century Europe*. Baltimore: Johns Hopkins University Press, 1973.

_____. *Tropics of Discourse: Essays in Cultural Criticism*. Baltimore: Johns Hopkins University Press, 1978.

Wilson, Kirt. "Emerson, Transcendental Prudence, and the Legacy of Senator Charles Sumner." *Rhetoric and Public Affairs* 2 (1999): 453–79.

Wilson, Major. "Republicanism and the Idea of Party in the Jacksonian Period." *Journal of the Early Republic* 8 (1988): 419–42.

Wood, Gordon S. "Conspiracy and the Paranoid Style: Causality and Deceit in the Eighteenth Century." *William and Mary Quarterly* 39 (1982): 401–41.

———. *The Creation of the American Republic.* New York: W. W. Norton, 1969.

Wooten, Cecil W. *Cicero's Philippics and Their Demosthenic Model: The Rhetoric of Crisis.* Chapel Hill: University of North Carolina Press, 1983.

Young, Marilyn J., Michael K. Launer, and Curtis C. Austin. "The Need for Evaluative Criteria: Conspiracy Argument Revisited." *Argumentation and Advocacy* 26 (1990): 89–107.

Zarefsky, David. "Conspiracy Arguments in the Lincoln-Douglas Debates." *Journal of the American Forensic Association* 21 (1984): 63–75.

———. *Lincoln, Douglas and Slavery: In the Crucible of Public Debate.* Chicago: University of Chicago Press, 1990.

Zarefsky, David, and Victoria J. Gallagher. "From 'Conflict' to 'Constitutional Question': Transformations in Early American Public Discourse." *Quarterly Journal of Speech* 76 (1990): 247–61.

Index